This book is dedicated to
RUTH MERSEBURGER-WHARRAM
1921-2013

GAIA

People of the Sea

JAMES WHARRAM *with Hanneke Boon*

Dec. 2020

To Georgia,

From one skipper to another,
Keep sailing

[James signature]

Hanneke Boon

Lodestar Books

Foreword

It's a grand thing for the planet that James Wharram has finished this wonderful book after having lived on its land masses, its islands, and notably its oceans, for well over ninety years.

This morning I cut myself a slice of good brown bread on a board whose corner carries a carving of the Polynesian Catamaran icon. It was made for me in 1970, the year I first met James. I was little more than a teenager, but James had already shaken the yachting establishment to its garboards with his Atlantic crossings in double canoes he built himself, inspired by the oceanic achievements of the Polynesian People of the Sea. I was naïve enough to imagine that some wealthy corporate would sponsor me for an OSTAR entry in one of his designs. James was surprisingly kind.

He invited me to visit *Tehini* where Ruth looked after me and the great man asked if I had any money. I hadn't a bean, of course, but we didn't give up. A month or two later, while I was still trying to raise the cash, James needed a bed for the night in Salisbury, where I lived. He duly showed up and, for some reason, it was decided that he and I would embark on a two-man trip to Southampton in a wreck of a MkII Ford Cortina under my command. As we went flying over the blind crest of a hill at flank speed on the old A36, an innocent van-man was turning right across our bows. I slammed on the anchors, only to hear the disappointing sound of worn-out pads sparking on pitted discs. With seamanlike intuition, I wrenched the wheel hard to the right. Passing port to port, we bounced off the van's nearside flank and finally lost way at the edge of a ditch. Miraculously, nobody was harmed. James took the events in a stride so cool that one could begin to understand how he had succeeded in some of life's more outrageous ventures. And thus it was that two lads from Manchester forged a relationship in the fire of real action.

Despite having known James for so long, it was only when I read this memoir that I came fully to realise quite how much more than a designer he really is. Half a century on, he remains an independent spirit. His refusal to compromise with the increasing bureaucracy that blights our times has made many a sailor in today's consumer-driven scene ponder on what really matters. The stream of designs from his board has set generations free, but with a set of Wharram plans you get so much more than the drawings. Running through the book like the rogue's yarn in a length of three-strand rope is the man's personal philosophy, and that is what makes it such a compelling read. His descriptions of the achievements of vernacular Polynesian navigators are compelling, but his commentary on their lifestyle and how it was torn apart by the representatives of our own is something every westerner should study. Page after page challenges readers to look hard at their own circumstances and do some serious re-evaluation before it's too late.

James Wharram's early rejection of the monogamous mores of the post-war years while still in south Manchester must have required a deal of courage. Such questions remain close to his heart, yet the way he talks about them is tinged not so much with anger at small-minded bigots, but with a wry smile. Perhaps this is the result of the wisdom that comes to a few with advancing years but, joyous to relate, one can wring the chapters inside out and still find no hint of compromise with the establishment.

As we progress through these pages, it is clear that although plagued by sea-sickness, James became a fine seaman, trained entirely in the school of hard knocks with the ocean as his chief instructor. His designs are criticized regularly by people who have not taken the trouble to hear what he says, and thus to discover their subtle excellence. The description of a major storm survived so ably by *Gaia* north of New Zealand while life on board retained its communal harmony is a revelation. The tale of a dead beat north up the Red Sea, a notoriously awful and difficult passage, is told in the almost throwaway manner of the sailor at peace in his own skin and with nothing to prove.

I sailed again with James and his companion Hanneke many years after our early meeting. I never did conjure up the funds for the race boat, but the world still turned and I found other ways of following the sea. James was a hero to me in those far-off days. He still is. There's absolutely nobody like him and there never will be.

Tom Cunliffe
July 2020

Contents

Illustrations

Preface

The fiftieth anniversary of my first offshore catamaran voyage, from Falmouth, England, 500 miles across the Bay of Biscay to Ribadeo in northern Spain, was in 2006. As it was also the fiftieth anniversary of the UK's first offshore voyage by catamaran, it led to yachting magazines writing articles on my life and career.

An English yachting writer, experienced sailor, and personal friend, Tom Cunliffe, began his article with: 'Who is James Wharram? Is he a philosopher, or a crackpot? A catamaran designer or a doodler? A lifestyle guru or a libertine? Could he be a madman or might he be, perhaps, unsettlingly sane? One thing is for sure. He is one of twentieth century seafaring's most iconic figures.'

But my favourite description came in 2012 when the French magazine *Chasse Marée* published a twelve-page article about me and my life's work, announced on the cover in these words: 'James Wharram, Architect Libre-Penseur'—'James Wharram, Architect Free-Thinker.'

I sent this article to my German friend Klaus Hympendahl in Germany, a well-known yachting author. His reply was to the point 'You must write a book!' I replied:

'Well I have written a book called *Two Girls, two Catamarans*, you translated it into German.' He retorted: 'That book, James, was of a time many years ago, write a book of now, of your designs, voyages and sailing philosophy.'

I have now passed the ripe old age of 90 and live a comfortable life in Devoran on the Fal Estuary in Cornwall. On the high tides the sea floods to within a few metres of the studio where I am writing. And as with these tides my memories come and go. They come with memories of youth and excitable ambition, dreams of adventure, love, discovery and learning… they go with the balanced reflection of success and failure, euphoria and disappointment, love and heartache, gain and loss.

But, most important of all, with the thought that my catamaran designs continue to inspire and give joy to a whole host of modern sailors and ocean travellers, while restoring credit to the ancient Polynesians who sailed and explored the Pacific on these remarkable craft.

James Wharram FRGS
May 2020

Cento

Much have I travelled in the realms of gold,

And many goodly states and kingdoms seen,

But still I long to learn tales, marvellous tales,

Of ships and stars and isles where good men rest,

How others fought to forge my world.

What mad pursuit? What struggle to escape? What wild ecstasy?

How far the unknown transcends the what we know.

We are the music-makers,

And we are the dreamers of dreams,

Step forward,

To feel the blood run through the veins and tingle

Where busy thought and blind sensation mingle.

Come, my friends, 'tis not too late,

For we are the movers and shakers

Of the world for ever, it seems;

To strive, to seek, to find and not to yield.

Alison Chisholm

MAN OF THE SEA

I wandered lonely as a cloud
That floats on high o'er vales and hills,

William Wordsworth

1   Formative years

I was born in 1928 in Manchester in the north of England, and from the age of ten grew up on the edge of the city, in the newly-built suburb of Wythenshawe. During my childhood I spent much of my time alone—I was an only child and both my parents worked. With my dog, a golden retriever, I roamed the fields and copses nearby. Further from home I explored the River Bolin, where I taught myself to swim, and I would walk to the ancient Roman mines of Alderley Edge; I liked being alone with nature, where I felt at home.

I don't remember much of my early schooling, but there was one trauma I still recall quite clearly. I was left-handed and in those days it was considered wrong to write with your left hand. I remember my grandmother forcing me to practise writing with my right hand. As a result my handwriting has been terrible throughout my life.

My secondary school years were during the war when the paper shortage restricted conventional learning; as a result we spent a lot of time debating. There I learned at an early age the art of public speaking, I learned to question things, and I developed an interest in politics. Fortunately I had some very good teachers. There was one teacher who took us on field trips, potholing in the Derbyshire hills. Nowadays that would have been forbidden on Health and Safety grounds, but we went down into the potholes without safety gear, in our daily clothes.

When the Second World War ended I was sixteen. As a teenager I was a libertarian, a dreamer, and at that time, according to my father, destined to end up a 'bloody labourer!' As a father myself now, with a dreamy son, I can understand his concern about me in my teens, for I was, in effect, three different personas: practical, political and mystical dreamer.

My father had followed *his* father's career and had moved from bricklayer to small-sized jobbing builder, to bigger construction jobs during the war. He had learned to handle major building projects, and to lead hundreds of men. His post-war ambition, in the then budding world of 'builder developers', was to build up a family firm handling major projects. My part was to study building engineering, and his ambition was that I would go on to study architecture.

At these studies I was, unfortunately, fairly useless and I never progressed to architecture. I realise that I did learn about construction—by osmosis. Being surrounded by my father's workmen and occasionally going with him to jobs, I was that being increasingly rare today, the apprentice craftsman; I learned by watching men of whom the highest accolade was 'he did a bloody good job'. Without my realising it, their attitudes became part of my approach to designing and building boats. And nevertheless, from my time at the engineering college, I did learn the basic laws of mechanics, technical drawing, and methods of calculation.

My second persona in the late 1940s was in politics. Nowadays politics is boring: run by party machines, selling shallow solutions to deep problems using advertising methods, sound-bites, spin, posture training. In the post-war 1940s, politics was a vibrant, believable subject. The British had just won a war for freedom from the fascist threat. I was mixing daily with men little older than me who had parachuted at Arnhem, fought in the jungles of Burma, endured the hell of kamikaze planes in the Pacific. They deserved freedom from poverty in old age, freedom from poverty when the economy fails, a good state education, and access to the best medical attention when sick.

The city of Manchester where I grew up was a 'radical city'; the city where a hundred years previously Marx and Engels had lived, studied, and formulated what came to be called 'Marxist economics'. In 1819 citizens had rioted and had been 'sabred down' in the famous 'Peterloo Massacre', just for demanding a political voice.

Manchester at this time was a city with its own notable newspaper, *The Manchester Guardian*—later moving to London and becoming just *The Guardian*. Manchester also had a massive central library, the equal of the (then) British Museum Library in London. There I learned to self-study; to go into any subject from the basics, with an open mind, guided by the library's marvellous card-index system. My political studies at the end of the Second World War included writers like H. G. Wells, George Bernard Shaw, Bertrand Russell, and William Morris, whose Arts and Crafts ideals are still an important part of my design philosophy. In addition I studied the economics of Adam Smith, Ricardo, Marx, and of course the great British economist John Maynard Keynes.

I became chairman of a Labour Party youth group; I gave lectures on H. G. Wells and George Bernard Shaw to women's guilds and co-operative groups; and I was ear-marked for training as a future Labour Member of Parliament.

What stopped me from becoming a bore or a politician is that I had a third persona. I was a 'bog-trotter', a rock climber, a hiker, a mountaineer. That is, every weekend and every longer holiday I took a bus out to the Pennine Moors, the hilly backbone of northern England; as I got older I travelled to the Lake District and to the Isle of Skye in Scotland, where in the words of the romantic poet Wordsworth 'I wandered lonely as a cloud'.

The 'simple living' aspects of my catamaran designs—sometimes referred to as Spartan—arise from these teenage experiences. Wandering the high moors, particularly in winter, is a survival exercise and has the very practical aspect that if you don't do it right, you die!

In the mid-1940s there was no camping gear industry supplying specialist tents, sleeping bags, cooking stoves or protective clothing (clothing was still rationed at that time). And come to think of it, it was actually illegal to roam the moors close to Manchester and Sheffield. In 1932 people were sent to prison for asserting their 'right to roam'. However, the desire to wander overcame the niceties of law or the need for specialised equipment. Our mountain boots were ex-army, so were our woollen trousers and pullovers ('our', for there were other roamers like me at the time). My mother, a strong feminist who supported my independent exploits, made me thick flannel shirts and she re-shaped an old cotton overcoat to make me an anorak with a hood. For the winter my father found me a naval duffel coat. It was heavy, but it kept out the snow and the rain. My cooking stove was a billycan over a fire. Rucksacks were a problem; the unattainable dream was a framed Bergen pack. I made a wooden Yukon pack-frame, based on photos from my library studies. Early on I learned to adapt what was economically available to achieve my dreams.

I also learned to adapt my body. Not having a tent, I slept in youth hostels, sheep-shelters, and increasingly in the open, finding wind shelter behind rocks, burying my sleeping bag in heather and bracken, and developing the ability to tune in to the natural forces of nature. This weekend and holiday life was totally different to my normal weekday life in the city. I was beginning to consider mountaineering as a future. Indeed two fellow 'bog-trotters', Don Whillans and Joe Brown, in later years became internationally renowned mountaineers.

I believe that my teenage years of bog-trotting and mountaineering either opened up areas of Carl Jung's 'archaic man' within my subconscious, or enabled me, like early man, to innately understand aspects of the natural world around me. It is this awareness that explains a great deal of my later sea craft design philosophy.

I can remember when my dreaming adventure life turned from mountaineering to the sea. I was rock climbing in the Cuillin mountains on the Isle of Skye. From high on the ridge I could see the sea lochs reaching like fingers into the heart of the island. I thought that sailing that sea would give me access to most of the world. It was not a blinding prophetic flash however, as I had been opening to the ideas of a sea-life for some time.

In Manchester Central Library, while studying 'the centrifugal forces acting on a gearwheel' for my technical college—why I had to learn that, I never understood—or reading books on politics for my political life, at times it did get boring. Then I discovered an alcove of delight. In addition to books on mountaineering there was a shelf of small-boat sea adventures. I was seduced by the exploits of Joshua Slocum, Captain Voss, Erling Tambs, Dwight Long, and William Albert Robinson.

There is seduction and there is lifelong love. On this sea adventure shelf I found *The Voyage of the Kamiloa* by Éric de Bisschop, a voyage by 'double canoe' catamaran from Hawaii to France in the late 1930s. This book has been my lifelong love; Éric de Bisschop was my inspiration to become a catamaran designer. It was not only his boat and his voyage that inspired me, but also his theories on the migrations of the Pacific islanders, of which more later.

Prosaically it was MacDonald the boatman from the Isle of Skye who gave me the practical impetus toward sailing the seas. He used to take his converted lifeboat into Glen Brittle at the foot of the Cuillin mountains to pick up charter guests. After I paid for one trip on his boat we did a deal: I would find him charter guests for a day's sail and in return I would get a free ride on his boat.

With all these conflicting ideas floating around in my head, something had to give. For my nineteenth birthday, my present was a passport. Within weeks, I was gone from my northern English adolescent world.

The transition from adolescence to adulthood is considered a major one in most societies; it certainly was for me. My passport present had been for a climbing holiday in Switzerland; within three weeks I was having my first love affair with a Swiss girl who was the same age as me to the day. When not 'in love' I worked to earn money on a Zurich building site, in my father's words 'as a bloody labourer'; this included a short sharp course in Schweizerdeutsch (Swiss German). I had entered the world of post-war Europe.

I had also entered a unique University of Life. The last time such universities existed was in the early Middle Ages, when students travelled Europe and attended those of Toledo, Paris, and later Oxford and Cambridge, to engage with philosophy, science, art and other potent subjects, echoing ancient Greece, where students gathered around famous philosophers in discussion and argument.

The post-war European cities were hummingly alive with young people, who had fought in the 'resistance' or were young Germans and Austrians who realised how savagely their ideals had been abused. Social ideas were a matter of strong debate in the cafés and youth hostels where we met. On politics I held my own, but I soon realised that in art, music and literature I was, as an Englishman, a 'peasant'.

During the war years women had found their sexual freedom, but there was still much macho sexuality around. Because of my youth and inexperience I did not have a strong macho attitude, so my guides into music, art, literature, and fashion were women, some a few years older than me, who did not have to surrender their valued independence to their young and questing lover.

I met Pat, an American woman ten years older than me, while she was on holiday in Switzerland. She had studied at Bryn Mawr and Vassar colleges in America, and at the time I had no idea of the importance of her studies. She was about to take a further degree in English Literature at Oxford. I read Shakespeare's poetry to her and we discussed literature. She saw me as a prospective writer to be encouraged and guided; as she was to become an editor at a prestigious American publishing house, who am I to dispute it?

After two years Pat returned to America, and realising where I wanted to go, sent me as a farewell present a seminal book in my development as a designer, *Boat Building in Your Own Back Yard* by S.S. Rabl, first published in 1947. This book, which I still own, showed a very simple traditional American style of boat construction; boats that could be built with care by anyone, without needing a seven-year apprenticeship. Through this book building a boat for myself became to me a practical possibility.

A major sexual and sensual input into my life, combined with an introduction into the artistic and cultural values of central Europe, came from a Viennese woman I met in Zurich. Again a few years older than me, Traudl was in her final stages of becoming a doctor. She was specialising in psychology, for which Zurich was then a centre. I think she saw me as a wild, primitive sexual animal, which she enjoyed and tried to civilise.

I followed Traudl to Vienna when it was still occupied by the Russians, with concession zones for the British and Americans. Wearing ex-army clothes and knee-boots of both British and American style I must have seemed from one of the exotic branches of some specialised military group. Most of my time in Vienna I was there illegally, yet nobody checked on me. Traudl took me around the emerging 'salons' where discussions were on Hitler's forbidden subjects: art, as in Klimt, music as in Smetana's *Moldau*, and the psychology of Freud and Jung. These were subjects of deep, often excited discussion. I was living the life of an early medieval scholar.

When not civilising me culturally, Traudl civilised me sexually by teaching me how sex leads to sensuality and on to a deeper meaning of life. These are the concepts that lie behind the philosophy of Tantric Yoga. Through Traudl I became aware of the 'Universal Female Aspect'.

In the Mediterranean and many parts of the world, the sea is seen as the female, the mother, the lover, the goddess. Later in my boat design life I brought in this female aspect. Yacht design is more than a bunch of formulae, it needs sensual lines to fully express itself.

Soon after Vienna I was hitchhiking through France, Germany and Denmark to the wartime neutral country of Sweden, where I had heard one could find simple, small fishing boats, which I could adapt to sail the oceans. There I learned another life lesson: boats, even small boats, cost money. My boyhood dream had not faced up to this essential truth, and it was to be a few more years before I finally woke up to this and achieved my first ocean-going catamaran.

My being an only child may explain a tension between my parents regarding my activities 'growing up'. Now in my mature years with two sons—one very much like me—I realise how much, in an inarticulate way, my father cared for me, though his advice was often terse to the point of sounding brutal: 'You say you want to sail the sea on a yacht. You have never been to sea. You want to get a bloody job on a boat and see what it is really like!'

My father was right; I had to stop being a medieval scholar, a writer, a poet, a dreamer, a lover. The sailboat dream must meet hard physical reality. At that time in 1949 I was living my scholar's dream in Pembrokeshire in South Wales, working at an agricultural camp picking potatoes. Milford Haven was then a major fishing port, so I went down to the docks and applied for a job on a trawler.

Looking back, the trawler skipper who employed me must have been desperate! Dressed in a flowered shirt, soft moccasin shoes, and wearing glasses, I was offered a job, albeit the lowest of the low as cook's assistant and 'decky' learner. Away I went to sea, down the Irish Sea, around Ireland and into the Atlantic ocean to the 'Porcupine Bank'. I was violently seasick, and after two days I was hauled out of my bunk and put to peeling buckets of potatoes. They gave me the nickname 'Longfellow' because I was 6ft 2in tall and kept a journal.

My vessel, the *Westcarr*, was one of the pre-war steam trawlers which had supplanted the old sailing kind; indeed some of the crew had begun their lives trawling under sail. I could write a tale of hardship aboard the *Westcarr*; on the Atlantic side of Ireland the autumn gales were ferocious. On one of the trips the news over the radio was of the capsize of two newly-designed trawlers off Iceland as a result of ice on the deck and rigging. What I cannot write is of difficulties with the crew of real hard working seamen—no cruelty, no hazing, no contempt from them. They took me into their company as one of them, and with their example I began to become a 'man of the sea'.

When I came to live in Milford Haven many years later I was welcomed back by *Westcarr*'s retired skipper. I let him use my office on the docks for National Union of Seamen business. The trawler experience left a deep impression on me, and I now knew I could endure what landsmen called 'the savage seas'.

I went back north for another short bout of carefree hedonism, but a few months later, in 1950, I approached a firm in Leicester called the Bell Boat Building Company with my usual opening: 'I would like to work here, I will accept any job.'

The company had started out making beehives and the owner was a keen sailor. He was one of the many young men released from the services in post-war Britain, who turned to sailing or mountaineering to mentally make a fresh start after the military horrors they had experienced.

At this time Bell was producing a hard-chine general purpose 14ft rowing and sailing dinghy promoted by *Yachting World* magazine: the GP14. For its time it was quite revolutionary, being made with flat sheets of plywood glued together, using the American hard-chine workboat construction techniques I had learned about from *Boat Building in Your Own Back Yard*.

Hard-chine boatbuilding had been developed by the early settlers in America. In Europe over hundreds of years many trades had developed that used wood as the main construction material. There were specialised furniture makers, house carpenters, barrel makers, wheelwrights, boatbuilders and so on. Traditional European boatbuilding with its many curves in wood was a highly skilled craft. In the pioneering days of America men who could handle a saw, plane, axe or adze had to be a Jack of many trades. As they were not trained boatbuilders, they developed simple hard-chine boats, which can be built with the minimum of complex curves in their individual pieces. European boatbuilders tended to look down their noses at such simple methods.

At this time the Bell Boat Building Company was building beehives on one side of its factory floor and the GP14 on the other. The company was later commissioned by the *Daily Mirror* to build the hard-chine 'Mirror Dinghy', of which at least 100,000 kits were sold. This boat introduced thousands of young people to sailing, so helping to democratise small boat ownership in Britain at that time.

I was fired from Bell because I was 'no good as a worker'. Ten years later, at the 1960 London Boat Show, after my first two Atlantic voyages, I approached the company's stand with a certain amount of smugness. They remembered me; 'James' they said, 'we later fired the foreman who fired you. He was offloading his mistakes onto you'.

2   Ruth

When I was fired from the Bell Boat Building Company it was easy for me to go back to my self indulgent, hedonistic way of life, and for a while I did; but it did not satisfy, so I went back to the hills to rethink my way. The hills I went to were the beautiful Lake District in northern England. After two or three days solo trekking I ended up outside a youth hostel, which in the early afternoon had yet to open, so I sat down, rested against my pack and began to read. Glancing up I saw a young woman leaning under the weight of her rucksack coming up the hill. That woman was Ruth Merseburger. Looking up at her in 1951 it never occurred to me that in a short time she would become a major force in my life and an inseparable partner for the next sixty-four years.

Ruth was German and seven years older than me. She was shy, but quietly strong and, as life was to show, a brilliant organiser. She came from a quiet middle class family in a small town in central Germany, Zeulenrhoda in Thuringia. Ruth's father owned the local bookshop. She was an ardent if infrequent skier and mountain walker.

In the early years of the war Ruth had studied 'publishing' in Leipzig. This field attracted intellectuals who did not want to join the Nazi party, hence could not hold jobs as teachers. Ruth was the youngest amongst this group of much older, more experienced students. Mixing with them developed many aspects of Ruth's outlook on life. In the last year of the war she was working under German conscription as a housemaid and child carer for a professor of law, a very discreet man but, like the students in Leipzig, with anti-Hitler, anti-Nazi views.

When the war ended Ruth was among German women who were known as the 'trümmel frauen'—'rubble women'. In post-war devastated Germany there were very few menfolk as many were either dead, prisoners of war, or broken, therefore it was these women who amongst the ruins started to rebuild Germany, with their bare hands removing heaps of bomb rubble from the roads.

Before I met Ruth she was studying art history in Marburg. Her money had run out so she came to England as an au pair to raise money for further studies and to improve her English. Crossing the Channel to England at the age of thirty was the first time she had seen the sea.

A general perception of the Germans is that they build superb motorcars, hold the EU together and have no sense of humour. What is not generally appreciated is that there is a deep mystical strand in the German subconscious. It shows in the work of their composers like Beethoven, poets like Goethe, painters like Caspar David Friedrich (one of Ruth's favourites) and in the concept of the 'wander-vogel', the wandering medieval type of student.

The teachings of Rudolf Steiner are a further example; he was a multi-faceted German philosopher known in the West for his educational ideas, anthroposophical medicine, performing and visual arts, social activism and biodynamic agriculture. Ruth, in her study groups, had mixed with people who followed his teachings, which were frowned on during the Hitler era.

My creative relationships with American Pat and Austrian Traudl had limitations, because they both lived in the established Western cultural boxes of Publishing and Medicine. They could 'look' out of their boxes, but they could not 'live' outside them. Ruth, like myself, wanted and needed to 'live outside the box'.

3   My first boats

L iving outside the box' has a fine romantic sound, however it has its own discipline, which I had to learn. The first year Ruth and I were together, we built, in my father's back garden, a 15ft 6in design from *Boat Building in Your Own Back Yard*. I made all the mistakes of many first-time builders—lengthening the design, changing the construction material, and increasing the size of the cabin. It was a failure.

Ruth did not walk out on me, but at the end of 1952 she took a job in Wimbledon, where she had previously been an au pair, to make some money. This job offered accommodation for the two of us, and as fate would have it, not far away on an island in the River Thames was a branch of Britain's then prestigious boat building firm, Thorneycroft.

Thorneycroft had built high quality wooden luxury yachts since the 1930s; they also built wooden craft for the Royal Navy. I turned up at their office and asked for a job. The bosses soon realised I had no acceptable qualifications. When I said I wanted to work there and would do *any* job eyebrows went up, then after a brief private discussion, they said 'We have a labourer's job in the stores helping the store keeper, Percy'. 'I'll take it', I said.

Percy was a wonderful, kind old man who was delighted to have a young, strong helper. The stores contained old-fashioned heaps of everything needed to build boats from 16 feet to over 100 feet. One dusty dark neglected storeroom, which I was asked to clean and sort out, held wooden models of past designs and experiments. I found there a model of a Hickman sea sled, an American double hull motor craft from before the war. There were also American yachting magazines, like *The Rudder,* I had not seen before. I was on an intensive learning curve.

As 'store man' I also had to deliver items all over the building areas. I kept my eyes open and learned a lot about high class, traditional wooden boat building. I learned that you never touch a craftsman's tools. Even with a 'please' they would often say 'wait', and move the tool themselves.

A younger boat builder who understood my motives for working at Thorneycroft took me under his wing. One day he said: 'If you want to learn about boat design, you must talk to old Jock.' Old Jock was a Scotsman; he told me that as a boy around 1905 he accompanied his father and uncle around Aberdeen harbour when the tide was out, to study the hull forms of the now legendary 'Zulu' lugsail herring fishing boats. To a landsman all hulls would have looked alike, but to builders and sailors there were subtle differences between each hull—Differences that improved speed, seaworthiness and load carrying. Old Jock's father had built a fast seaworthy Zulu and Jock told me a model of it hung in Aberdeen. Talking to Jock taught me early on a valuable lesson as a designer and later as a marine archaeologist—be humble, look and listen, learn from the past and respect your tools, then try to improve and move on.

After working at Thorneycroft for six months, by springtime I was ready to build my own boat. During my studies at Manchester Central Library I had come across the works of G. R. G. Worcester on the junks of China. As a marine archaeologist I can write that the historical development of sail-shapes and hull-forms of offshore sailing vessels in northern Europe and the Mediterranean was different from the sailing craft of Asia and the Pacific. One important difference in sail shape in particular was the 'sunblind type' of fully-battened sails of the Chinese junk. For some time I had been considering building a junk as our means of going to sea.

I learned that for the sum of £15, plus £5 delivery cost, I could have a 20ft ex-ship's wooden lifeboat delivered to me, complete with its lugsail. This was it, I was going to convert a lifeboat into a small junk-rigged vessel and sail the seas.

First I had to resign from Thorneycroft and it was a sad parting on both sides. It was made clear that there was a place for me on the management side. I had learned so much and had made many friends at every level. I was leaving security behind, but this obsession with sailing the oceans was driving me on.

The lifeboat arrived on the back of a lorry at Thames Ditton on the river Thames, where there was space to convert and launch our boat. It was, like most of the lifeboats of that era, a sturdy double-ended wooden clinker hull, held in shape by wooden thwarts. I ripped the thwarts out and put deckbeams across the gunwales. In the middle of the ship I built a commodious cabin—far too big for the size of the hull. Then to limit leeway I made leeboards, as on Thames barges and Dutch traditional

Jim and Ruth in 1952

sailing vessels, out of the old thwarts. I made a junk sail out of the lugsail that came with the boat. With two mattress sacks stuffed with hay for beds, a primus stove, kettle, frying pan, and saucepans, away we went to sea.

'Away we went to sea' was not as romantic or as easy as it sounds. From Thames Ditton through London to the open sea there are twenty-two bridges, we had no engine, and we could only proceed down the Thames when the tide was with us. Even hauling hard on our two oars, in the strong swirling tide we often came out of the other side of a bridge stern first. In two to three days we were through the bridges and had reached Hole Haven, a then desolate creek by Canvey Island in the Thames estuary. Ruth was a wonderful, brave companion, never criticizing me for my ineptitude, always encouraging. Together we started to adapt to sea life on a small boat.

In the early 1950s 'yachting' was very much a minority activity, so there were no moorings, no pontoons. As we had no dinghy we either ploughed ashore knee-deep through soft mud when the tide was out, or when the tide was in swam ashore. There were 'odd' people who lived on old fishing boats, or ex-navy motorboats, who befriended us and gave us advice.

From Canvey Island we worked over to the Swale, between the Isle of Sheppey and the mainland on the south side of the Thames estuary, sometimes in adverse or no wind. I walked along the muddy shore towing the boat with a rope over my shoulder, Ruth steering the boat clear of the shore until we reached Whitstable, and then in the open sea coasted around the North Foreland to Ramsgate. Our plan was to cross the English Channel, sail up the coast of Belgium, and Holland, then up the river Rhine to Düsseldorf in the heart of Germany, where Ruth had relatives. Then sail back down and onwards etc., etc. Boy, did we have a lot to learn!

We spent a week in Ramsgate, foster-fathered by an old Thames sailing barge skipper called Tom; he simplified my complicated junk rig, taught me how to sail efficiently, then when the tide and weather was right told me: 'Go now.'

In the early 1950s the English Channel was not the densely ship-packed, tightly controlled waterway that it is now. Patriotically, for the British, it was the seaway that kept European invaders out of Britain. On one side was home, on the other the Continentals. Sailing across the Channel was a major step in seagoing.

Of course I had my own Continental in the person of Ruth, who was showing great aptitude as a navigator. So, we continued the voyage of the *Annie E. Evans*—we had named the boat after a dear old Quaker friend of ours—from Ramsgate to Calais, working up the French coast to Belgium, to Zeebrugge, then into the Schelde and through the Dutch islands to Dordrecht, heading up the river Rhine to Düsseldorf. When we ran out of favourable tidal currents we relied on friendly tows from the numerous small river barges.

We had completed our planned voyage, we had learned a great deal about our abilities to sail together, we also knew our 20ft junk-rigged lifeboat was not going to be suitable to sail the seas. Ruth, with a certain amount of exasperation said 'What are you going to do now, what do you really want?'

4   Archaeology and history

Archaeology and the early history of man—where he came from, his development into modern man, his tools and social organisation—is now a rich, deep, many-tiered subject in modern universities. It often features in TV programmes and many informative articles are written in newspapers and magazines on the latest revelations about our origins and early social behaviour.

Archaeology as a science began to develop in the late 1800s, when wealthy men with enquiring minds employed gangs of labourers to dig into ancient mounds. For example Heinrich Schliemann started to excavate Troy in 1868, Flinders Petrie began controlled and scientifically recording excavations in Egypt in 1880, and Arthur Evans excavated the palace at Knossos, Crete from 1900–1905. Archaeology at that time was a rich gentleman's hobby.

In 1949 Carbon-14 dating was developed to enable a recovered object to be accurately dated. From that time archaeology, as a university subject with strict and precise rules and disciplines, began to emerge.

Separate from this, at around the same time another aspect of archaeology was being developed, 'experimental archaeology'—recreating an ancient object and using it to find out its function and possibilities. Thor Heyerdahl was one of the first people to use this technique to prove his theories on the migrations of the Polynesians.

Thor Heyerdahl was a Norwegian. The Norwegians, living on the furthest North Atlantic coast in Europe, are a hard, highly individualistic people of the sea. In the late 1800s their unique attitude to living and adapting to nature was demonstrated by their great explorers: Fridtjof Nansen, who explored Greenland and the Arctic in the 1880s–90s, and Roald Amundsen, leader of the expedition first to reach the South Pole in 1911. They respected, and adapted to, the lifestyle of the Inuit people of the Arctic. The British expedition to the South Pole, led by Captain Scott at the same time, tragically failed because Scott and his men could not, or would not, adapt to the Inuit lifestyle. Tragically and with great personal courage their expedition failed.

Thor Heyerdahl was born in Larvik in 1914, the proud Norwegian stories of Nansen and Amundsen being part of his youth. In his book *Fatu Hiva*, first published in 1974, after his famous post war *Kon-Tiki* voyage, Heyerdahl describes how in 1936, aged just twenty-two, he persuaded his family and university to back his plan to go to a South Sea Island in the Marquesas to study botany! He also managed to persuade a twenty-year-old fellow student, a girl called Liv, to go with him; he married her, the convention at that time.

In *Fatu Hiva* he stresses more than once 'I was not a hippy' as he described the joys and hardships of living naked, foraging for plants, fish and crayfish in the streams. I can understand Heyerdahl's irritation at people being pointed in the wrong direction by the word 'hippy' when viewing his work—the same thing happened to me.

In 1936, whilst living on Fatu Hiva, and recognising the devastation, in numbers and culture, of the original Polynesian people through Western contact which brought disease and the intrusion of missionaries, he began to think about a serious archaeological problem: Where was the original homeland of these mid-oceanic island people and how did they get here?

The Heyerdahls were having a tough time surviving. It is very hard for a Westerner to go back totally to stone age living. Fortunately they gained the helpful friendship of one of the last pure-blooded Polynesian chiefs Tei Tetua. One sunset, as they sat with Tei Tetua, musing over where his ancestors had come from, the chief went into a semi-trance singing an ancient song, which led to further discussions on where had the ancestors of the Polynesian island settlers come from, and on what type of water craft. Rock carvings and other archaeological remains in the Marquesas suggested connections with South America.

Intrigued by his findings on Fatu Hiva, Heyerdahl continued to research Polynesian history back in Norway and in North America and, based on archaeological and ethnographic data available at that time, came to the conclusion that the origin of the Polynesian peoples was to the east, i.e. the American continent. And that the sea craft that made these migrations across approximately 4000 miles of ocean must have been balsa log sailing rafts from Peru. These native sailing craft dated from before the Spanish invasion—in 1528—and were still in use as coastal workboats into the beginning of the twentieth century.

Then came the 1939–45 war and this peaceful, dreaming, simple-living young man had to take up arms to defend his country, living in the snows of Arctic Norway with a gun in his hand fighting young Germans, many of whom, under different circumstances, would have been his brothers in thought. Heyerdahl was the type of young man I had met and learned from in my early wandering years just after the war.

It is clear from how quickly Heyerdahl organised his post war *Kon-Tiki* raft expedition in 1947 that in his 'dream' time while fighting for his life and country, he was already planning a major sea voyage to prove the theories he had started to evolve on Fatu Hiva. The 'would-be botanist' was about to become one of the first experimental marine archaeologists.

If you love the sea, if you love adventure, if you are interested in the history of early man, you should read *The Kon-Tiki Voyage*. The first chapter, with its sub-heading *A theory; who peopled the Polynesian Islands; riddle of the South Seas; theories and facts; legend of Kontiki and the white race*, gives an overview of Heyerdahl's studies on which he based his theories. But in addition to his archaeological theories and the technical details of sailing the deep ocean on an ancient sailing craft, Heyerdahl again and again described the beauty and spiritual awareness that comes from ocean sailing, particularly on a small non-Western craft. The book was so popular that it has been translated into seventy languages. The documentary film about the expedition won an Academy Award in 1951.

Sitting on the Rhine pontoon in 1953 outside Düsseldorf, aged twenty-five, by my to-be-abandoned 20ft converted lifeboat, Ruth as my partner had a perfect right to query my future ideas and way of life. She was aware of my reservations regarding Heyerdahl's claim that the American balsa sailing raft was the only seagoing craft used for the settlement of the central Pacific islands. After all, not long after we met we had hitchhiked to London together and stood in a long queue to see the *Kon-Tiki* film. While watching it I had been muttering to Ruth: 'He is wrong... he is wrong, why hasn't he studied Éric de Bisschop's voyages and theories?'

So when she asked 'What are we going to do now?' meaning 'what are you...', I answered 'I want to build a double canoe and sail it across the Atlantic to prove Heyerdahl wrong and Éric de Bisschop right'. For a twenty-five year old this was quite a statement, but fortunately my partner, a German woman of the 'trümmel frau' era, had the courage to listen and not immediately walk away.

Éric de Bisschop's *The Voyage of the Kaimiloa,* first encountered in Manchester Central Library, became the first book in my own sea library; I still have it.

It was the book that first opened my mind to a life of sea adventure; it was the book that made me aware of the sea, not as a barrier, but a pathway to the world; it was the book that made me aware of the Pacific and its amazing 'people of the sea'. In the nine opening years of my adult life, from age sixteen to twenty-five, its idea was a *leitmotif,* always on the edge of my dreamtime unconsciousness.

In the book de Bisschop tells of his two incredible small-boat journeys that began in Shanghai, China, in the early 1930s. The first was on a 40-ton, approximately 60ft long, Chinese junk he built some 1000km up the Yangtze river. She was subsequently wrecked in a typhoon off Taiwan. Undaunted, however, with his friend and year-long crew, Tatibouet (a Breton) he returned to China and within three months built a 40ft junk, *Fou Po II*. De Bisschop and his friend sailed her through the Philippines, the Dutch East Indies, North Australia, Papua New Guinea, Melanesia and then on to the atoll of Jaluit in the Marshall Islands. The purpose of this voyage was to study ocean currents and the possible migration routes of the people who had settled in the Pacific islands.

This was in the 1930s, a period when the Marshall Islands were under Japanese control. Knowing nothing of sailing heroes they jailed de Bisschop and Tatibouet as spies. But somehow de Bisschop talked his way into release, enabling them to continue their 2500-mile voyage to Hawaii.

De Bisschop's determination to study ocean currents meant slow progress, which almost resulted in disaster. Unbeknown to the two Frenchmen, in their search for evidence of spying the Japanese had opened Eric's sealed food containers. This was only discovered one and a half months into the voyage when the smell in the food lockers revealed that their basic food stores had rotted. Over a month of near starvation followed, and on reaching the Hawaiian islands, they managed to anchor off the leper colony of Kalaupapa, from where the locals carried de Bisschop and his friend into the hospital.

De Bisshop and Tatibouet had sailed over 10,000 miles against the prevailing wind and currents of the Pacific Ocean. For this reason alone they should be honoured as great pioneering small-boat sailors.

Having inflicted much hardship during their voyage to Hawaii, fate was to administer yet another blow. In his hospital bed Éric de Bisschop received news from a friend that the previous night's storm had broken loose the anchored *Fou Po II* and had smashed her to pieces on the rocks. He had lost everything including his precious notes of his ethnographic studies. Tatibouet offered to build the distraught Eric a new junk to which he answered, 'Oh, my good Tati, not a junk this time, we are going to build a Polynesian double canoe… the type of sailing ship Polynesians used in former days to cross the Pacific'.

The book goes on to describe him arriving in Honolulu and being greeted by an excited American press; how in twelve months he designed and built his 38ft double canoe *Kaimiloa*; and how he met and fell in love with a beautiful Hawaiian princess, Papaleaiaina.

As a young man I was more interested in his double canoe. I wanted to know in detail precisely how he had designed and built the first modern catamaran. With hindsight, however, I now understand that de Bisschop was, in fact, describing not so much his double canoe, but his head-on conflict with 'academics' of the Bernice P. Bishop Museum of Hawaii. He disagreed with their opinions and derided the canoe models exhibited in the Museum, describing them as: 'Picturesque models manufactured to please the inquisitive tourist.' He did not seem to care that he had made bitter academic enemies who would later help to write him out of sailing history.

After the launching of *Kaimiloa* in 1938, the story continues to describe the incredible voyage they made across three oceans to France via the Torres Straight and South Africa in the winter. *Kaimiloa* proved to be incredibly seaworthy and survived several severe storms.

The academic issue of the 1920s and '30s was the origin of the central Pacific peoples, the same issue that Heyerdahl started to explore on Fatu Hiva in 1936. How had they arrived in those mid-ocean islands? They certainly had not walked—the only way was by watercraft. If they had come from Asia, they must have sailed thousands of miles against the prevailing winds and currents—this is the route Éric de Bisschop had sailed aboard his *Fou Po II* in his personal attempt to prove it was possible.

Eighteenth century European sailors had accepted the Polynesian outrigger and double canoes as seagoing craft, able to sail to windward, but by the twentieth century, under the influence of missionaries and colonial administration, those same canoe craft were being described as *unseaworthy* and *unable* to sail to windward. It was this premise that contributed to Heyerdahl's theory that the peoples must have come from South America on sailing rafts. What Heyerdahl either did not know, or chose to ignore, was that Éric de Bisschop had made his voyage half way round the world on a Polynesian double canoe in the late 1930s, just after Heyerdahl's sojourn on Fatu Hiva, and had thereby proven that such boats could have made the west-to-east migrations into the Pacific.

Sitting on that pontoon in Düsseldorf, Ruth listened quietly as I poured out my thoughts on Heyerdahl and Éric de Bisschop and ancient Polynesian migrations. Ending with 'I want to prove Éric de Bisschop right by building a double canoe and sailing it across the Atlantic!'

5 Tangaroa

L ooking back in time, my 'I want to' seems ridiculous, a juvenile fantasy. I was twenty-five years old, I had no inherited money, no trade, no profession; I was a dreamer. Ruth sat quietly and replied, 'I will help you, but only if you put all your best effort and all your abilities into the project', 'Discipline' had entered into my life. Then being practical she asked 'How much will it cost?' Around that time there was a small book on sailing by Weston Martyr called *The £200 Millionaire* so I quickly said: 'Oh about £200', (£200 in 1954 is approximately equal to £5500 in 2019). We sold our *Annie E. Evans* to two river policemen and returned to England.

On the way back to my parents' home in Manchester we stayed in London to visit the Science Museum in south Kensington, with its marvellous collection of Chinese junk and Pacific canoe models. There I found exhibited a model of a twenty-four-foot double canoe with a beautiful hull shape made in 1935 by an old Polynesian islander in the Society Islands. I bought a photograph of this model and decided to use this boat as a base for my Polynesian double canoe. At twenty-four feet it could be built within my limited budget.

The hull shape of the model was quite slender so with this as a starting point I had to redesign the hull shape for loading up with sufficient stores to cross the Atlantic from Britain to the tropical isles of the West Indies, a voyage which would be of similar distance and sea conditions as a long Pacific sea voyage.

A great help in my design research was that Manchester Central Library sought out for me a book entitled *Canoes of Oceania* written by Haddon and Hornell, published in Hawaii in 1936. It was a compendium of all that was known of Pacific canoe-form craft, from the past and still in existence in the 1930s, with drawings and descriptions of their construction and sailing observations by the early explorers.

Strangely, the book that gave the minimum design information to me was *The Voyage of the Kamiloa* by my hero Éric de Bisschop! His brief description of ancient Polynesian design was:

...instinctively I realize why Polynesian sailing craft of old like those of many islands of today, are shaped like half-moons with lines obviously as fine as possible on account of leeway, but with their submerged lines increasing the displacement...

...it is not so very idiotic; to preserve the mode of construction of the Polynesians, who in their seagoing craft started from the initial principle of the dug-out, adding to it, in order to increase freeboard, as many planks as were necessary.... I have discarded the usual keel; in its stead, a thick beam carved to shape, on the top of which we have nailed the planking of the hull.

With the scant knowledge and experience I had at this time, this gave me no help at all, so I Westernised the beautiful curved Tahitian canoe, which I had seen in the Museum, into a hard edged, long, narrow American dory style hull. I decided to call my double canoe *Tangaroa* after the father god in the Polynesian pantheon.

For building material I decided to use 4ft by ⅝in pine planks, beautiful clear red pine, which were available at reasonable cost; marine grade plywood was still hard to get and expensive. As they were shorter than the boat, I placed them diagonally on the hull sides—inspired by my sojourn at Thorneycroft, where they built motor torpedo boats using diagonal planking—and crosswise on the flat bottom. Looking now at the structural aspects of the design I am amazed how much I already understood of the subject. The edge-glued planked hulls, the watertight bulkheads—as used on Chinese Junks and on *Kuimiloa* the diagonal bracing on the inner hull sides to prevent hogging, the outer wales to tie it all together, all gave strength with lightness as well as the safety of watertight compartments.

Throughout my wandering years my father had kept a despairing eye on his disappearing dream of a major Wharram construction firm. Whenever I needed money, he would casually mention that 'so and so building firm is setting up a major project. As a labourer you will be sure to get a job' and I would always get taken on when I applied. Many years later I realised that he must have 'put in a word' to the inner group of building project managers. I also suspect the word was 'give him a hard time'. I was always at first given the nasty jobs, but when I would say I was leaving, there was frequently a hanging silence that said, I should stay, prospects were there.

The building job that I took to raise the money for my *Tangaroa* was at the

Ruth and Jim, **Tangaroa** *build*

construction site of an office block, where they were making a framework of rein-forced concrete floors and pillars to be walled in later. In the mid-1950s concrete was delivered from the mixer to the wooden forms by a large two-wheeled barrow, and as a labourer that was my job. When they saw that I understood 'structure', I was moved to being a part of the wood-working team that made the forms out of thick plywood to pour the liquid concrete into. I was unaware at the time that I was learning about the strength and possibilities of plywood, as an easy to use, hardwearing, load-bearing material.

The ply they used for the concrete shuttering was of Douglas Fir; it looked rough and often had voids in its inner layers. Seeing it covered with releasing oil and con-crete, at no time did I think of it as a suitable boat building material. At that time in 1954 plywood was being used for boatbuilding, but it was always very expensive, tropical hardwood ply, with guaranteed glue and wood specifications, bearing a British Standard kite mark. Such plywood was too expensive for my dreamboat.

In our lunch break we would sit in the site office and while the other navvies were fooling around throwing crusts of bread, I would sit in the corner studying my pre-cious library book *Canoes of Oceania*. These men may have been rough, but they had kind hearts and always treated me respectfully; they called me the 'professor' as I wore glasses and always had my nose in a book.

Working high up on the office block, which was on the edge of town, I could see a small farm. Passing it on my way home one evening I asked the young farmer 'do you have a shed I could build a small boat in?' He thought it was a great joke, but for a small weekly sum he would clear the chickens out of the loft and I would have a boat shed, 'Providing you can get the boat out of the shed without damaging it'.

Whilst I was pushing loads of cement around, dismantling and re-assembling giant plywood mould boxes, Ruth, with the constraints on her work choices through being an 'enemy alien', worked as a domestic cleaner in the nurses' accommodation in a nearby hospital. She subsequently said 'It was the easiest job I ever had'.

By March of 1954 we had enough money for me to stop working and begin build-ing in the farm loft. I cleared the chicken shit out, blocked up the gaps in the walls and levelled the floor. Building a small boat alone is like an exercise in meditation; through-out the summer I worked on my dream. The boat could have been built faster, but my father along with his head carpenter would occasionally visit to see my progress. This head carpenter was of the same ilk as the boat builders I had worked with at Thorneycroft. Each visit was like an examination.

On her days off, Ruth would come to sand, paint and put her feminine spirit into the boat. She was not the only feminine spirit; another young German girl, Jutta, visiting my English friends came to the boatshed and asked: 'Can I help?' To test her sincerity I gave her the unpleasant job of painting inside the small end hold. She did it without complaint. Then one day she said: 'I would like to sail the oceans with you'. I knew that my planned voyage across the Atlantic on this small double canoe, to prove Thor Heyerdahl's theories wrong, could be very hard and possibly very dangerous for a young outsider. Éric de Bisschop had shown that the double canoe was seaworthy, however his *Kaimiloa* was 38ft long; my little double canoe was only 23ft 6in. Éric had sailed thousands of miles across oceans even before his double canoe voyage. I was a beginner at offshore sailing and to encourage a young girl to join as crew was not sensible. I pointed out the hardships and danger that we might meet on the voyage. Her answer was: 'I was in Berlin when the Russians came, I know and have seen hardships'. At that time the story of these wartime hardships and horrors was not generally known outside Germany. I did not fully realise what, as a girl of nine, she had seen and experienced. So I gave a grudging promise of 'maybe' and she returned to Germany.

By September I had finished the boat in the barn loft, got it down to ground level without damaging the loft or the boat, and assembled the two red painted hulls, with their uniting beams on which I laid the slatted decks, into my darling little *Tangaroa*.

Compared to my adventurous hard living in the mountains, the accommodation on *Tangaroa* seemed luxurious. Others described it as living in two coffins, or more politely two wardrobes on their sides. I decided to launch *Tangaroa* on the Thames estuary. From Manchester to Burnham-on-Crouch in Essex was about 200 miles. Some young friends who were starting up in the building trade said if I gave them some help to finish a contract, they would load up *Tangaroa* on their lorry and transport the boat, Ruth and myself 'free' to Burnham.

We loaded up, collected our last gear from my parents' house and said our goodbyes. Driving down the road I realised I had forgotten something and went back to find my strong, powerful mother weeping. Adventure for sons can be anxiety and sorrow for mothers. However I grabbed my forgotten gear, joined Ruth and my friends on the

lorry and off we went. My building friends had a great time unloading the boat, assembling it and launching it. They drank the launching beer and sped back to Manchester to their next week's work.

I climbed on board alone. 'Hello *Tangaroa*' I whispered. Ruth joined me. We looked into the hull compartments—no leaks! Next day Ruth and I together struggled to raise the tall mast. Still sweating we hoisted the sails, truthfully quite small compared to my later boats. *Tangaroa* 'took off', she leaped forward out of control; I had never experienced such rapid boat acceleration—and, out of control, we rammed her into a mud bank.

Dejectedly I hauled the sails down, bitterly thinking my design was a failure, and who was I to recover the lost art of Polynesian double canoe sailing? Ruth made me a cup of tea and began the woman's job of rebuilding a man's ego. Encouraged, we hauled off the mud waist deep in cold muddy water and tried again. This time *Tangaroa* tacked and tacked again—we had a sailing boat.

But it was late in the autumn and to sail down the English Channel and across the Bay of Biscay would have been tempting the sea gods. On advice we sailed up the River Colne to spend the winter in the waterside village of Wivenhoe, to get jobs and wait until springtime.

I have described how step-by-step I learned aspects of life, boat design and boat building. By chance Wivenhoe gave me my final study course in the attitudes I needed to become an ocean sailor.

Sailing up the river Colne we passed a tall shed-like building, behind which the village of Wivenhoe came into view. We spotted a simple wooden walkway over the mud, to which we tied up, and went ashore to a row of small cottages. One had the message 'Notice—boats and gear stored at owner's risk' beside the door.

Out of the cottage came a small, alert white-haired man, wearing a peaked cap and a dark blue fisherman's sweater, bearded with pipe in mouth. Bob Eves, eighty years old, was a retired legendary barge skipper who first went to sea at the age of twelve in 1886. He spent most of his life sailing flat-bottomed, leeboard, spritsail barges up to 80 feet long. Such sea craft were once a major transport system in the Thames and coastal waters. Their captains were men of legend.

Interviewing him in his small living room as to whether we could moor our boat on his pontoon for the winter, we struck an immediate rapport. He later came to refer to me as his 'Mate'. This was an honour. Ruth impressed him just as much, as he later told us she reminded him of his beloved late wife.

Ruth got a job in a small sardine-canning factory; I got a job in the nearby town of Colchester as machine moulder in an iron foundry, a job I had done years earlier when I had looked for my dream boat in Sweden. When both of us returned 'home' Bob would have kettles of hot water ready so we could wash off the grime and fish oil. Then would begin the discussions and reminiscences; from Bob I learned to think as a 'Sailorman'.

Bob was not the only man of the sea in Wivenhoe. There was a solicitor in the village, John Donnelly, who in the immediate pre-war years had sailed around the world as bosun on a 118-foot engineless barquentine called the *Cap Pilar*. He was a traditional square-rigger ocean sailor. We used to babysit for him and he showed the concerned attitude of an older brother towards our sailing dreams.

Soon after we arrived in Wivenhoe, the cottage next door to Bob was bought by a tall, grey haired Mr Cully, as his retreat from a 'somewhere upcountry' wife and domesticity. He had been a judge in Siam—now Thailand—where, at the same time as the *Cap Pilar* was circumnavigating the world, he had a 45ft schooner built in the finest teak, from the board of the great American schooner designer John Alden. With a crew of four Malays he sailed her to Britain via the Red Sea and the Suez Canal, just before the 1939–45 war broke out. At that time not many yachts had made such a voyage. He made his at the same time as Éric de Bisschop was sailing his *Kaimiloa* from the Pacific to France via the Cape of Good Hope.

There was also a dear old man in the village called 'Tiny' (John) Howlett, being looked after by his devoted Chinese servant. I still have a copy of his book, *Mostly about Boats*.

All these men circulated around the Nottage Institute, set up in the 1890s to train local working boat sailors and transform them into professional yacht crews. There, during that winter, Ruth and I learned how to sew sails in the traditional method, stitching by hand. These experienced small boat sailors treated us as serious-minded pupils, indeed Wivenhoe at that time was a sea version of the early medieval universities I have described earlier.

PEOPLE OF THE SEA

What shall we tell you? Tales, marvellous tales

Of ships and stars and isles where good men rest,

Where nevermore the rose of sunset pales,

And winds and shadows fall towards the West.

James Elroy Flecker

6 First pioneering voyage

I n spring 1955 Ruth and I hoisted the sails on *Tangaroa* and left Wivenhoe. In September of that year, one thousand miles later, we sailed into Falmouth. We were not alone: Jutta had corresponded with us throughout the winter making it quite clear she too wanted to live 'outside the box' so *Tangaroa*'s first thousand-mile voyage had included retracing the voyage of *Annie E. Evans* across the English channel, up the Rhine to Emmerich, just over the German border from the Netherlands, where Jutta Shultze Rhonhof was waiting to be given her chance to sail on our tiny ship of legend.

I had been accustomed to more than one woman in my life at the same time, not in secrecy, but never together. However sailing a small boat is a totally different lifestyle than living on the land in a city—it creates a very close bond. Jutta integrated quickly, the two girls got on well together. They were happy to share 'their man'; there was no jealousy. By the time we were sailing into Falmouth we were that special inter-dependent unit, a 'small sail-boat crew'.

Sailing down the English coast we had attracted little interest, but in Falmouth we were starting to get noticed. Falmouth was, and is, the last major port before you sail away from England into the Bay of Biscay and onward to the oceans of the world. Biscay has a fearsome reputation, even more so in the mid-1950s, before the advent of modern electronic navigation. There is quite a list of people who have set out from Falmouth to sail the seas and returned a few days later, overwhelmed by the vastness and ferocity of the ocean.

The small, odd shaped double canoe with her two-girl crew attracted immediate attention from holidaymakers. The local boatmen would, in loud voices, prophesy break-up of the ship, drowning of the crew, and the waste of attractive women. Then they would syphon some of the crowd off for trips around the bay. However, national cinema Pathé News did interview me; a clip of the film (on YouTube) shows me young, gangly and telling the world I was a 'marine archaeologist' trying to prove the ancient Polynesian double canoe was a seaworthy craft. As the concept of 'marine archaeology' did not yet exist, it was quite a statement.

What kept my confidence up was that one night on the beach when the tide was out a quiet, gentle, but firm man came to the boat and asked me questions. He introduced himself as Captain Dell of the New Zealand shipping line. 'What flares do you have to attract attention?' I showed him my simple flare system, a paraffin soaked rag on a metal shaft, I also showed him my charts, water, food and so on. I passed his inspections. Then he said, 'I will tell you when the weather conditions are right to get you clear of the land and into the Bay of Biscay'. Then, one evening, he came down to *Tangaroa* and said: 'Go early in the morning'.

Crossing the Bay of Biscay was hard, *Tangaroa* did not sail fast, we had head winds and endured a moderate gale, and so it took us ten days to arrive off the northern coast of Spain. Biscay is the sea test of many aspiring ocean sailors. It can be a miserable, frightening experience and many turn back, never to attempt it again. I could have given up after the first awful couple of days, but persevered. I discovered I would get terribly seasick, and so did Jutta. Ruth, the woman who had never seen the sea before the age of thirty, had an iron stomach and never got sick. She did a fantastic job in navigating us across to Spain, with minimal instruments. This tough voyage gave us the confidence that little *Tangaroa* was a fit ocean-going boat.

As it was late in the year and the winter gales soon started, we spent the winter in Ribadeo, Galicia, Spain. This part of my life is described in my book *Two Girls Two Catamarans*, so I will keep it brief.

In 1955 Spain was still exhausted from its civil war. The Guardia Civil was an ever-looming presence, they thought at first we were spies having sailed in by night on our small boat. Fortunately we found a friend in Pepe de Sela y de Torres, a local man from an ancient noble family impoverished by the civil war, who stood guarantor for us. We were absorbed into the Sela household, and Pepe and his family became my lifelong friends. Though we could not speak each other's language, in general outlook and life interests Pepe and I had so much in common that we could communicate via a dictionary, hand waving and sketches. Ruth and Jutta were immersed into the feminine household of the three Sela sisters and Pepe's wife, the impish, ever-smiling, quick moving Marichu.

Ribadeo was incredibly beautiful. Workboats still used lateen sails. Sea-going

Jim with Jutta and Ruth at Falmouth

tunny-fishing boats fifty to sixty feet long were being built out of the local Gallego pine. Trees were hand sawn in a sawpit into planks. Final shaping was done skilfully by that ancient tool of man, developed thousands of years ago in the Stone Age, the hand adze, now made of steel with a short wooden handle. Ox carts with solid wooden wheels and axles were still in use.

By spring 1956 the winter storms were over; we had to part from our Spanish family and sail on, out of the Bay of Biscay, around Cape Finisterre and down the Portuguese coast to Lisbon. The spring weather was not perfect: our log records that we rounded the Sisarga Islands (where Nelson lost one of his ships) heading out against the Atlantic seas close hauled in winds of force 5–6. Our tiny, crude flat-bottomed double canoe proved that such Polynesian type craft could sail to windward. We sailed down the Iberian coast from one small fishing port to the next.

Over the centuries local fishing boat types have evolved depending on the kind of beach they would land on. Boats were developed on the Spanish and Portuguese coasts that could surf in on the big Atlantic waves. Landing on a beach from a surfing wave in a small boat needs every hand to push and pull it out of the waves to dry land. As a sailor and one-time fisherman myself, I would be there, thigh deep to give the final lift and heave. I was able to say in my then adequate Spanish 'soy un pescador'; if there was a good catch of fish I was given a token share. At the same time I was learning more about boat design.

Nowadays you can learn small boat design academically, but for thousands of years all over the world one learned design by visual observation and 'feel', learning to sense through your whole body the dynamic forces exerted on a boat. Aspects of these 'off the beach' coastal fishing craft sank into my design consciousness; I became aware of how overhangs and flare in the bow and stern gave lift over the waves. These elements of design, learned 'through the skin' on the beaches of Portugal, I later applied to my second catamaran design, *Rongo*, which I designed after sailing *Tangaroa* across the Atlantic.

Continuing our voyage on *Tangaroa* we arrived in Las Palmas on Gran Canaria, this being the main departure point for an Atlantic crossing. Today the Canary Islands are a major holiday destination. Las Palmas harbour is full of boats from northern Europe and the Mediterranean waiting for the end of the hurricane season in the West Indies to sail across the Atlantic. Some join the Atlantic Rally for Cruisers (ARC) to sail in a fleet, all in constant touch with each other and their homelands through modern electronics.

In 1955, Gran Canaria was a sleepy island, impoverished from the Spanish Civil War. There was no tourist trade, no marina, no palatial yacht club. The island was a poor outpost of Franco's Spain. In the harbour at Las Palmas were three or four large British yachts flying the naval blue ensign granted only to the most exalted. They completely ignored us under our plebeian merchant 'red duster'.

Also in the harbour were two fishing boats with crews of Latvian and Austrian former SS officers who were heading to South America for immunity and safety. Then there was an American workboat known as a Tancook Whaler sailed by Fin, a singlehander. He had fought the Russians, but when drunk, which was often, he made it clear he did not like the SS men. Also in the harbour paddling around in a Klepper folding canoe was a young German, Dr Hannes Lindemann, who had also fought in Russia. We discovered he was planning to cross the Atlantic in his canoe.

Later in our stay arrived a Dane, Walter Westborg, a member of the Danish underground who with a boat had helped Danish Jews escape to Sweden. His boat was a small steel lifeboat totally enclosed with a cabin. He was ocean testing this lifeboat for a Danish shipping magnate. It was the ancestor of all enclosed modern lifeboats today.

Where the British yachtsmen snubbed us, these hard war-seasoned men treated my girls, Ruth and Jutta, in a polite and respectful way. There was something about the combined womanliness of Ruth and Jutta that brought out the best in these hard men. All over the world women have been associated with water and sea deities; as sea women my girls carried some emotional essence of this type of femininity.

There had been serious discussions between us as to 'should we sail?' for Jutta, with a soft happy smile on her face had announced: 'I think I am pregnant!'. It seemed to me my *Tangaroa* Polynesian dream was over; Jutta and her baby would have to come first. 'Don't be a fool' said Jutta confidently, 'It will be months before the baby is due, by then we will have sailed the Atlantic'.

Without engines to power away from the Canaries we had to wait for the trade winds to 'set in'. The trade winds are the regular ocean winds caused by the rotation of the earth. It was by sailing from one trade wind system to another that our Western ancestors began their discovery of the world in the sixteenth century.

Those with engines had sailed when we finally set off two weeks before Christmas in light variable winds, hoping to reach the trade wind belt offshore, or that it would catch up with us. Overladen with food and water we crept out of Las Palmas.

In my life I have made seven Atlantic crossings, *Tangaroa* being my first ocean voyage and also the worst. Depending on the year, the Atlantic trade winds can be gentle, kind and a sailing joy, or they can be hard and cruel to small boats, with large waves tipped with foaming, crashing crests under cloudy skies. 1956–57 was such a year; *Tangaroa* was so burdened with stores that when steering I could reach sideways and trail my fingers in the sea.

The Atlantic crossing to Trinidad took over five exhausting weeks, during which we experienced problems with the two deep rudders. The steel rods through the gudgeons kept breaking, and repairing them was hard work and stressful. We also discovered the bottom of one of the hulls, which was built from pine planking, was being eaten by teredo worms, which must have got in during our long sojourn in Las Palmas. An improvised repair kept this sealed for the remainder of the voyage, but by the time we arrived in Trinidad, *Tangaroa* was no longer fit for more voyaging.

Our voyage on *Tangaroa* had taken sixteen months. We had sailed four thousand miles from Falmouth, across the Bay of Biscay, down the Spanish and Portuguese coasts to the Canary Islands, and across the Atlantic Ocean to Trinidad. We had sailed the first British catamaran, and also the smallest, across the Atlantic. We had proven that a simple twin-hulled sailing boat could take on a major ocean crossing and deliver her crew safely to their destination.

Before the days of yachting electronics—SSB radio, GPS, plotter, internet, satellite phone—once out of sight of land one was alone. For us the vastness of the sea space, the feeling of changes in the wind, the cloud patterns, resonated in our inner consciousness. In my sailing life I have met a number of single-handed ocean cruising sailors who behind their onshore banter carry a stillness with them that radiates inner calm, a special awareness, and strength. They are like shamans.

I had sailed with two women, one young, the other more mature. Due to their experiences during the war years both had seen male boasting masculinity fail. During our long and arduous voyage my male energies intertwined with their female energies, which were responding to the wildness of the seas and the power of the wind. This awareness and respect of these deep female energies would explain my later life attitudes.

7   Trinidad, a raft, and a new catamaran

On the Atlantic voyage I had learned a lot. My inner self had absorbed the 'feel' of the ocean. With this new knowledge, combined with my studies of the seagoing fishing boats in Portugal and Spain, Éric de Bisschop's book, and my earlier studies of *Canoes of Oceania*, I was ready to design another double canoe: a bigger one that could better withstand the hardships that we had suffered on *Tangaroa*. But first we had to find somewhere to live.

On arrival in Port of Spain it was very soon made clear that aspects of colonial rule still existed, as Customs and Immigration asked us for a 'bond' of £100 each for permission to stay on the island. I refused to pay this and challenged the customs officer: 'I will pay this bond only if Trinidadians pay the same when they come to live in Britain.'

Trinidad at that time was a vibrant, humming society; along with the other Caribbean islands of Jamaica and Barbados it had just been given its independence, and there was hope that there should be a Caribbean Federation, consisting of all the former British Caribbean island colonies.

That ideal was failing. Politicians excepted, people in Trinidad did not care. Trinidad was a racial melting-pot; as well as native Americans there were Africans descended from slaves, Portuguese, Chinese, and Indians imported from the British Empire to labour on the sugar plantations; together they produced a lively racially-mixed group of people. Everywhere people were hammering out 45-gallon oil drums into wonderful percussion instruments and forming 'steel bands'. Alongside, but separate, there was the old English colonial class, who lived expensively in 'white areas', where we could not afford to live.

The first person we met on landing at Port of Spain was a Chinese-Indian young man, who introduced himself as Ken Ali. He was a keen small-boat racing sailor. Ken Ali advised us to up-anchor and move up the coast to his and other young Trinidadians' new mixed (race) yacht club along the coast at Cocorite. The officials in Port

Rongo's voyage from Trinidad to UK, 1958-59

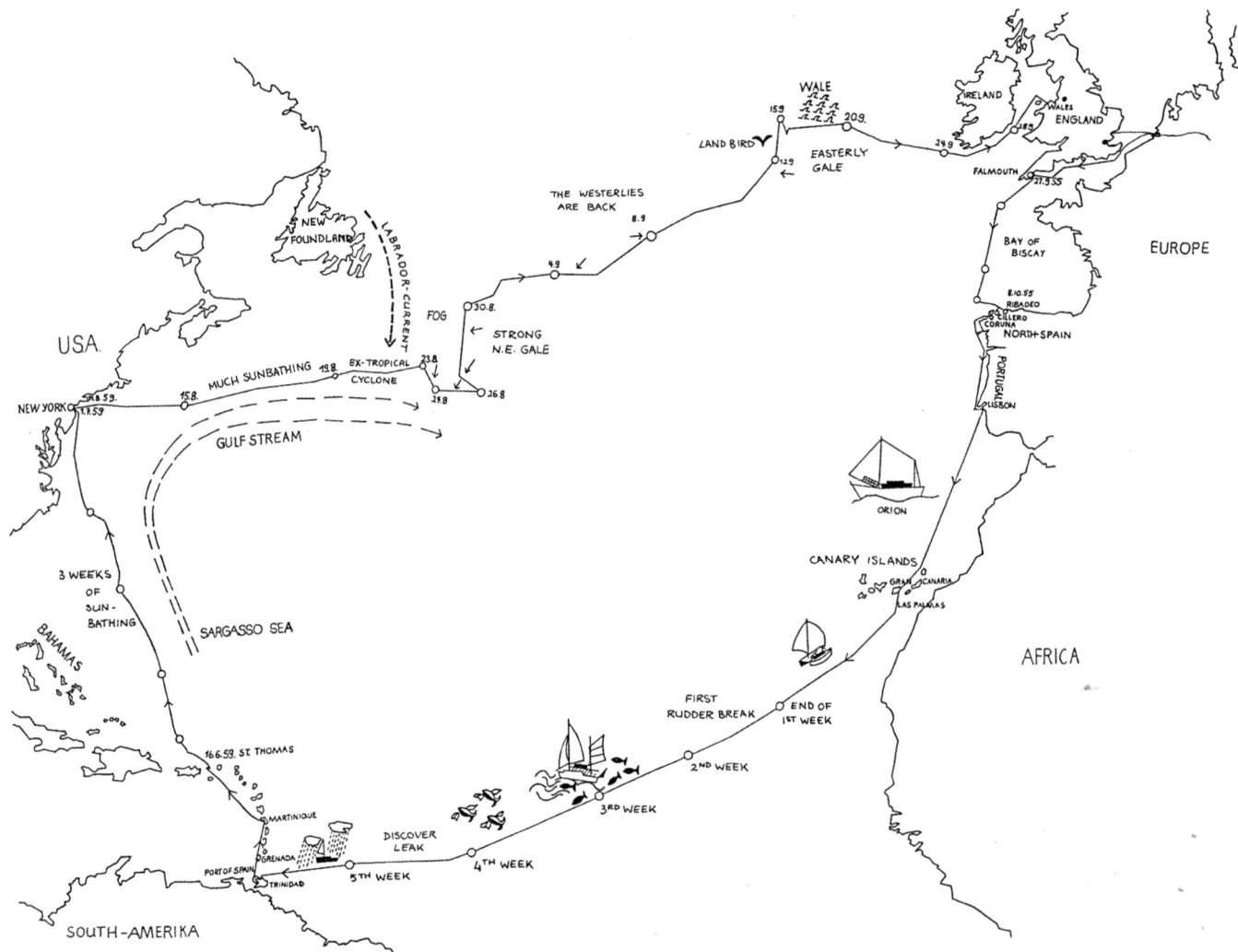

WALE
159   209.
LAND BIRD
EASTERLY
GALE
12.9

THE WESTERLIES
ARE BACK
8.9

IRELAND
WALES
ENGLAND
8.9
24.9
FALMOUTH
21.3.55

BAY OF
BISCAY

EUROPE

NEW
FOUNDLAND
LABRADOR-CURRENT
FOG
4.9

30.8.
STRONG
N.E. GALE

USA.

MUCH SUNBATHING 13.8.
EX-TROPICAL
CYCLONE 23.8.
21.8   26.8.

NEW YORK
24.6.59.
1.7.59
15.8.

GULF STREAM

8.10.55
RIBADEO
LILLERO
CORUNA
NORTH-SPAIN

PORTUGAL
LISBON

ORION

3 WEEKS
OF
SUN-
BATHING

SARGASSO SEA

CANARY ISLANDS
GRAN CANARIA
LAS PALMAS

AFRICA

BAHAMAS

16.6.59. ST. THOMAS

MARTINIQUE
DISCOVER
LEAK
GRENADA
PORT OF SPAIN
TRINIDAD   5TH WEEK   4TH WEEK

3RD WEEK

2ND WEEK

FIRST
RUDDER BREAK   END OF
1ST WEEK

SOUTH-AMERIKA

Tangaroa's voyage from UK to Trinidad, 1955-56

of Spain were glad to see the back of us. In Cocorite, we met Ken's Chinese mother and Indian father. Jutta's pregnancy was discussed and was seen as 'no problem', but where to live *was* a problem. The sea-battered 23ft 6in *Tangaroa* under a hot tropical sun was not a place for a young expectant mother.

I decided to build a houseboat to moor off the yacht club, but the cheap wood I was promised was useless. Fortunately a new white friend, Cliff Potter, offered for us to stay at his house a while and in return asked me to help him build a 16ft Shearwater catamaran from a kit he had bought from the Prout brothers in England.

In the comfort of the Potters' house I read in a *Time* magazine about my hero Éric de Bisschop making a voyage across the Pacific on a bamboo sailing raft. This gave me inspiration. With bamboo growing thick and fast on Trinidad I decided I could build a Kon-Tiki style raft for us to live on. Using a machete I chopped loads of 50ft bamboos, to lash into bundles to make bamboo-logs for my raft. Ruth and I started to build it while Jutta stayed at the Potters' preparing for her baby to be born.

Around that time there was a new birthing theory by a Doctor Grantley Dick Read, which advocated that the father should be part of the birth. The face of the matron of the private nursing home expressed her horror at such a new concept, but I out-faced her and was present at the birth of our son Hannes, who was named after Dr Hannes Lindemann who we had met in Las Palmas on his Klepper canoe. On arrival in Trinidad we received a letter telling us he had managed to successfully cross the Atlantic. He had capsized many times, but had survived due to the outrigger float he had built at my insistence.

Jutta and baby Hannes went back to the 'white luxury' of the Potters' house, while Ruth and I finished building the raft. We then moored it offshore near the Cocorite Yacht Club in crystal clear water where the on-shore land breezes kept us cool—and away from the mosquitos. It was paradise!

A week or so after the birth Jutta, with her baby, was rowed out to her new home. She collapsed into tears. 'It's beautiful', she said, 'Just beautiful!' And so it was; with its thick cooling coconut-fronded roof, and split bamboo woven walls letting in dappled light and cool air, it was magical.

I had sold the story of our Atlantic crossing to an English newspaper for £1000— we had money! And after many hard years, I drifted. We swam in the sea, enjoyed living and our new baby. Sometimes we did not go ashore for days. I started to write a book about our voyages and Polynesian Pacific migrations in which I would show the theories of Thor Heyerdahl were wrong and those of Éric de Bisschop right. I was also drawing a new catamaran design on which to continue our ocean voyages.

Then one day two battered small yachts dropped anchor beside our 'raft' home. They had just sailed in from South Africa. They had the same problem on arrival in Port of Spain as we had had, being asked for a 'financial bond' to stay in Trinidad. When they, like us, refused to pay, they were given the advice: 'go further up the coast and anchor near that raft at Cocorite.' The single-handers that sailed these two yachts were Bernard Moitessier and Henry Wakelam.

The Frenchman Bernard Moitessier was one of the first 'ocean wanderers'. Some of them are like Christian monks, anchorites, or the Hindu and Buddhist holy men, who wander the earth in search of God and infinity. They use being alone on the vast ocean on their small sailing boats to find their inner spiritual connection with the infinite. Bernard was such an ocean wanderer. In contrast, on the other small boat was Harry Wakelam— a practical engineer, with a heartening grin—a lover of food, wine and women.

Aboard our raft, Bernard very quickly appraised my mental situation. He looked at the sun-dappled golden beauty of the raft interior, the goddess-like women, the pile of manuscript of the book I was writing, nearby an easel with a drawing board on which I had drafted out my next dreamboat to sail back on the ocean. With clear sharp French logic, Bernard summed up the situation: 'You must build that boat and sail, otherwise you will rot here in this paradise.'

Bernard made the decision for me, but it was Harry Wakelam who pushed and helped to make the first practical steps to make a base on which to build my new 40ft design, to be called *Rongo* after another Polynesian god. With the aid of Ken Ali and his friends we located large timbers for the base. We also found a perfect place to build the boat—under the shade of a mango tree, outside the house of Ken Ali's parents. With a place to build, Harry Wakelam's physical drive and Bernard's mental enthusiasm, we soon had the first bulkheads up and the vision was becoming the reality.

Secure that I was on the right path, Bernard and Harry sailed off again on their voyages. I carried on helped by a professional Barbadian boat builder, Mr. Gaskin, and Jutta's practical artistic abilities, as she was freed from continuous mother-care by Ken Ali's Chinese mother Ma and her daughters, who all loved baby Hannes.

In designing *Rongo* I combined all I had learned in the previous years of ocean

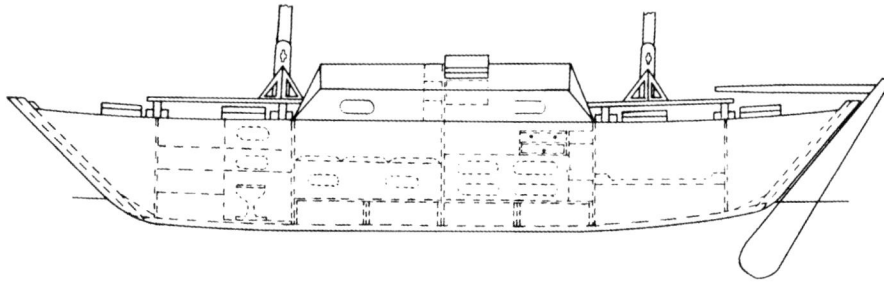

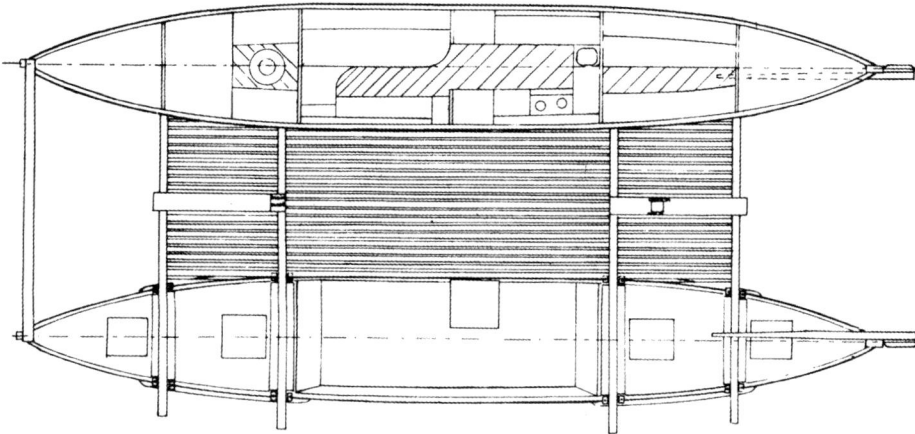

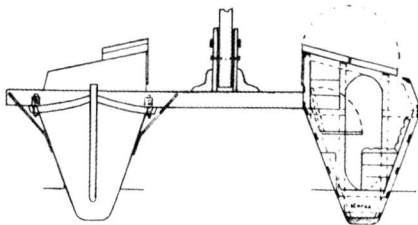

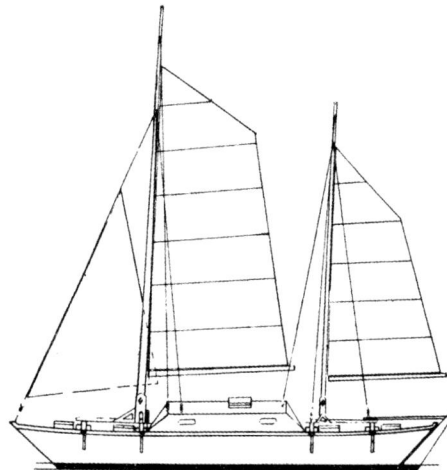

Rongo design

sailing and studying boats I had seen on the way. I now understood the descriptions Éric de Bisschop had given in his book, so I adopted a hull profile similar to Éric's *Kaimiloa*, with a rockered keel, raked stem and stern posts with good overhangs, and flare to give lift when riding large ocean waves. I remembered how the flaring hulls of the Portuguese fishing boats had helped them to ride the large surf coming in to the beaches. I gave the hulls canoe sterns so they would be able to take the large following breaking waves I had seen smashing into the sterns of *Tangaroa*.

The flat bottoms of little *Tangaroa* had pounded in rough seas and her centreboard had created a lot of drag, so the hull cross section of my new *Rongo* would be a Vee'd section that would cut through the water and not need a keel or centreboard to sail to windward. I drew a narrower V than *Kaimiloa*, which had a 90 degree angle at the keel, for better windward efficiency.

I mounted the crossbeams with flexible connections as Éric had done on *Kaimiloa*. I devised metal fittings with rubber blocks that would compress like car shock absorbers when the boat strained over large waves. This would reduce stresses on the hulls and the beams. To be doubly safe I added some rope lashings from the beam ends to the hull sides as well.

With more money, which I had earned writing articles, than when I had started to build *Tangaroa* I was able to buy high quality Bruynzeel marine plywood, which was imported from Holland. *Rongo* was to be a far superior boat to little *Tangaroa*.

Back in England 'catamarans'*, as double canoes were now being called, were being designed and built by other designers. The Prout brothers, Roland and Francis, who came from a background in canoeing, had built the first Shearwater catamaran. This was a small 16ft day-racing craft and they were selling it in kit form. Clive Potter had bought a kit and I had helped him build it whilst living at his house. Then there was Bill O'Brien, an Irish aviation engineer, who was also designing small chined-hulled catamarans for day racing. His hull shapes were inspired by the floats of sea planes. Around this racing scene a new organisation was set up by a Dr John Morwood: the Amateur Yacht Research Society—AYRS. I had started a correspondence with Morwood from Spain after crossing the Bay of Biscay and continued writing to

---

*   The word catamaran is in fact a misnomer. Catamaran is a Tamil (South Indian) word meaning 'tied logs'; it was a word used by the British navy for the small rafts they used to work on the outside of naval ships.

him from Trinidad, telling him about my successful crossing of the Atlantic by catamaran. However I became disappointed and even angry when he delayed publishing anything about my Atlantic crossing in his magazine.

As we were building *Rongo* I heard about another 40ft catamaran, sailed by a Captain Butt, who was attempting the first crossing by catamaran of the Atlantic from North America to the UK. This was a setback, as I was planning to make this much harder Atlantic crossing and had wanted to be the first to do so in a catamaran. An even greater shock was that Captain Butt never arrived, proving how hazardous the North Atlantic crossing could be.

The full story of my voyage with *Rongo* has been written in my book *Two Girls Two Catamarans*. To be brief, *Rongo* immediately proved to be a fast and capable craft, outsailing a similar size racing monohull on her trial sails in Trinidad. After a few weeks of test sails we set off up the Caribbean to St Thomas.

In St Thomas we met up with a new 40ft catamaran called *Ay-Ay* by an American designer called Dick Newick. He was on board and invited me for a sail on her to nearby St Croix. Also on board was an American professor of psychology, a Dr John Lilly, who told me that after several years studying dolphins in his laboratory and aquarium, he had come to the conclusion that these sea-mammals were very much more intelligent than anyone had ever suspected. He was convinced that the intelligence of these cetaceans was higher than that of chimpanzees or gorillas, in some respects terrifyingly close to man. I quizzed him on the purpose of his studies and suggested it was for the US military. His answer to this was: 'classified'. I was to remember this conversation with John Lilly later on our *Rongo* voyage when we were surrounded by a huge pod of pilot whales.

From St Thomas we sailed 2000nm non-stop to New York, to an amazing welcome. As members of the Slocum Society—of ocean sailors, set up in 1955—we contacted John Pflieger, the Commodore, who straight away invited us to a dinner where the first person we met was Boris Lauer-Leonardi, the editor of *Rudder* magazine, who had published my articles on the voyages of *Tangaroa*. Many other famous ocean sailors attended this dinner, Count Grabowski, Jean Lacombe, Bruce Robinson, as well another budding catamaran designer, Bob Harris. This meeting led to other invitations and parties. After the struggle of the previous years it was good to feel honoured and appreciated.

First Jutta then I were invited on a popular television quiz show, 'Tell the Truth', where I met Sir Edmund Hillary. The audience had to choose who was the real Hillary from three contestants posing as the mountaineer, I being one. Ed helped me win, so I could buy a radio for our Atlantic crossing with the prize money.

I remember one cocktail party at the Smithsonian Institute where there was a discussion on whether the Vikings could have reached North America. The firm opinion was that Viking ships with their shallow draft could not sail to windward. I commented: 'I have just sailed a shallow draft double canoe 2000nm from Trinidad to New York', but the next cocktail was more interesting than pithy observations, so I moved on.

My mother flew out to New York to collect our son Hannes, as we felt we could not risk the life of a two year old on the dangerous voyage we were about to undertake.

Our crossing of the North Atlantic, like our crossing on little *Tangaroa*, was particularly hard. We encountered an ex-tropical cyclone and weeks of easterly winds, but *Rongo* proved the storm-riding, seagoing, and windward abilities of the double canoe of the ancient Pacific. We again had trouble with our deep rudders, even though I had made these much stronger than on *Tangaroa*. I had to cut the bottom off one of them in order to rehang it, which showed me that I did not need deep rudders to steer. It took us six weeks of hard sailing to reach the east coast of Ireland, and we became the first people to have crossed the North Atlantic from West to East in a multihull.

I will sum up our voyage with these quotes from *Two Girls Two Catamarans*, observations I wrote with the voyage still fresh in my mind:

Rongo rode powerfully over waves that would have had *Tangaroa* struggling. Jutta's favourite game was to sit astride the bow, trailing her legs in the sea. As we surfed down the face of the wave, the rushing seas would rise round her legs and thighs. She looked like a glowing figurehead as the water sparkled off her golden skin.

…How will a catamaran go to windward? How can a boat with only two feet draught without centreboards or fin keels, work its way against the wind and seas without sliding sideways more than going forward? These were the questions single-hulled yachtsmen had asked. *Rongo* showed us how it was done; she piled up on the lee-side of each bow a wedge of water and resting, as it were, her shoulders against this wedge, she fought her way forward, day after day.

...At last I began to understand the reason for my constant rudder difficulties. Deep rudders, sticking below the bottom of the hull like a fin, are common on single-hulled boats. They not only steer the boat well, they are also considered hydro-dynamically efficient and help to prevent leeway. For this reason I had used them on the *Rongo*. From the beginning I had regarded a catamaran as a superior raft made out of two canoe-shaped hulls, giving a craft the stability of a raft and the speed of a slim, narrow, canoe-shape. What was not apparent to Western sailors until I had sailed a few thousand miles, was that the behaviour of a raft or catamaran on the sea was different from that of a deep-keeled boat. When a wave hits the side of a keelboat, it rolls on its side and slithers sideways, dragging the keel and long rudder at an angle through the water, thus reducing the shearing strain. A catamaran, because it is a raft shape, cannot heel, so any projecting fin or rudder takes the full twisting strain as the craft gets knocked sideways by large storm waves.

...During our North Atlantic crossing I studied the action of Rongo's bows meeting the seas and watching how the overhangs of the boat and the 'flare' of the hulls (the Vee'd outward shape of the hull) first sliced the wave, then with increasing buoyancy lifted the hulls of Rongo over the wave tops without the sea washing over the bows. Rongo was like a living intellect 'thinking' its way through the seas. Perhaps the flexibility between the two hulls added to the feeling of a mobile life force supremely confident at its task.

...The masts, too, came under my scrutiny. I had made them solid with a big taper from the bottom end to the top, so that they could bend like a fishing rod under the wind gusts. As Rongo hammered into the sea, instead of a disrupting shockwave from the jerks of the hull, plus the wind gusts, tearing the conventional, rigidly built, hollow mast apart, my flexible masts nodded like trees absorbing the stresses and strains, then releasing them in a controlled flow.

...During the voyage I remembered Captain Butt. He had been last seen a year before on his forty-foot catamaran, Ocean Clipper, seven hundred miles out from England. After that he was never seen again. If we made it across the Atlantic we would be the first multihull to have done so.

Four years previously we had abandoned the land and like the ancient Polynesians turned to the sea. It had not been easy for us to adapt ourselves to the wide, featureless ocean but we had done it. The sea had remoulded our inner souls and on approaching the mainland of Europe, when we had a beautiful visitation of hundreds of pilot whales, we felt that this was perhaps the 'official' recognition of our status as 'People of the Sea'.

In my account of the North Atlantic crossing I already made comments on designing further catamarans. At one time I told Ruth when she relieved me during a night watch:

'Don't laugh, I have been designing in my head a little catamaran, bigger than our Tangaroa but smaller than the Rongo, in which other people can sail the seas.'

'At a time like this!' she said. 'You are a strange man, sometimes I think you are not of this world. That's probably why I love you'.

8   Planning to sail round the world

My father's positive evaluation of the quality of *Rongo*'s construction following her 4500-mile voyage from New York to Britain should have been sufficient praise, but in 1959 my arrival home as a sailing pioneer and ocean adventurer received a very mixed reception. I had unknowingly made one big mistake in New York whilst being interviewed by a British journalist on my proposed Atlantic voyage. He had asked me about my 'relationship' with the two girls. 'Oh, I love both of them equally' was my quick answer and then carried on with my explanations of Thor Heyerdahl, Éric de Bisschop and ancient sailing craft of the Pacific and so on. But still the resulting headline printed in a British national newspaper was 'Love Tangle on a Raft'.

In late 1959 the sexual revolution had not really got going in Britain. My return with two German 'fräuleins' overshadowed the two pioneering ocean voyages we had made: pioneering voyages that were the opening of a new chapter in yacht design—'the development of the multihull'. Still, I did get an article published in the *Manchester Guardian*, which soon after moved to London and became *The Guardian*; also an article in a delightful magazine called *The Yachtsman*. Apart from that our voyages were largely ignored.

Whether it was my 'too early' path into the sexual revolution of the '60s and '70s by living openly with two women, or my insistence on basing my designs on the sailing canoes of the ancient Pacific, it is so long ago I can't be certain. Added to this I was from the north of England and 'yachting' was largely the province of the southern privileged classes.

The result was that the English concept of the catamaran, exhibited at the January 1960 London Boat Show, was *Misty Miller* designed by Michael Henderson. It had two semi-circular section hulls similar in shape to those used by the Prout brothers for their 16ft Shearwater design, which were mounted on deep ballasted fin keels 'to prevent capsize', and had a mushroom float mounted on the top of the mast, just in case. As a design it was a dog's dinner of arrogant Western concepts imposed on the ocean-tested Polynesian double canoe of the Pacific seafarers. One American designer at that time referred to the Polynesians with 'what have we to learn of a bunch of bare arsed natives, riding on canoes tied together with bamboo poles?' *Misty Miller,* when subsequently sail tested, promptly capsized. Later, when the Prout brothers, who had made their name with their 16ft *Shearwater,* started to design cruising catamarans they produced the 27ft and 31ft *Ranger* class, which did not have deep keels and which had a high resistance against capsize through better worked out design.

On our arrival in Britain we had sailed *Rongo* up to North Wales, to the sheltered estuary of the Conwy river. This was not too far from my parents' house in Manchester, where we spent that winter of 1959–60. During this winter Jutta, who was an artist and had technical drawing skills, drew up a set of building plans of *Rongo,* which we offered for sale, so others could also build her. I think three sets were sold and two of them actually got built many years later, but this was not yet the start of my career as a 'multihull designer'.

After a winter in Manchester our dream plan was to sail once more across the Atlantic and into the Pacific via the Panama Canal, to sail to lonely Polynesian islands unspoilt by missionaries, and to study any remaining Pacific canoe craft. We wanted to explore the islands as Thor Heyerdahl and Éric de Bisschop had done and to learn all we could about these ancient Pacific explorers and sailors before the last of the elders died out.

The reason I was looking for islands 'unspoilt by missionaries' was that in 1820 the London Missionary Society was formed to go out to the newly discovered Pacific islands with the aim to 'convert the natives to Godly ways'. This meant making the women wear ankle-length shift dresses, even when swimming, and to put a stop to their guilt-free sex. This was cultural arrogance and blindness at a time when London, due to the poverty of the lower social classes, had thousands of prostitutes. Many of them were children, they lived in degradation and brutality, and often suffered an early death through disease.

When Captain Cook for Britain and Admiral Bougainville for France discovered the islands of the central Pacific in the late 1770s they found beautiful, naked people swimming around their anchored craft. They found a tolerant, happy, accepting, joyous sex culture.

Rongo refitted, with new rig, and Mayor of Conwy aboard

France at that time was moving towards social revolution. French philosophers saw the physical beauty and open, guilt-free sex as a survival of a 'mythical golden age' of man.

But less than fifty years later the British were sending protestant Christian missionaries into the Pacific to bring these Polynesian people 'to God', which meant 'their God', i.e. no nakedness or open sex. The French, in competition, were sending out catholic missionaries at the same time. Both were preaching the same message and in addition were saying: 'Polynesian sailing craft are dangerous.' To stamp them out they built Western style boats, which they controlled and were the only ships permitted to voyage between islands. They totally denigrated the indigenous double canoe craft, as these represented the islanders' freedom and sexual customs. What should be remembered here is that the Polynesian population had suffered terrible losses through diseases brought by the Europeans, hence did not have the strength to stand up for their culture.

This claim of the unseaworthiness of the Pacific canoe-form craft was still upheld over 100 years later by Andrew Sharp, a retired New Zealand civil servant, who in the mid-1950s wrote the book *Ancient Voyages in the Pacific*, still in my boat library, a book that when I read it in 1960 made my blood boil and gave me even more reason to prove the seaworthiness and ocean voyaging abilities of the Polynesian double canoe.

In this book Sharp wrote that the Pacific canoe craft could not sail to windward, waves would wash over their decks, and they would break up in storm conditions. He also denied there was any evidence their sailors could navigate over long distances. His opinion was that all migrations in the Pacific had been accidental drift voyages.

Hence my dream in 1960 to sail to the Pacific, to find islands free from missionaries as Heyerdahl and de Bisschop had done, and to study what I hoped was left of the canoe sailing culture.

At that time in Manchester there was a magazine on textiles called *Skinner's Silk and Rayon Record*. A friend advised me to write an article for them about *Rongo* and my use of a new synthetic rope (first on the world market) called 'Courlene'. When building *Rongo* in Trinidad I had used two or three hanks for my beam lashings. Mentioning this rope in my article brought the then great firm of Courtaulds, the makers of Courlene, down to visit me. Courtaulds also made new synthetic paints and they produced a new man-made material called 'Gannex' used for wind and waterproof clothing. The Courtaulds rep. did all he could to give us materials to fit out *Rongo* for her proposed exploratory voyage into the Pacific. We repainted her with the new synthetic paints and replaced all the rope with new man-made fibre. We were also given a lot of clothing made of the new nylon fabrics, indestructible stuff that we still owned many years later.

We also decided to change *Rongo*'s rig. The cotton fully-battened sails I had rigged her with in Trinidad were worn out and they were also hard to lower in a gale, as we had experienced on our North Atlantic crossing. I designed a new rig, inspired by the Polynesian rigs I had seen in drawings. Instead of a single mainsail, I divided this area up using a mizzen staysail above which I set an upside down triangular mainsail on a sprit. I called it a 'Polynesian sprit rig'. This upper triangular sail was fitted with brails, the use of which I had studied on Thames barges during my time in Wivenhoe, which meant we could brail up the sail in any wind conditions. It could then be lowered to the deck as a bundle.

In springtime 1960 Jutta, Ruth and I went back to Deganwy in the Conwy estuary in North Wales to start the refit of our *Rongo* for the proposed voyage. Even my parents joined us to help with burning and scraping off the old oil paint so we could apply the new synthetic paint.

During our refit I met Roger Murray, who has played a major part in my life and who is still my dear friend. He belongs to the treasured group of men who have given me help and advice; I have been very lucky in my male friendships. Roger was a gifted artist and worked in advertising at the *Empire News* in Manchester; he was negotiating a contract with his paper for my expedition, which would have covered expenses. Besides this he went out of his way to use his contacts to get other firms to sponsor me. Through him the Dunlop rubber company gave us one of the first inflatable life rafts for small boats. He also obtained for us steel bows and arrows for hunting in the jungles. Then sadly his newspaper collapsed and with it the chance of sponsorship.

Roger later moved to London to become advertising editor on *The Observer*. Roger still remembers me that first time I walked into his office; his first impression was of 'a tall, intense young man with strong charisma and determination'. Roger in his life since has worked as an artist, painting in Spain and Robin Hood's Bay in north Yorkshire; owned steam engines—which made him a close friend of Fred Dibnah (the famous steeplejack, who made many TV documentaries on Victorian engineering);

worked in the Ocean Youth Club; owned many boats, including canal boats; motor cycled across the Sahara desert—in other words he is a man of many talents; he is also a brilliant cartoonist and raconteur.

While looking for a new sponsor I became aware of David Attenborough, a new personality in nature programmes at the BBC, so I wrote to him, enclosing a film of me rock climbing in Derbyshire (taken by Ruth on a new clockwork Bolex 16mm cine camera), and explaining my dream of sailing the Pacific and learning from Polynesian elders the sailing stories of their ancestors. He wrote back that unfortunately his department was short of money, but he did send us an encouraging letter and 30,000 feet of 16mm colour cine film stock.

Deganwy was a beautiful place to be working on a boat on the beach; we looked out across the bay at the magnificent Conwy Castle, symbol of the medieval conquest of Wales by England. Above Deganwy dock was the distinctive hill called the 'Vardre', where it is said the great magical poet of history Taliesin meditated and wrote.

Rongo's refit was done and the mayor of Conwy said: 'I want to give your proposed voyage a civic mayoral send off '; this was an honour. The crowd was there, and the mayor in his valuable mayoral chain. The sky was dark and stormy looking. While on board for the official goodbye the mayor slipped and his prized chain disappeared into the sea, never to be seen again. Looking back I think it was an omen. Anchor up, dressed in our new 'Gannex' waterproofs, we were soon speeding out to the open sea. It was late in the autumn; soon it was dark as we headed from Wales westward into the Irish Sea.

During the night and the following day in rising winds and seas, I found *Rongo* would not steer straight. Easy steering is essential for an ocean sailing boat. In those days under stress, my mind would go into overdrive; I reflected on my former deep rudders, which had caused so many structural problems on my first two transatlantic crossings. In Wales I had sawed them off level with the keel. I concluded that the stern end of *Rongo*'s keel, which curved up to the sternpost, needed a skeg placed in front of the shortened rudder, just as an arrow needs feathers at its end to fly straight and true. To make and fit those skegs I needed a port, and to go back to Wales after the send-off was not an option; but to starboard lay the sheltered waters of the Irish coast, and Dublin, which with a following wind we reached easily. Sailing through the rain squalls into Dublin bay then into the port of Dún Laoghaire I was moving into another chapter of 'growing up' in my life.

9 Fate intervenes

In 1960 southern Ireland was still like Spain, a monolithic Catholic state. Yet behind the 'walls', and as in Spain, there were men and women beginning to 'question', like my friend Pepe de Selas in Galicia. The Irish are inherently a warm, friendly people, so I soon made friends. Dún Laoghaire harbour when the tide was out, with me working on my back under a blocked-up *Rongo* to attach the new skegs, was a great place to begin new friendships. It was hard work, not helped by the onset of the winter gales sending a swell into the inner harbour, but it was done. With the winter gales beginning, sailing across the Bay of Biscay was not a wise plan so we decided to wait for springtime.

I, as a male, was invited to use the Royal George Yacht Club's library. The Irish Naval guardian of the famous gun-running yacht *Asgard* had me aboard, yarning about the ship and how and where it carried rifles to start the 1916 rebellion. On shore we had friends who had fought as officers in the English army during the Second World War and friends who were members of the 'old' IRA in Northern Ireland who had fought against the English in the war. Then there was John De Courcy-Ireland, a friend whose ambition was to establish an Irish maritime museum (and after years of work he succeeded).

Everything seemed positive, then the Belgians decided to pull out of their African empire in the Congo and chaos erupted. As I have written, Ireland at that time was a monolithic catholic country; the TV and newspapers heavily reported on the rape of many white women, particularly the nuns. Over two to three days, hearing and seeing this news our quiet, gifted Jutta broke down. She had to be restrained from wishing to jump into the harbour and swim out to sea to join 'our friends' the dolphins we had met on the Atlantic voyage the year before.

I knew that Jutta as a nine-year-old girl had been living near Berlin with her nurse, sister and mother when the Russians came in, in 1945. She had told me the Russians gave her food. I only realised the full horror, degradation and rape of the women of

eastern Germany at the end of the war much later on, reading the book *Hour of the Women* by Christian von Krockow. Many Russians acted in revenge for the Russian women who had been raped by Germans.

I guessed that Jutta's breakdown was due to her war experiences, so I called in my Irish and English officer friends, and they answered 'Yes' to my query of the possibility of delayed post-war trauma. One officer had been an army doctor and now had a mental trauma clinic in Dublin where she could get treatment. I visited Jutta every day; the doctors and matron of the clinic warmed to this beautiful, adventurous, strong young girl. Ruth as always 'managed the crises' and Irish friends pointed out where I would be welcome as a boatyard manager with my practical and sailing experience.

Jutta was officially diagnosed as schizophrenic. The specialists at the clinic, after much consultation, were convinced that it would be best for Jutta if she carried on with her sea life. Her despair could be controlled and eventually cured by a new 'super drug' on the market called 'stelazine'. I told the matron Jutta would be cared for, but her reply was 'Keep her working, do not let her brood'.

So in the spring of 1961 we sailed away from Dún Laoghaire down the Irish coast, out into the Bay of Biscay, and towards Galician Spain and my friends in Ribadeo. With her new sail rig and her underwater-reconfigured skegs and rudders, *Rongo* sailed in a confident, dreamlike hiss. In my 'wander years' when I had lived with and was taught by Traudl in Vienna, I had learned a lot about the teachings of the psychologist philosopher Carl Jung and the 'archaic man' that is within us all. Sailing with two lovely women and a beautiful four-year-old son on a newly configured ocean-going double canoe, I reconnected with the inner archaic dream-self that I had known in my solo, teenage, moor and mountain wandering days.

In Ribadeo the Selas three sisters, Pepe, and his wife Marichu greeted us in the warm Spanish way as family. Our blond blue-eyed Hannes was admired and loved. Clothes were found for him and he was adopted into the Selas family. I discussed Jutta's withdrawn emotions with Pepe, my older 'brother-friend'. He gave me support and understanding. Little did I know that Pepe himself carried within him deep mental war wounds, from his experiences as a young man in the Spanish Civil War; wounds that resurfaced much later in his life as severe depression.

As in 1956 on *Tangaroa,* the sea dream brought an end to our stay. We left Ribadeo and sailed on down the Spanish and Portuguese coast as we had done five years earlier, stopping in Cadiz. There an old Jesuit priest befriended me. He was fascinated with *Rongo*, and in discussion with him I discovered his main boat interest was in the 'Zebec' (or Xebec), the ship type used from the sixteenth to eighteenth centuries by Algerian pirates, who in King Charles' reign were raiding southern Britain and Ireland for slaves. I have found an innate love of the sea and sailing craft in many very different people.

From Cadiz we sailed on and out to sea, well off the Moroccan coast, 700 sea miles to Las Palmas in Gran Canaria. It was five years since we had left there aboard *Tangaroa*. The port now had a small fleet of transatlantic yachts planning to sail off together once the winter trade winds had arrived and steadied.

On the day they departed, Ruth and I in our dinghy went out to sea to film them with the film stock given to us by David Attenborough. Jutta went shopping to the market. We had been told in Ireland at the nursing home to encourage her in activities. The fleet did not come out on time; in fact it was three hours before, one by one, they came before the lens of Ruth's camera. Arriving back at the harbour we found our bag of vegetables on the quay but no Jutta. We were agitated, but soon even more so. Our young friend Antonio arrived 'are you looking for Jutta? There has been an accident with a young woman!' Antonio led me to an unfinished building and there I found the broken body of my beautiful, golden haired, golden skinned Jutta. I had slept out in the winter snow, given public lectures and pioneered ocean sailing in an ancient sea craft, but in my inner self I was still a boy. I had never witnessed suffering or death and I went to pieces.

What had happened? Jutta had done her shopping and had sat waiting for us; close by was a partially finished building, which in its unfinished state, resembled wartime bomb damage. After the Russian army moved through Prussia in 1945 there was mass rape of German women (repaying many of the horrors visited on their own women). I learned years later that many German women, after the horrors of being raped, had leapt to their deaths from high buildings, and in Jutta's family an aunt or family friend with her two daughters had done just this. Left too long alone looking at the incomplete building Jutta had slipped back into the lost state she had developed in Ireland. Guided by horrific childhood memories, she had climbed the building and jumped.

While writing this book nearly sixty years after Jutta's death I discussed her illness with a German psychologist friend—she had read *Two Girls Two Catamarans* many times and identified with Jutta. Her assessment, on learning of Jutta's symptoms and suicide, was that she had not suffered from schizophrenia, but that it must have been delayed Post Traumatic Stress Disorder, caused by her experiences at the end of the war and triggered by the atrocities in the Belgian Congo. Maybe with present day knowledge of PTSD she could have had therapy and recovered. At the time such therapy did not exist.

Looking back on those horrific days I realised that I got incredible support. First from Ruth, who had successfully avoided much trauma during the Second World War, yet soon after became the quiet leader of four fellow female students at Tübingen University who, when it rained, had studied with umbrellas held over their heads as most of the roof tiles had disappeared during the bombing. Some of these women had seen and experienced terrible things.

With the stoicism of a war-experienced woman, Ruth took over, assisted by some people on other yachts, one of whom was Jewish, and I must record the generous help from the British Consul, who arranged to have Jutta buried at the English cemetery.

Some weeks later, with an Englishman, Clive, as crew, guided to us by the British Consul, we left Las Palmas and began our third voyage across the Atlantic. It was a beautiful voyage, the 40ft *Rongo* lifting easily over the seas that had battered the earlier, smaller *Tangaroa*.

Arriving in Trinidad was like 'coming home'. During our previous stay, when building *Rongo* we had made many friends; from Denis Solomon the son of the Prime Minister, to local fishermen and many people in the developing yachting scene. Trinidad with its newly invented steel bands and vibrant calypso songs was an exciting country. Indeed our son was a Trinidadian and there were possibilities here for me to take up a new life, but in my mental state they did not tempt me. After the death of Jutta, emotionally and practically our original plan of sailing on into the Pacific to study the descendants of the ancient settlers was unthinkable.

Waiting for us in Trinidad was a letter from Ernie and Peggy, with whom we had spent happy days sailing, swimming and sunbathing in the beautiful and then undeveloped American Virgin Islands before we sailed on to New York in 1959 on our first epic voyage across the north Atlantic in *Rongo*. The letter said 'sympathy, come to us in St Thomas to think things over'. Denis Solomon the Prime Minister's son and his fiancée Sheila offered to sail with us as crew the 500 sea miles non-stop north to St Thomas.

Thank God they did; the Caribbean is presented to the present-day tourist as golden beaches and gentle seas, but as Denis was later to write in an article: 'Most people think of the Caribbean outside of the hurricane season as sunny and placid, sunny it is, but during the first two or three months of the year the trades can blow half a gale for weeks on end. Eric Hiscock, a great English pioneering post war sailor, wrote in the April 1960 issue of *Yachting World* that he lay hove-to for two days in a gale force wind in the Caribbean'. Ours was a hard windward voyage from Trinidad to St Thomas. Denis and Sheila were a magnificent cheery crew; they needed to be.

Charlotte Amalie Harbor was a bit too crowded for me. I was soon offered a job to skipper a 50ft traditional American schooner, but the American woman owner, rightly or wrongly, presented likely emotional problems for me. The marina of St Thomas with all its facilities and comforts and the friendliness of its people were too much; I wanted time to reflect and I needed solitude. I was advised by Peggy and Ernie to sail to the windward side of St Thomas, so we sailed to where a chain of islands formed a great sea lake called Pillsbury Sound.

In one of the beautiful bays, called Red Hook, we anchored on top of a shoal of white coral sand with a distant view of the islands of Thatch Cay, Grass Cay, Mingo Cay, Lovango Cay, the names alone reading like a poem. Close by an American lawyer had bought a beach and was establishing the new concept of a Beach Hotel. On his beach he had a fleet of the new sailing surfboard type 'Sunfish' dinghies. I watched his guests, most of whom were rather plump New York ladies who treated me as older sisters might, getting on one of these easily capsizable craft and then drifting, whilst rotating rapidly, towards a reef which was covered in spiny, stinging sea urchins. I drew the beach owner's attention to this. 'Would you become the beach master and teach these people to sail?' he asked.

So I ended up with a delightful job teaching interesting people, and with the healing love of Ruth and baby love of Hannes I began to accept a life without Jutta. But as anyone who has lost a deeply loved person will know, as you start to heal from the loss on the outside, on the hidden inside of one's personality it takes much longer.

So when April arrived, a good time for sailing home to Britain, I wanted to move on and return to Ireland and Wales. When I told the owner of the Sapphire Beach Club I was sailing on and away, as an older man he pointed out a future I could have developing the beach. But he was a landsman, I had become a man of the sea; sailing

Jim and Hannes on Rongo, mid-Atlantic, 1961

DELICATE INSTRUMENT
TO BE HANDLED WITH
GREAT CARE

the ocean answered a deep inner urge in me. Fortunately Ruth also had this inner urge. She as a German had the philosophical outlook of the 'wander vogel'; she loved the immensity of ocean sailing as much as me.

First we needed to clean and antifoul the bottom of *Rongo* for the long voyage home. It would be cheaper to do this in Antigua, 200 miles to the east-south-east. I had heard of a bunch of mad English sailors who had 'colonised' the derelict dockyard of Lord Nelson's West Indian fleet in English Harbour. An English wartime naval officer, called commander Nicholson, had appeared after the war on a proposed voyage around the world, called into English Harbour and fallen in love with the place. Then came other English ex-war officers happy to live in the equivalent of an officers' mess.

The English Navy's approach to 'psychological care' at that time was to drink heavily, go wild, then to continue with one's 'duties' the next day; a tough regime. In English Harbour, I not only raised *Rongo* on blocks with a lorry jack to paint her bottom with antifouling, but also made good friends, and the accolade from Commander Nicholson 'why not stay here and work with us as a charter skipper?'

So five months after Jutta's death and the collapse of my dream to sail to the Pacific, a new life, developing the new concept of yacht charters in the tropical islands of the Caribbean, was being offered to me. But again I did not give in to the temptation. On 5 June we—*Rongo*, Ruth, Hannes and I—left English Harbour and Antigua to sail first 920 miles to Bermuda, then 3000 miles across the Atlantic back to Britain. Since our last north Atlantic crossing in 1959 from New York there had still been no other multihull to sail this hard west-to-east north Atlantic route.

Ruth was a skilled, seasoned navigator by now and we discussed the routes we might take. Instead of the more northern great circle route, which was the shortest, but also the riskiest (as we had experienced on our first *Rongo* crossing in 1959), we decided on one that would skirt the Azores high. First we would sail to Bermuda and start our crossing from there.

This book is not an account of sailing voyages, but one about my life as a designer. I wrote a a long article about this voyage, called 'The Way Back', I would have liked to use large chunks of this account, but just a few quotes will have to do, to give a feel of what it was like to make another long and arduous ocean crossing:

Whilst most of my body and brain suffered in shivering misery, a small section of it exulted in *Rongo* riding the storm. It was magnificent. I remembered the question that I am frequently asked; 'What would you change in the design of *Rongo*?' 'Nothing' would still be the only answer. After thirty-six hours of gale force winds the sea really built up. Normally during summer gales in the North Atlantic the seas are steep and not particularly high, but on the crest of one wave I looked behind me and there was a real monster snarling high in the sky. Abruptly the stern rose and I braced my feet to stop myself from sliding forward. I looked astern at the mountain of water. The face of it was streaked with creamy foam and as it began to overtake us, *Rongo* rose. But the force of gravity slid her forward and down so that she accelerated until the twin wakes spewed up a rooster tail, which indicated we were moving faster than 12 knots. I did not dare call Ruth as she was just putting a new film into her cine camera. Four times we rode those great combers, then Ruth's head emerged from the cabin with her cine camera ready, but it was too late. There were no more waves to equal them.

After that the wind began to moderate. We were at the edge of the BBC weather forecast areas. A few hours later we heard the forecaster announce the arrival of 'our' gale into their areas; NW winds up to force 9.

So we struggled on. August 1962 was one of the worst in yachtsmen's memory. We tasted each depression and front to the full as it passed over us, before it lashed the British coastline. Hannes, whom we had feared to be a liability, turned out to be a real blessing. Always cheerful, he kept up the spirit of the ship. When one us came below off watch, tired, just wanting to sleep, he played quietly until one opened one's eyes again. Then he would tell about his own little world, an imaginary family of chickens living in our cabin. Without Hannes it would have been an utterly dreary voyage.

Rongo's new 'Polynesian spritsail rig' had worked really well; Ruth and I could handle it with ease. The smaller sails were easily lowered or brailed. Having no battens and the sails being laced to the masts meant we could lower sails with the wind from any direction.

It had been thirteen months since we left Ireland, during which time we had sailed around the North Atlantic, a total of 10,000 miles. It would be another thirty-three years before we finally sailed into the Pacific, on another bigger catamaran, to study the canoe craft I had hoped to study on this failed round the world voyage.

THE DESIGNER

We are the music-makers,

And we are the dreamers of dreams,

Wandering by lone sea-breakers,

And sitting by desolate streams.

World-losers and world-forsakers,

Upon whom the pale moon gleams;

Yet we are the movers and shakers,

Of the world forever, it seems.

Arthur William Edgar O'Shaughnessy

10   The dark years

The 'old young' man who sailed into Dún Laoghaire harbour in August 1962 was a very different one from the boy who had built a twenty-four-foot double canoe and with two German girls sailed it across the Atlantic six years before. He had been hammered by the sea into a competent ocean sailor, he had pioneered the basics of offshore multihull design and sailing, but he had lost two dreams, his golden girl Jutta and his dream to sail into the Pacific and immerse himself in the Polynesian past before it vanished. It was to take three confused, sometimes dark, sometimes exciting years to turn him into a major catamaran designer.

Since my first visit to the London boat show in 1960 a strong interest in what came to be called multihulls was developing in Britain. There were two influential men in this development; one was Dr John Morwood, a medical doctor and armchair sailor with whom I had had an on-going heated correspondence since my first stay in Trinidad in 1957–58; the other person who had given multihulls status was Prince Phillip, the Duke of Edinburgh, who had sailed on the 16ft *Endeavour* during the 1955 speed trials in Cowes. This was the first small racing catamaran, engineered by it's owner Ken Pierce with hulls built by the Prouts. Due to his enthusiasm the Prince became President of the Amateur Yacht Research Society (AYRS), which had been set up by Dr Morwood.

At the 1960 London boat show as a deep sea catamaran designer and sailor I had scorned the exhibited catamaran with its deep fixed ballast keels and its large buoyancy saucer on the mast to prevent total capsize, but by 1962 common sense, following practical experience, was beginning to lay down sensible design principles. However the designers doing this were not looking to the historic Pacific Vee'd hull shape, which had been proven by Éric de Bisschop on his epic ocean voyage and my Atlantic crossings with *Rongo*. The preferred hull shape in Britain, propounded by John Morwood, was the round bottom as developed by the Prout brothers from Canvey island in the Thames estuary.

The Prouts were Olympic canoeists and had been building paddling canoes in the late 1940s. Some time in the early 1950s they had experimented with combining two canoes into a sailing catamaran, which had led to the 16ft racing 'Shearwater' design, which out-sailed any of the fast sailing monohull dinghies of that date. It was made in moulded plywood and sold in kit form; I had helped a friend in Trinidad build one of the first in 1958. It is strange that later, when I became good friends with the brothers, I never asked them what inspired their basic hull design; I expect it was the round bilge on their paddling canoes, which were designed with minimum wetted surface, essential for winning races. Of course the drawback of this hull shape is that for sailing to windward it needs dagger boards or keels for lateral resistance, which my Vee'd hulls don't.

However it is sufficient to write that the majority of catamarans in the world today use the basic underwater hull shape as developed by the Prouts in the 1950s. The only othershape developed at this time in Britain was the chined type, designed by Bill O'Brien, who had a background in flying boats. Bill O'Brien was very active in the 1950s in racing dinghies and later small racing catamarans; he designed the 16ft 'Jumpahead' for the same racing scene as the Prouts' 'Shearwater'. He went on to design the successful 'Bobcat' and 'Oceanic' cruising catamarans, which eventually were reworked into the GRP 'Catalac', which remained popular well into the 1990s.

As I wrote before, Ireland was like Spain a state controlled by the Catholic church, however it was not a total dictatorship; cracks were appearing and in those cracks excited discussions took place, based on ideas that could be freely read in English newspapers or heard on English radio. The Irish Republic was a place of warm-hearted friendship and exciting ideas all of which were extended to Ruth and myself. You can drift a long way on exciting cultural ideas; my father, sensing this, gave me a new practical beginning. 'Son' he wrote 'I want you to design and build me a 20ft catamaran I can tow behind a car!'

Sailing *Rongo* into Deganwy in North Wales in the summer of 1963, from where we had so confidently left three years before to sail to the Pacific, was an emotional experience. However, on the end of a towrope was the beginning of a new life, the 22ft 'Wharcat', which I had designed for my father, who hoped with it to set me up in a new life direction as a multihull designer and boat builder. I had built it with my father's money out of quality plywood in a friend's furniture factory in Ireland, putting in my best skills to impress him. It was a narrow catamaran, only 8ft wide, so it could be trailed behind a car, with a low bridge deck cuddy-cabin to give shelter.

Deganwy at that time was a row of shops and a small estate of 1930s suburban homes. A coastal railway line ran past the village and branched onto a massive pier that had been built in the 1880s for the transportation of slate; behind this pier was a sheltered silted-up dock. We moored *Rongo* on the beach in this dock. It was the place where we had refitted her in 1960, and we again enjoyed the beautiful views across the estuary to Conwy Castle with wild Welsh hills in the distance. Walking these hills was for me a return to the 'teenage James' who had begun his wandering dreams on the northern hills and moors of England and Scotland. It was good for my still very bruised soul.

Then in the autumn came the first test sail of the new 22ft car-trailer Wharcat with my father on board. The boat sailed beautifully past the row of shops, the channel widening on the other side, to the view of the wide open sea over mud-flats. Then came a gust of wind from the open sea. The Wharcat picked up an exciting speed and promptly capsized! We climbed on to the centre platform of the upside-down vessel; I was shocked, horrified that I had wasted my father's money. My father just put his hand into his builder's donkey jacket pocket, he pulled out his packet of cigarettes for a smoke and said disgustedly, with no criticism, no emotion: 'and my bloody cigarettes are wet too'.

Almost immediately an observant shore friend was there in a rowboat. We left the Wharcat with its mast stuck on the bottom and trudged dripping back to *Rongo*. I remember some passers-by asking us if there had been an accident; my father just pointed back to where we had come from and calmly said: 'Yes over there.' The Wharcat was easily righted, did sail again and eventually a saw down the middle and a 2ft widening of the beam gave her the needed stability to sail successfully for many years.

That capsize deeply disturbed me, it brought to the forefront of my consciousness 'who or what was I?' The last three years had hit me hard with the loss of Jutta, the abandonment of our ocean voyaging dreams, my inability or unwillingness to enter the developing word of yacht charter, and the rejection by the yachting establishment of me as a serious designer of multihulls. And now this capsize!

Fortunately I had my ever-magnificent, caring companion, honed to shape by the best aspects of German culture and the hardships of war, my Ruth. She said: 'You must write a book'. 'We have no money', I answered. 'Do not worry' she insisted, 'I can get a job, we can survive'.

So early in 1964 I began to write my 'love story' of Ruth, Jutta, the ocean and our first double canoe/catamaran voyages across the Atlantic. Today reading *Two Girls Two Catamarans,* published in 1968, is like looking into a golden age of innocence.

Of course, in the wider world there was the lingering Cold War and the 'Iron Curtain' with behind it the Communist empires of Russia and China and the threat of nuclear war. These were major concerns, but in the day-to-day foreground, life was full of exciting hope and ideas for the future. The Second World War had been over for nineteen years, the men who as young soldiers, sailors and airmen had regularly faced death or boring monotony waiting for action, were now approaching middle age (I was thirty-six). These men were willing to work, what they were not willing to become, were 'wage slaves', driven by necessity. It was a very tolerant time open to many ideas.

It was a magical world too. From my own sea and mountain experiences I had accepted, in a modified way, Carl Jung's concepts of the archaic man or woman within us. From *Rongo*'s mooring on the beach, across the railway line, a short walk up the hill, there were the ruins of an ancient hill fort—known as Taliesin's Castle. Taliesin was an ancient Welsh poet and magician. I would climb up that hill to clarify my next pages of writing for my book. My poetic Welsh friends believed that Taliesin was the guiding spirit of my book.

I had my dark spells, where Jutta's death was still a deep wound. I still have diaries from that time, carefully preserved by my archivist-trained Ruthy, in which I dare not look now at many pages of dark thoughts and despair. To try to pull myself out of this I tried meditation. For this I was looking for a suitable focus; I was not attracted to Indian mandalas, certainly not the Christian cross, which I abhorred as a symbol of cruel death. When leafing through a book on the art of early man, I came across a symbol that drew me in. It was from the period when people still worshipped the mother goddess; it was a representation of the bird goddess as two eyes with eyebrows connected into the shape of birds wings. The owl of the Greek goddess Pallas Athena was a later manifestation of this symbol. I took a piece of paper and drew the 'eye symbol' on it. It was immensely powerful and I have since adopted it to identify my designs.

But in those diaries were also some positive thoughts: I was thinking about new designs and had big dreams of setting up a community of Sea People on a new 52ft catamaran I would build. This is what I wrote:

3 March 1964

So far since late August my journals have recorded chiefly my anguish and pain. Yet out of all this pain and suffering has come much.

Out of my deep turmoil is coming the future, for I have in the last 6 weeks designed a new 35ft Tangaroa.

A 50% increase will give me the 52ft Tehini. Tehini will be a charter ship, which will realize my dreams.

Tehini can be built for £4000. She can earn that in a year. I propose to charter both sides of the Atlantic. The Areoi, the People of the Sea, shall live.

So in 3 months I have moved from deep desperation, from being lost in soul and direction, to finding myself and my way.

This is perhaps the only way that was ever open to me. Our lives are I believe a mixture of dreams (?) and forces. Indeed the Greeks were right in mixing the affairs of Gods and Men.

My People of the Sea concept will work. In its simplest it is a holiday venture, a kind of glorified Outward Bound holidays in the sun. Because of its essential simplicity it will be accepted.

Many men have created a movement to give themselves wealth. It is funny I intend to create a business to create a movement.

Essentially we must raise the money for the first Tehini. That will in a year pay for the next boat and so on.

If I cannot get the money by my 'Two Girls Two Catamarans' book I shall return and beach charter in the West Indies and build Tehini myself.

Six months later I returned to this theme:

Monday 28 September 1964

I am making a deliberate attempt to make a fresh beginning, to control my thoughts after a deep spiritual collapse last Thursday. I have Friday, Saturday and today practised meditation and concentration.

For concentration I use the sign of the Goddess [eye symbol]

It does seem as if I am getting a little control on the wild horses of my passions.

So each day I intend to meditate and write in the morning, work on Rongo in the afternoon.

For as I wrote in one of my journals about 12 years ago, my ambition is to sail the seas with two girls. Now I write my ambition is to create the People of the Sea, a new Areoi.

11   Start of my career as a designer

L iving on Deganwy beach was a great way to meet people; walkers would stop and chat, and one was Eric Jones, a railway engineer from Crewe, where many of Britain's magnificent steam locomotives had been built. Eric, like so many men of his era, had also served in the War, in a special unit in Italy known as 'Popski's Private Army'. Chats lead to friendship. Eric and his wife would turn up at weekends with flagons of home-made cider or beer. One day sitting on the deck of *Rongo* he said: 'I wish I could have a boat like this'. 'How much money can you raise?' He thought, then said: 'I could sell my canal boat for £600'—'I will design you a boat like this that you can build for about £600'. With my design and building experience, and four Atlantic crossings behind me, I felt confident I could design him such a boat.

What made this design for Eric unique was *how* it was to be built. Before this new 35ft Tangaroa design, the accepted method of building was as had been depicted in (you guessed it) *Boat Building in Your Own Backyard* by S. S. Rabl, starting with a carefully levelled building base made out of heavy timbers, onto which bulkheads would be squared and levelled up. I had used this method for building *Rongo* in Trinidad.

For Eric, I developed what I called the 'egg box principle', making a backbone out of plywood and timber framing to the exact shape of the keel, stem and stern profile of the hull and slotting bulkheads on to this. It removed the heavy building base structure out of the cycle; the fixed backbone and bulkhead structure could be stood up on any type of floor and squared up with a string through the centreline. The bulkheads would be levelled with wedges to the floor. It was a simple but radical step in design for self-building. It looks a simple idea but at the time, as far as I know, it was unique.

Another feature of the design was the two separate slim 'canoe' hulls joined together by flexibly mounted beams with an open slatted deck between them, as on the ancient Polynesian double canoes, Éric de Bisschop's *Kaimiloa*, my 23ft 6in

Lines drawing

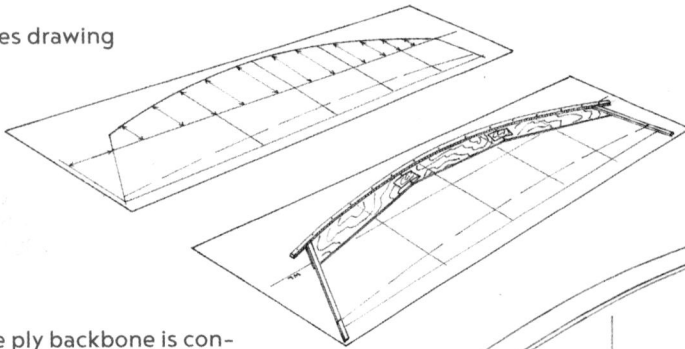

T-girder formed by
backbone and
inner keel plank

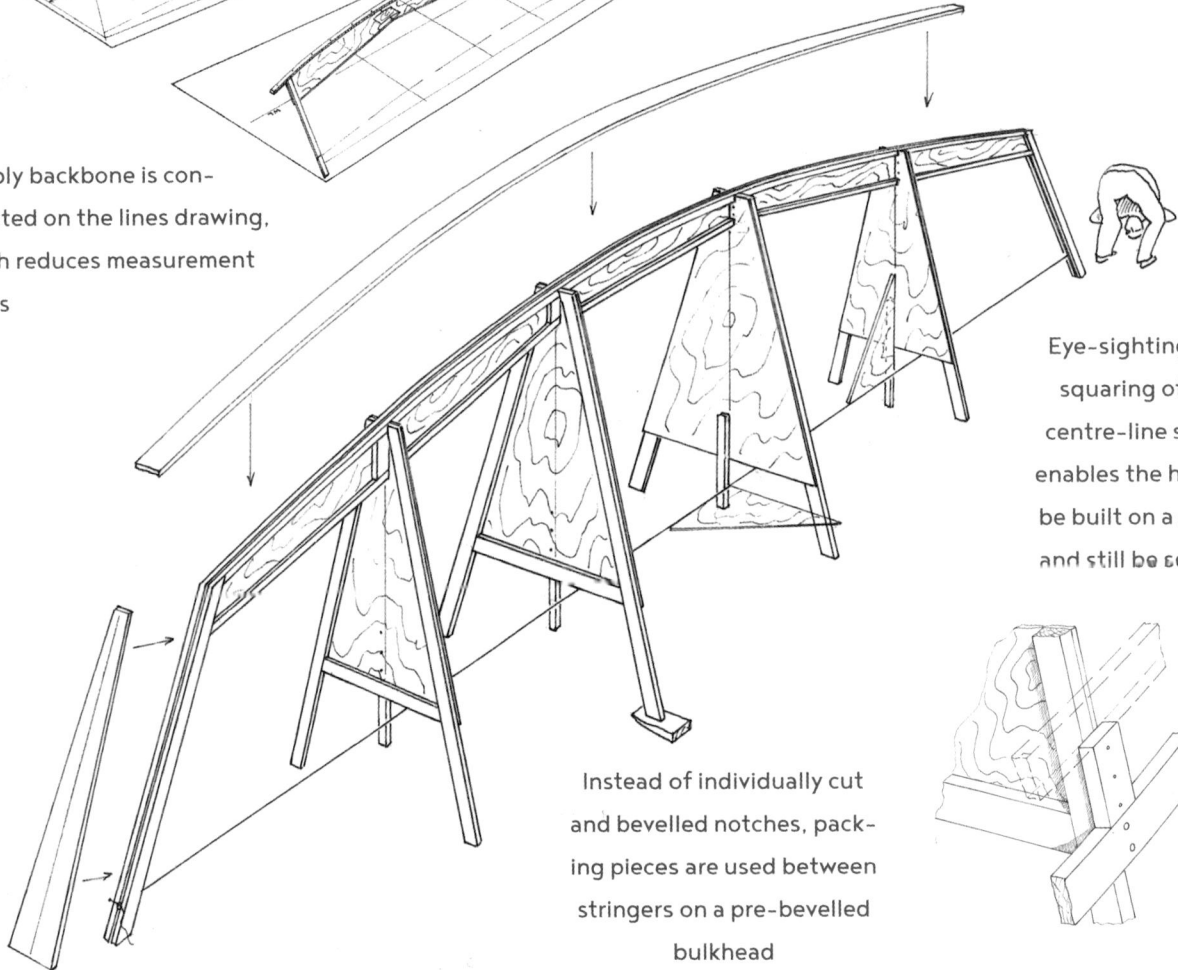

The ply backbone is con-
structed on the lines drawing,
which reduces measurement
errors

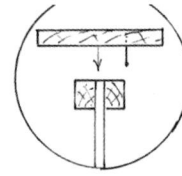

Eye-sighting and
squaring off the
centre-line string
enables the hull to
be built on a slope
and still be square

Instead of individually cut
and bevelled notches, pack-
ing pieces are used between
stringers on a pre-bevelled
bulkhead

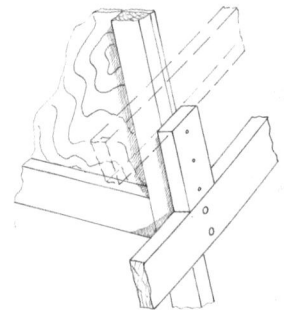

Wharram 'Backbone and Bulkheads' building method

Tangaroa and 40ft *Rongo*. This flexible structure of two separate hulls and a wash-through centre deck had been fully proven for its seaworthiness on my four pioneering ocean voyages. But there was a hidden deficiency in this design arrangement: Western Social Comfort!

Our north European ancestors lived in huts or halls that animals could freely enter; they had mud floors that would be fouled by the animals and also the people. As a result deep in our Western culture is the concept of tables and chairs. Around these tables has developed the convivial social custom of sitting and eating while looking across at the happy faces of your friends. However in what we call the East of our globe, people traditionally sit on the floor. Japanese traditional culture shows the elegance of this sitting style. Yoga students attest to the spiritual aspects of sitting cross-legged. Early in my mountaineering days, I had got used to sitting on the ground, also I had been practicing yoga, so for me the table-and-chairs concept was not a necessity.

The narrow hulls of Pacific canoe-form craft did not have the width for the table and benches as are standard on monohull sailing yachts. The early 'Western' catamaran designers of the 1960s solved this problem by adding a bridge deck cabin, which was connected to the hulls to form a single rigid structure. I had seen how huge ocean waves could batter the catamaran and had seen how the flexibility of *Rongo* had taken up these stresses. I could never design an oceangoing catamaran that did not have this flexibility, nor one on which the waves could not drain through the centre deck. My ocean-trained eyes could see a wave breaking into the cockpit of the deck-cabin catamaran and flooding the cabin.

Within the narrow hulls of the new 35ft Tangaroa I designed the living space in the centre of each hull, for cooking and navigating, where motion is least, as I had done on *Rongo*. Fore and aft of this space I placed berths that are like wombs, in which the crew can feel sheltered from the vastness of the ocean outside. I did not design big windows to look out of, like those of the deck-cabin designs; one can see enough ocean when out on deck.

My rigs were low and flexible, to 'give' before strong wind gusts. In my studies of books on yacht design, like those by the American Howard Chappelle, I was aware that the double canoe was a 'form-stable' boat, and that form-stable boats should keep the rig low to have maximum stability. Chappelle had written: 'to increase the sail area on a shallow draft, form-stable boat one should increase it horizontally, not vertically', hence my use of two masts, and sails with a low centre of effort. Chappelle also supplied 'rules of thumb' for the ratios of sail area to weight, and freeboard to hull length, in line with traditional practice. To me stability, to be free from the risk of capsize,was of eminent importance.

In designing Eric's 35ft catamaran, which I called Tangaroa after my first double canoe, it was like opening a door into a new inner mind world that had been growing within me, since my first Atlantic voyage on my little 23ft 6in *Tangaroa*; a mind world shaped by ocean waves and winds. When designing I see/dream the boat in its actuality sailing in all weather. However turning these dream images into drawings, that strangers in a far off land can build from, is not one of my gifts. Ruth and I became aware of this, and she contacted a friend in Germany, who put us in touch with a young woman in Hamburg called Helga, who was trained in architecture, and she was also a sailor. I was able to work with Helga at a distance by sending her my rough ideas, structural solutions and sketches, which she then turned into beautiful classic drawings a self-builder could work from. I owe a great deal to Helga.

In 1964, to bring in some extra income I had started to write regular articles for a journal called *Yachting and Boating*. So in early 1965, when the new Tangaroa design was drawn up by Helga, I sent an article about it to the editor, who published it. It immediately drew a response and people wanted to buy the plans and build her. Soon there were others who wanted a bigger design and those who wanted one smaller, so over the next year my design career suddenly took off, with Helga working hard to keep up with drawings and producing our first design brochure: *Build Yourself Your Own Polynesian Catamaran*.

In 1965 when my design sales were taking off, I heard about plans to hold a yacht race to sail in stages around the British Isles, starting from Plymouth in the summer of 1966. This was to be some tough race! I saw this as my chance to prove myself in the eyes of other yachtsmen. I needed a boat to enter.

So far, I have only written about the Pacific double canoe being adopted and adapted by Westerners. However in south-east Asia and the Indian Ocean another multi-hulled craft had been in wide usage, the double outrigger canoe, i.e. one canoe hull stabilised by an outrigger float on each side. To enter this race, I decided to build such a double outrigger (nowadays called a trimaran). It was cheaper to build one hull,

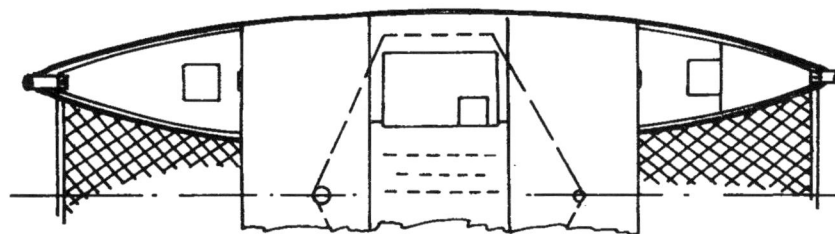

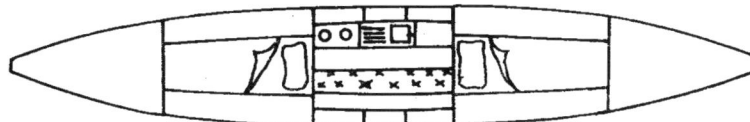

Tangaroa Mk I (drg: Helga Hempel)

and in theory with one hull stabilised by a minimum wave drag float on each side, it should be faster than a catamaran.

To save time I adapted one hull of my newly designed 35ft Tangaroa, and designed two smaller and slimmer Vee'd hulls as outriggers. It took me seven months to build this boat in a nearby barn. I built it out of low-cost beautiful Canadian Douglas fir plywood and rigged it with two masts and sprit sails. My ocean experiences had dictated a flexible rig with low centre of effort, which I could handle easily.

The race stipulated two crew. Ruth declined to be my crew, she did not like the idea of racing, so it was agreed that Helga, whom I had met only on her two brief visits to Wales, would be my crew. She had been attending a course in navigation.

With little time to spare I arrived in Plymouth with my new 36ft double outrigger, which I had called *Tikiroa,* on a truck. With no time to test her we set sail with the rest of the fleet. I did not get very far in the race, when with a large bang the wooden centre board I had deemed necessary to sail against the wind, broke in half. I entered Falmouth to make a new one, losing us time. With the new board I hoped that the speed of the boat would enable me to catch up with the racing fleet. Then, moving on fast, I had another problem: I had designed the floats to be buoyant for stability. In big cross-seas off Land's End, with speeds touching thirteen knots, the buoyancy in the floats set the boat oscillating wildly from side to side.

I retired from that race in what must have been a towering rage, against myself, with fallout on whoever was near me, which happened to be poor Helga, who did not have the strength and resilience of my tough Ruth; she ran back to Germany and a more peaceful life.

So first the capsize of my father's boat and now this boat. I was a top ocean sailor, but in boat design was I just a 'dreamer?'

I sailed into St Ives and moored *Tikiroa* on the beach in the harbour of this old Cornish fishing village. St Ives was then a centre for artists, not yet dominated by the present day floods of tourists. Barbara Hepworth, the sculptor, had her studio here. On the beach I met the artist Francis Codrill and discussed my 'failure' in the race with him. He said: 'The boat is beautiful, have faith in yourself, you are a designer.'

Sailing back with Ruth to Deganwy, she gave me 'conditional' support. I write conditional, because Ruth's gentle caring presence was not 'airy-fairy', it was balanced by her post-war German practicality. She saw male racing competitiveness

with the eyes of a woman, who had seen male posturing destroy continents and kill millions. She knew my inner self; she gently redirected my focus back to designing cruising catamarans, based on my proven *Rongo* design, for people who wanted to find adventure and freedom by building an ocean-going boat that could take them anywhere in the world. She was right; more and more people came asking me for designs.

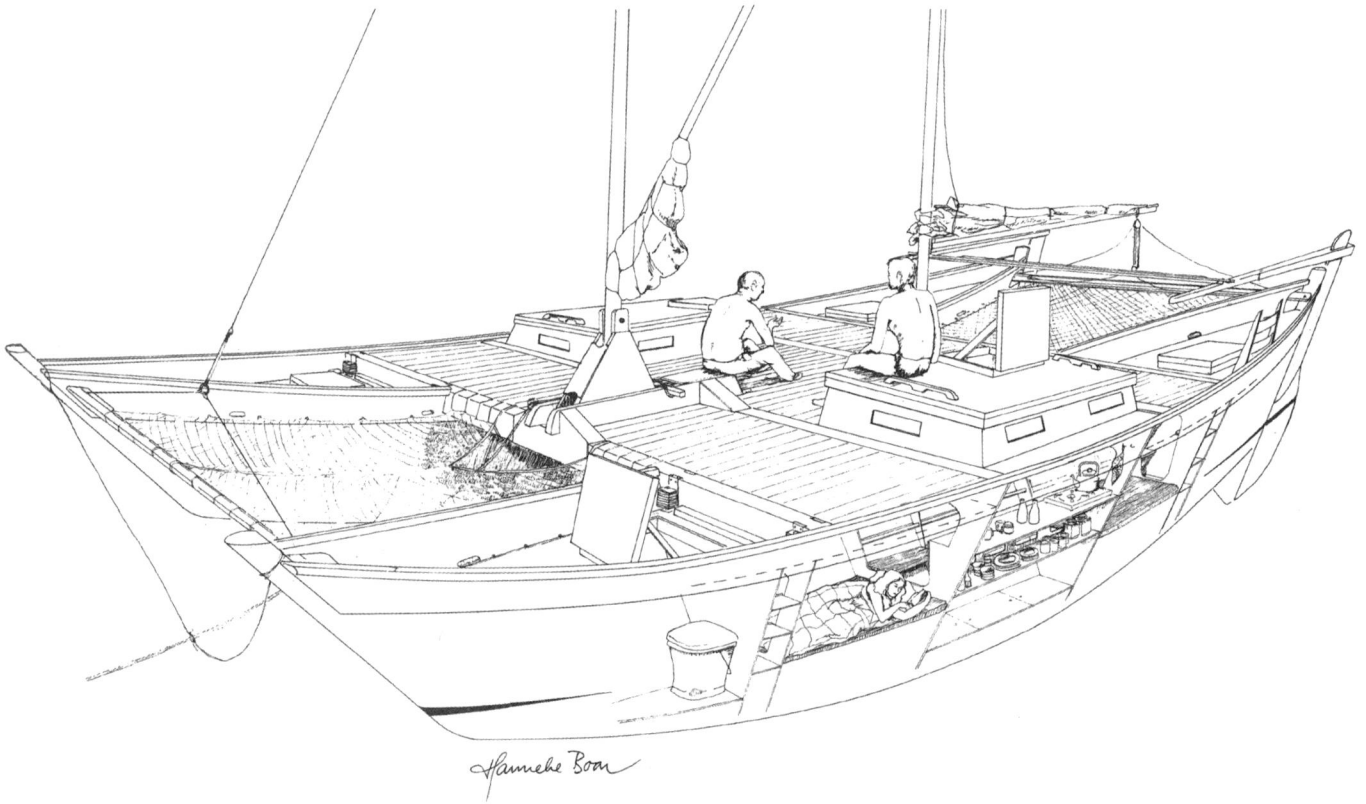

Narai Mk I

12　On the beach

L iving on that beach in Deganwy was a crucial turning point in my life, which hitherto could be seen as a lead-up, a learning period, a maturing period that culminated in a burst of creativity that was of value to others: a new beginning.

Where there was the advent of new designs in my practical life, in my mystical life there was a girl called Maggie. I have written how Deganwy beach was a wonderful place to meet and talk to walkers. At the same time as one, Eric, was inspiring me to design, another walker was inspiring the magic, creative, sexual side of my Jungian archetype. In the summer of 1964 two London girls were on a walking holiday in Wales, and they walked along Deganwy beach. One of them was Maggie, and we had an immediate connection, but it was not until the following year, when she returned during her college holidays to help me with the building of *Tikiroa,* that she started to fill the hole left by Jutta's death.

I suppose by living openly with two women, Jutta and Ruth, I could be described as an early exponent of the later 1960s sexual revolution. At the time living a sea-life, I did not feel related to a social movement. I was living in a natural or open ancient Polynesian way, as first recorded by Captain Cook and Bougainville after their exploring visits to Tahiti.

My first recognition of this sexual revolution was soon after I settled in Deganwy one dark evening. I was filling my water tank behind a wooden fence when I heard a young girl's voice on the other side singing a line from an early Beatles song as she walked home. The line she was singing, repeated over and over again, was 'she loves you yeah, yeah, yeah'. To me, it was like a wild sexual ancient chant. Beyond that fence, there was a new freer and exciting world developing.

During the 1939–45 war millions of people had been uprooted, as soldiers, war workers and refugees. The then standard moral concept of the unity of one man and one woman (i.e. the woman would lose her virginity to her husband and be his only partner for life) had broken down. Many people had affairs, or short sexual flings.

To illustrate the loosening of sexual attitudes during the war, there is a novel written and published in the 1980s called *The Camomile Lawn* written by Mary Wesley, who had been a young woman in the war. It was more recently made into a BBC television series. It is a lovely, open-minded novel about a group of middle class people, young and middle aged, before and during Word War II. It describes their wartime life experiences: a young wife living in London during the Blitz who has various lovers, whilst her husband is away at the war; her cousin going boldly to a contraceptive clinic, so she can have sex with two twins, whom she loves equally, on their brief spells of leave as Air Force pilots; a fifteen year old girl's first sex, with an exciting German Jewish musician, who is also the lover of her aunt—who had swapped husbands with the wife of the German musician in an amicable way.

The book ends in the 1970s as all the characters re-meet around the funeral of the leading character, the musician. It gives a vivid picture of how sexual attitudes changed during the war, how the stress of bombing, and the proximity of death, made people let go of established social constrictions. It was these people that after the war were the parents of the young people of the 1960s, who were more tolerant of their children's behaviour, as they had done wild and exciting things themselves in their youth.

Maggie was one of those children, now often referred to as 'baby boomers', born in the late 1940s. Many of them went looking for adventure in the outdoors. They had no great expectations of comfort; they were happy to live simply on a boat, with no running water or showers, no electricity; the 'needs' of young people in the twenty-first century were not yet invented. They did not look for excitement in the world of the 'Internet', they went looking in the 'Outernet', in nature, for situations that offered adventure and different ways of living.

Whilst working on my designs for other people, my dream of building 51ft *Tehini* and starting a community of Sea People, which I had written about in my diary several years earlier, now became a possibility. We had the money, I had a place I could build her, and with Maggie's eager support we started building *Tehini* on the end of Deganwy pier, in the shelter of a stone shed, in the spring of 1968.

The length of 51ft gave room inside for six private bunk spaces, a large galley in the centre of one hull, and a spacious chart room in the other. The longer length would also give higher average speeds, particularly as I had kept her hull width to a minimum, so her underwater length to beam ratio was slimmer than my *Rongo* and my new 35ft Tangaroa, 40ft Narai and 46ft Oro designs. However, the design problem was what sail rig I should use to power the boat?

The 'Bermudan rig', which was the most common rig used on yachts at that time, requires a high mast and lots of rigging and a large headsail with powerful and expensive winches to hoist the sails and sheet them in. It is still the dominant sail rig on most boats today. I had rigged *Rongo* with a Bermudan ketch rig with fully battened sails in Trinidad, but I had changed it to an easier to handle rig, which I had called the 'Polynesian Spritsail Rig', on which the mainsail could be brailed into the mast in a squall. Ruth and I could handle this rig with ease on our second circuit of the Atlantic in 1961–62. From this experience I had drawn this rig on my new 40ft Narai and 46ft Oro designs. However the sprit would be big and heavy on a 51ft boat.

Éric de Bisschop when building his *Kaimiloa* in 1937–38 had used the very ancient Chinese junk rig, which he loved. This rig is cheap to construct and easy to handle in sudden squall conditions, which I had experienced on my two north Atlantic voyages. The sail is easy to raise and when lowering or reefing just falls down like a blind. I decided to use the junk rig on *Tehini*.

I had been struggling for this book to describe the technical ideas behind the *Tehini* design for several days, then my long-term partner Hanneke went in to our files and produced an article I had written about *Tehini* soon after she was launched, which was published in the venerable British magazine *Yachting Monthly* in 1970. It's a highly combative article in which I was reacting against the British yachting establishment's ideas on multihulls, which were developing at that time. However it did also describe the beauty of the boat:

> The inside of Tehini is lightly polished fir. The shapes of the entry ports into the bunk cabins and clothes lockers are Archetype shapes. Window ports are as small as possible and require a positive glance to see out at the sea. Only low sun angles can shine directly into the cabins, and lit by soft sun, the fir glows golden. Because of the wood grain and the angle the boat is lying to the sun, the permutations of shapes, colours, light and textures are endless compared to the very limited range of variables available with synthetic materials and large windows.

When I built *Rongo* in Trinidad, I had used expensive high quality Dutch Bruynzeel plywood, laminated from beautiful mahogany veneers. For *Tehini* I chose to build with the much cheaper Douglas fir plywood imported from Canada and the USA, which at that time was of high quality and came in different grades. I used the top grade called 'Two sides good.' This plywood was of much better quality than the Douglas fir plywood that is now sold as 'shuttering ply', and as I described in the article, it made a beautiful interior finish.

Soon our *Tehini* building project started to attract other young people, women and men, all drawn by the adventure of building this beautiful boat. There was a French mathematics student, Jean-Pierre, who later became a yacht designer in his own right, then we were joined by Nuala and later Lesley and Jan.

Jan—in a privately published picture book she recently wrote of her time with me—described life while building *Tehini*:

> It was such a stimulating environment in which creativity abounded. The boat attracted artists, writers, fellow designers and craftspeople from all over the world. James, 'us girls' and the catamaran mystique were like a creative magnet.
>
> It was a hugely creative time for me—I was encouraged to design and execute the art work for the bulwarks on *Tehini*. I was also carving wood trim for the tops of the cabin doors and creating sculptural forms of women.
>
> This creativity carried over to college where I had decided to concentrate on sculpture. I was also welding, designing mobiles and painting.

In the eighteen months it took to build *Tehini* we became a team, a boat crew of me as captain and the five girls. Jan enjoyed her three years of building and sailing *Tehini* with us immensely, but had been encouraged by me to continue her college training, after which she followed her dream of travelling across America and there found her partner in life.

In her book she concludes:

> Einar [Jan's husband of forty years] has always been grateful to Jim for setting me on the course of my life, we have both benefited from the freedoms,

sexual and otherwise, that I embraced at nineteen.

During the building of *Tehini*, there was also a shy sixteen-year-old girl who came with her sailing family from Holland to help during their summer holidays. I quickly noticed her artistic talent and asked her to make some carvings to decorate *Tehini*'s chartroom. Three years later she returned, drawn by the atmosphere of love, creativity and sailing adventure. This was Hanneke, who now, nearly fifty years later, is still working with me as co-designer.

Hanneke describes her first years with us on *Tehini*:

The *Tehini* crew of James and us five girls was an incredibly 'loving' group into which I was accepted and protected as the youngest member. James, who we all called 'Jimmy', was in the prime of his life, a very powerful, magnetic person, too big in every way for one woman to handle and not be overwhelmed. His multifaceted persona—political, mystical, creative, practical—was enhanced and balanced by the strong, sensual, 'mother goddess' figure of Maggie and the practical, sensible Ruth. Lesley, who loved to be a domestic provider, added funny banter and verbal puns and could draw wonderful cartoon sketches of people. Nuala, a great reader and conversationalist, resonated with Jim's political persona. When I joined the 'family' aged nineteen, I was shy and didn't say much, but loved the sense of 'group feeling'. I didn't just fall in love with Jim, I fell in love with all of them.

People often ask—were you not jealous? Somehow this was never an issue. James managed to make us all feel special. He brought out our innate abilities and encouraged them. By being totally open, nothing was kept secret, we all felt secure.

13   Tehini

In the autumn of 1969 we launched *Tehini* by dramatically pushing her over the edge of the stone pier into the sea. We now had a boat and a crew. We rigged her and did the finishing details on the beach, next to our now old and tired *Rongo*. I had arranged to leave *Rongo* behind in the hands of the local Sea Scout group, so they could use it as their headquarters, with the strong admonition that she was no longer seaworthy and not to take her out to sea. Sadly they decided to ignore this advice and after patching up the leaking bilge with concrete took her out to sea and… sank her off the coast of North Wales. The crew of scouts fortunately were rescued.

After a brief period of test sailing *Tehini* around the Conwy estuary, we sailed away down the Irish Sea. We did not get far; an imminent gale forecast and rising winds forced us to take shelter in Milford Haven, the fishing port from where I had first set out to sea as a young man on a trawler in 1947. In the twenty-two years since, Milford Haven had declined as a fishing port, its dock buildings now mostly abandoned. We spent the winter in the fish docks, preparing for our first big voyage down to Spain the next year.

In the spring of 1970 I had the boat of my dreams and with four girls as crew (Jan was back at college and Hanneke had not yet joined us) and my son Hannes, who was now twelve, we set sail across the Bay of Biscay, to Ribadeo in northern Spain once more, to meet my dear friend Pepe and family, who had done so much for us on the original *Tangaroa* voyage. Ruth and I had last seen them in 1961, a few months before Jutta's death on our voyage south on *Rongo*.

On our return to Milford Haven we prepared *Tehini* to take part in the second 'Round Britain Race'. My failure in the first race, with my double outrigger *Tikiroa*, made me determined to try again and prove myself and my boat to the established yachting fraternity. Maggie, who had become a strong boatwoman, would be my crew. Sadly the junk rig combined with my innate caution as a deep-sea cruising sailor led again to failure. The rig, in spite of its easy handling possibilities, was just too slow and inefficient for the inherent speed-potential of *Tehini*. We retired from the race after arriving at Crosshaven in Ireland's Cork Harbour.

Back in Milford Haven I decided to change the junk rig to a more efficient, faster Bermudan schooner, and was persuaded by its makers to use a new simple small-diameter aluminium mast concept, called 'Needle Spar'—a six-inch circular section with ¼in wall thickness. I regretted this choice later as the small diameter made the masts very flexible and seeing them form an S-bend under strain used to scare me into reducing sail, and thereby I was never able to achieve the true speed potential of the slim hulled *Tehini*.

Like many yachtsmen, I wanted a fast-sailing, close to the wind, easy-to-handle rig. This ideal has been a perpetual dream of my design life, and ten years later led us to design the 'Wharram Wingsail Rig' that is now a distinguishing feature of all my designs.

We were now successfully selling many self-build designs and we needed an office. We found an ideal building on the water's edge in Milford Docks, it had a fine ground floor workshop, with offices and a small meeting hall above. It was perfect for us—the monthly rent minimal. We called it 'The Longhouse'.

We did not like living on *Tehini* in Milford Docks, but we had discovered a few miles west of Milford Haven a sheltered tidal creek called Sandy Haven, an ideal place to moor her; it was beautiful and sheltered from the winter gales. Maggie learned to drive and we bought a Bedford van for our transport from our 'boat home' to our 'office'.

Milford Haven also had a first class grammar school for my son Hannes to start his secondary education. Even though Hannes had a far from usual upbringing living a Bohemian lifestyle on a boat, he excelled in school and later studied medicine at St Bart's hospital in London.

In The Longhouse we set up business as designers of 'Polynesian Catamarans'. As on the boat we worked as a team, I guided Ruth with her clever mathematical brain in the drawing office where we produced more drawings of new designs, with Lesley, who had artistic drawing skills as her assistant. Maggie was my personal assistant typing all the letters I dictated, as well as organising our social life. Nuala was in charge of sending the drawings to our customers. By now we had a range of ten designs, from 16ft to 50ft, with more being drawn. It became clear that there was a great demand for

my designs in the open-thinking world of the early 1970s, and hundreds were being built worldwide; many had started to make long ocean voyages.

While we were building *Tehini* a builder's group had formed called the 'Polynesian Catamaran Association', with a magazine called *The Sailorman*, which soon gathered a large membership. In the days before the internet and social media this was where people shared their experiences building and sailing their catamarans.

While these days in the early 1970s in Milford Haven were happy and prosperous ones for us, the rest of the World was in turmoil. The Vietnam War was at its peak and people felt the threat of nuclear war hanging over their heads.

In America in reaction to the war in Vietnam, but also in Britain and Europe, young people were re-evaluating their life through song, literature and by choosing to live a different, freer life style. This was the hippy movement with its concept of free love. These young people were not just looking for changes sexually, but also changes in working hours, demanding more holiday time and public support in sickness and in old age.

In America and elsewhere, people were setting up lifestyle communes, experimenting with group living, building their own low-cost houses—pole buildings, geodesic domes, A-frames and nomadic tents. I still have the books full of quirky, inventive ideas published in those years. Iconic amongst them was an American publication which assembled all these 'alternative' ideas in one volume, called *The Whole Earth Catalog*, first published in 1968; my designs, which expressed alternative living on the sea, had a section in this seminal work.

The next year, 1971, we made a voyage to Holland, where Hanneke still lived and where there was a large group of Wharram catamaran builders. We sailed from Milford Haven round Land's End, along the south coast and up the North Sea. Entering Holland at IJmuiden, we were met by the Boons who as a family had helped to build *Tehini* in Deganwy during their summer holidays. Nico Boon, Hanneke's father, had become my agent in Holland. He arrived with his eldest daughter Marijke and her new boyfriend Ronald, a ship's engineer who had just bought a set of 40ft Narai plans and the man who over the years has become a close and encouraging friend to me.

Arriving in Amsterdam, I was down below in the galley, naked in the midst of washing myself in a bowl of water on the step below the hatch, when the hatch suddenly slid back and there was Hanneke. She was full of enthusiasm to be back on the boat she had helped to build two years earlier. Now nearly fifty years later, as I am writing this with her assistance, that same enthusiasm is still glowing hot!

In Amsterdam, where we were able to moor right behind the Central Station, most of the members of the new Dutch Catamaran & Trimaran Club (CTC) crowded on board *Tehini*. Many of its members were building or had built Wharram catamarans. Holland at that time was a leading European country in the new concept of multihulls.

From Amsterdam we had a dreamlike 'light wind, drifting sail' to Volendam with a large group of friends on board. There two other Wharram catamarans met us. It was a wonderful welcome and a great feeling for me that there were so many people out there building and enjoying my designs.

The next day we sailed across the IJsselmeer to Friesland from where we all travelled by train to Groningen where the Boon family, who had lived in a flat in Amsterdam, had just bought an old farmhouse with a shed big enough to build boats in. During that trip, young Hanneke quietly made it clear she saw a future sailing, living, designing, and building boats with me.

14   Another voyage to the West Indies

On return from our voyage to Holland we spent two years in Milford Haven working on new designs and new construction methods, which I will come back to in a later chapter.

However, we wanted to make further voyages on *Tehini*, after all that is what I had promised the girls when we were building her. Hanneke had now joined the crew and we had made further improvements to *Tehini*'s rig by cutting down her aft mast and turning her from a schooner into a ketch. In September 1973 the first 'Whitbread Round the World Yacht Race' was starting from Portsmouth with boats including Éric Tabarly's *Pen Duick VI* and Chay Blyth's *Great Britain II* taking part, and as multihulls were excluded I had the great plan to enter our 51ft *Tehini* unofficially in the race. I was again driven by my need to prove my designs by doing well in races. It took me many years and much heartache to learn this was not the way for me.

The Bay of Biscay and a short sharp gale taught me a lesson. Two hundred miles south-west of the Spanish Cape Finisterre we discovered a weakness in *Tehini*'s construction. When building the beam attachment points, I had foolishly not fitted a set of bolts holding the structural timbers in place, relying purely on the glue joints, even though I had drawn these bolts on all my building plans. This led to the glue joints starting to strain open and could have led to major structural failure. The joint first showing signs of strain was in Hanneke's bunk right above her face and it was worrying looking up and seeing movement as the boat rose on every wave. We changed course and ran before the gale to La Coruña.

It was a simple, but difficult to access, repair job, where we not only fitted the missing bolts, but also reinforced the whole area around these fixing points, a modification we later added to all our 'Classic' designs. The work took two weeks, and we were now way behind in the racing fleet—what to do? Continue the race, and perhaps find out further weaknesses in the design? Or simply sail on to Las Palmas in the Canaries, then on to Trinidad and the West Indies? i.e., forget racing around

Tehini on the Atlantic, self-steering sail

the world. Whilst in Spain it also became clear that all was not well politically in the UK, in fact this became the famous 'Winter of Discontent', with strikes leading to the 'Three Day Week' in early 1974. I, as my political self, worried about this and did not want to be too far away from home.

With the agreement of the girls, I decided to forget the race and carry on to Trinidad. *Tehini* seemed relieved at the decision. She lifted easily and lightly over the Atlantic waves that had so battered the 23ft 6in *Tangaroa* seventeen years before. Arriving in Trinidad was even better; all our friends from the past were there to welcome us. Ruth and I enjoyed showing the other girls Trinidad, and Carnival was on its way, so we stayed to take part. The magic sound of Trinidadian steel bands practising for the carnival was everywhere. We were invited to join one of the carnival dancing bands through the streets of Port of Spain and we joined in with the big 'Jump-up' night-time parties.

In 1973 the Caribbean still had the natural charm of when I had left there on *Rongo* twelve years earlier, before the start of the mass tourist influx. From Trinidad we sailed up the islands, the girls delighted in learning to snorkel in the clear waters of the Grenadines. We stopped at most of the islands up the Windward chain, meeting the famous Norwegian sailor Peter Tangvald and his new young wife Lydia in Martinique on *l'Artemis,* the new boat he had built in the South American jungle. We sailed up to Antigua where we anchored in English Harbour.

English Harbour at this date was still undeveloped, with the old warehouses from Nelson's time standing empty. Hanneke spent time in the cool of the old Copper & Lumber Store sewing sails, and she learned to make hats from coconut leaves.

My old friends of twelve years before were still there, including Peter Deeth, who had sailed with us on *Rongo* on her maiden voyage from Trinidad to Grenada in 1959 and who now owned two hotels in English Harbour. There was old Ian Spencer, an experienced ocean sailor, whom I had met on my last visit, who lived in the 'Officer's Quarters' in a room full of fascinating artefacts. We went for picnics on the beach with him in a borrowed beach buggy. There was a South African woman, Rena, who had opened up a sail repair loft. It seemed natural to them that their friend James should arrive with a large catamaran crewed by a bunch of very capable women. Parties were organised. A magic day was spent on Jol Byerley's luxury charter boat swimming naked over the reef with the *Tehini* girls, Jol's wife, ex-wife and teenage daughter; for a short time Antigua resembled the scene that Captain Cook and the

French Captain Bougainville had described on their arrival in Tahiti in the late eighteenth century, with beautiful naked women swimming round their ships.

After Jol and I had discussed ancient Polynesian ship designs and social concepts, he introduced me to Edward Dodd, an American publisher visiting Antigua. Dodd was ill with 'flu at the time, but prepared to see us. I learned that he had recently written and published a book called *Polynesian Seafaring*, which I later bought for my library. This book is still a valuable source for understanding Polynesian sailing culture as observed by Europe's first Pacific explorers, Cook for the English and Bougainville for the French.

The final paragraph in Dodd's book reads:

Then one day, in another generation or so, some young dreamer in Tahaa, or Hivaoa, in Mangareva or Manihiki, would start wondering about those old myths. He might take to watching the migrating birds on a spring evening. After a while he might go up in the mountains to search out a tree… suitable someday perhaps for a sea-going canoe.

On reflection—that 'young dreamer' could be me, who could look over one shoulder and see the ships of my Viking ancestors, but was free enough of Western culture to see over the other shoulder the sea-going ships of the Polynesians.

During our visit Edward Dodd gave me a prospectus, just published by the newly established Polynesian Voyaging Society, with first proposals for the building of the Hawaiian double canoe *Hokule'a*. Little did I know how we would become embroiled, many years later, in the politics of this project.

When we started on our voyage we left our 'Polynesian Catamaran' design business in the care of two close friends, Lieutenant-Commander Bob Evans of the British Fleet Air Arm (a branch of the Royal Navy) and his very organised wife Anthea.

The British Navy at that time was adopting new types of jet fighter that could take off from the flight decks of aircraft carriers, which were originally designed for slow propeller aircraft. The taking off and landing of these new jets had to be tested; it was a very dangerous enterprise. It could be rightly said that the young test pilots who did this had to be slightly mad! Bob Evans was one of these mad young men. He was building one of my 40ft Narai designs at his naval base and he had offered, with Anthea, to look after the Wharram design office while we sailed off into the wide world. They were overwhelmed with design enquiries. The Antigua idyll was over and we had to set sail back to Milford Haven to relieve these two very good friends. We loaded up with stores. 'You are not sailing back to Britain already?' was the puzzled enquiry from all our Antiguan friends, meaning why are you leaving this island paradise—stay here, there is a happy future for you.

The voyage back was straightforward with calms in the Sargasso Sea and mixed weather getting colder as we moved north and east. *Tehini* was a capable ocean-going boat, so making this voyage was relatively easy. Our worst weather came at the end of the voyage, sailing under storm jib before a following gale up the Western Approaches. Hanneke still remembers being at the wheel when a set of three much larger waves broke under *Tehini*'s sterns. She gripped the wheel as the boat was picked up and started to race down the front of the waves, then watched as the two bows shot forwards and downwards, water rising up to deck level, but soon realised how the flare and overhangs of those powerful bows kept the boat from submerging into the wave in front, preventing the possibility of pitch poling.

Our *Tehini* had proved herself as an ocean-going ship, now I wanted to show once more she was also capable of doing well in racing. I knew she was good, we had taken part in the Crystal Trophy Race in 1973 and done really well, particularly when ghosting in very light winds. We had passed the Apache catamaran of Michael Butterfield, the keen racing Chairman of MOCRA (the British multihull association), off Cherbourg buoy in barely any wind, much to his annoyance.

July 1974 was the start of the next Round Britain Race. This time *Tehini* would be sailed by our friend Bob Evans as skipper with Maggie for crew. We just had time to get *Tehini* hauled out on the slip in Milford Docks and work done to smooth her battered keels and apply a new coat of antifouling. But once again my bad luck in racing held. They made good progress, but during the second leg in the rough seas off the north-west of Ireland disaster struck. One of the crossbeams suddenly cracked with a load bang, followed by similar cracking in another beam. A quick decision to make for the sheltered passage behind Achill Island saved the ship. *Tehini* was beached and Bob and Maggie jumped into action to make repairs. By the time I and the other girls arrived to help, the masts were already lowered. New beams were quickly made by our then Irish agent, Jarlath Cunnane, who fortuitously lived not far away in Knock

in county Mayo. He was in charge of building the new Knock cathedral, so had all the building skills and materials to hand. It took less than a week to get the boat back together and we sailed her back to Milford Haven.

The only problem was a navigational one: should we sail north-about or south-about Ireland? The distance was approximately the same. Bob insisted on south, I on north, and we nearly had a major row, but I decided to give in and let Bob have his way. He later told me he was privately terrified the weather would turn against us off the rugged south-west of Ireland and force us to turn back, but his luck held.

What had caused this failure of the beams? On examination it turned out to be rot. When building *Tehini* I had used solid hemlock for some of the beams. I knew it was not very durable, so I had laminated plywood on all the surfaces to stop water getting to the timber. Over time this had not been sufficient protection and rot had developed out of sight in the core of the beam. I have never made beams like that again, always recommending laminating them from layers of quality Douglas fir, which is a much more durable timber.

15 The multihull scene in the UK

As I write, four decades plus after we sailed back from the West Indies into Milford Haven, the picture I have of myself at that time is how stupid and stubborn I could be. For with our wonderful office on the docks, *Tehini* moored in a lovely sheltered creek, several lovely women living and working with me, I still was not satisfied. My 'build yourself' designs were selling well all over the world—but I wanted more. I wanted the approval of the English yachting establishment. This was a world with at one end Cowes on the Isle of Wight and at the other end London and the Thames Estuary. I probably could have got their approval, had I tried to conform; I could have studiously modified my north-country accent (English yachting society at that time spoke in the accepted 'clipped' public school voices, and northern accents were looked down upon). I could have turned up at various sailing venues looking like a yachtsman, with a hard drinking masculine crew, I could have restrained myself from giving criticism of other catamaran designs… instead I was turning up at such venues with an attractive, well-trained, highly vocal all female crew. What really got 'them' was that 'my girls' were not only good at sailing and navigation, but very good at building boats too—and in addition they looked beautiful!

The epicentre of Britain's new multihull group was MOCRA (Multihull Offshore Cruising and Racing Association). I became a member from the start in 1969 and was a committee member for many years. Here was a coming together of opposing attitudes and always I came up against social prejudice. I still remember being in the toilets one day and another committee member in the stall next to me saying: 'Jim, you design boats that bus drivers can build.' I think he meant it as a compliment, but it typified the class-ridden attitudes that were rife in the yachting establishment of that time. Another comment I remember is: 'Jim, why do you always live in the Celtic fringes?' meaning, why did I not move to the yachting areas of the south coast and behave like one of them. The final straw came one day when I was once again addressed as 'Jimmy boy' (a condescending term in Britain) and I thumped the table and said: 'The only people that can call me Jimmy are the women I go to bed with!' to a shocked silence. From then on I started to call myself 'James' and abandoned my northern name of 'Jim'. This class division was a particularly British phenomenon. I found that where the working classes were building my catamarans in Britain, in Holland—where some of the first Wharram catamarans were built—it was the doctors, engineers and other professionals that were attracted to the simplicity of my designs.

I was also a member of the AYRS (Amateur Yacht Research Society) founded in 1955 by Dr John Morwood, with whom I had had many a letter argument about the design of multihulls, starting from the time I arrived in northern Spain on *Tangaroa* in 1955. Morwood edited the AYRS magazine and I frequently became incensed over his (often biased) presentation of the development of multihulls.

Here I also managed to be at odds with other members. I was once invited to speak at a gathering which would be attended by Prince Phillip, who was the president of this Society. There were several speakers and we were all carefully instructed to speak for twenty minutes and to watch out for the nod from Prince Phillip to indicate when to stop. I was the last speaker and was never given the nod—I think he liked what I was saying—so I spoke for half an hour, to the annoyance of the others. I liked Prince Phillip, he certainly had an eye for women and he appreciated mine.

In spite of being sidelined by class as a Northerner, I was a powerful voice in multihull circles in those years. In 1973–74 an under-the-table deal had been done by John Fisk of the IYRU (International Yacht Racing Union—a subsidiary of the RYA) to get the Tornado catamaran accepted as an Olympic class in return for the British accepting a new multihull rating rule propagated by a Californian, Dr Vic Stern. It was not a case of whether this rule was any good—though it was mathematically complex, requiring every boat to be weighed, and no-one in MOCRA understood it—its acceptance without democratic discussion with MOCRA was wrong. The other MOCRA committee members had basically rolled over and accepted the IYRU/RYA decisions. The fact it could affect multihull design for many years to come incensed me to write a 'minority report' exposing the whole affair. I sent it to 'everyone'. I think it was the aftermath of this report and my correspondence with Prince Phillip that eventually led to an invitation to the Royal Thames Yacht Club in Knightsbridge for an interview, for me to be considered as a member of the new RYA Cruising Committee. I was accepted as multihull representative in 1977 and served on it for fourteen years.

16   Years of plenty – research & development

In those years of the early 1970s our Milford Haven 'Longhouse', staffed by highly intelligent sailing women, became a 'Mecca' for would-be dreaming sailors. From all over the world, people with building or sailing dreams would turn up to discuss, to learn, or gain the confidence to construct their own projects.

At this time we had a range of thirteen designs from the 12ft Surfcat to the 51ft Tehini, which were all selling well, and for the first time we had a surplus of money. So much so, that for the first time I was able to take the girls on a shopping spree in a leading fashion shop in Haverford West. An hour or so later—with a bill of £1000 we emerged with each girl laden with bags—each of them containing beautiful dresses. They certainly deserved this significant treat in reward for their many months of tireless hard work and commitment. That evening the girls made a celebratory feast in our Longhouse.

What should be realised is that our group of me and the five girls was never a 'harem', with the man ruling over the women. The women were strong and independent and we all worked as a group of equals to achieve our goals. The girls also had the freedom to occasionally explore and expand their sexuality within our known group of friends. But as most men want to lead their 'own' lives, men never became a part of our core crew. We kept this side of our life discreet. My reputation in the outside world as a man living with several women was enough; leading a very public life in the world of yachting, the girls' reputation needed to be protected. This protection was in the form of a business partnership of six equal partners under the name of 'James Wharram Associates'.

Sexual freedom for women was coming into the public eye in the 1970s with as its most vocal proponent the Australian academic and writer Germaine Greer, who was outspoken regarding her many affairs with men, and whose first book *The Female Eunuch* sold in vast numbers. But my girls had other interests to pursue than sexual politics; their public image as sailors and boatbuilders first was what mattered most.

The increased income from the sales of my self-built designs, combined with our large Milford Haven workshop, enabled me to experiment with new hull shapes and new materials. Other multihull designers of that time were using fibreglass construction. One way was to make a 'female' mould with a perfect glossy interior surface in which layers of glass cloth and resin were laminated, left to harden, then lifted out as a complete hull of a boat; messy and unpleasant for the builder but, if made with care, reliable and strong. We had several of our 22ft Hinemoa designs built in this way, by a reliable company near London called Bromley Boats. We were using two of them as charter boats in Milford Haven. It is an expensive method to set up and only becomes economical when selling boats in large numbers.

A simpler method, ideal for one-off designs, was to use GRP foam sandwich construction, which could be done on a much simpler and cheaper male mould. This male mould was similar to my backbone, bulkheads and stringers structure, which formed the basis of my plywood hull designs. Foam sheeting is attached over the surface of this mould instead of plywood, followed by several layers of fibreglass. When set, the shell is lifted off and turned over; then one must laminate the inside of this foam shell with more structural glass laminations and add bulkheads. It was a horribly messy, unhealthy way of building a boat, but could turn out hulls quickly if one was not too concerned with durability or finish, so was a fast way to create a racing multihull.

At that time, the major selling point of multihulls in the eyes of the yachting public was their potential speed in racing. Many racing multihulls were built quickly and rigged with large, tall sails and would do well in races, sailed by experienced racing crew. Often these boats were not very durable—I heard of one older foam sandwich racing trimaran that had water pouring out of the foam core when drilling a hole to mount a barometer—and in the hands of the less experienced they could capsize. I knew how to design strong tough boats to ride out ocean storms, but inwardly I could not abandon the concepts of durability and safe stability for my designs, hence would always be handicapped when it came to winning races.

The designs I was selling at that time for self-building were all built in plywood, held together with either urea-formaldehyde glue, which had been developed in World War II to build the hugely successful de Havilland 'Mosquito' plywood fighter/bomber, or resorcinol glue where extra strength was needed. It was a tested method of building, with which I knew self-builders would achieve good results. The other building methods I had to first try myself, before I could design in them for others.

᰿᰿

At Christmas 1971 I received in the post a Tide Calendar, published in Hawaii by the Dillingham Corporation—it was sent to me by one of my builders there. It was inspirational; here for the first time since I had studied *Canoes of Oceania* (published in 1939) as a young man in Manchester Central Library, I saw a collection of the ancient Polynesian canoes from that book sailing the ocean waves in exciting, lifelike paintings.

Inside the cover was an inspiring description of how the Polynesians had migrated from south-east Asia on their canoes and populated all the islands of the Pacific. In fact it described everything I had been dreaming and talking about since I had read Éric de Bisschop's book at the age of sixteen and made my first Atlantic crossing by double canoe to prove his migration theories. Here was no longer the doubt seeded by the missionaries and spread by Andrew Sharp, but a new belief in the seaworthiness of the Polynesian canoes as I had been proving with my pioneering Atlantic voyages. At the end of this description is this text:

> Since its inception several years ago, the Dillingham Corporation's Tide Calendar has become a labour of love for those who plan and assemble it. The 1972 calendar is no exception. Original paintings and drawings by Hawaii-born artist Herb Kawainui Kane illustrate it, wedding early Polynesians with you who live, work or play near Hawaii's timeless tides. Its charts precisely record their ceaseless movement.

This artist, Herb Kane, had the genius to take the drawings of Captain Cook and Admiral Paris and turn them into modern-day bright coloured art illustrations, with the vividness of the now highly collectable advertising posters for railways and steamships in 1930s Britain. As an experienced ocean sailor and student of the drawings Paris and Cook made on their first visits to the Polynesian islands, I can only write that Kane's interpretation of these drawings was the work of a figurative genius.

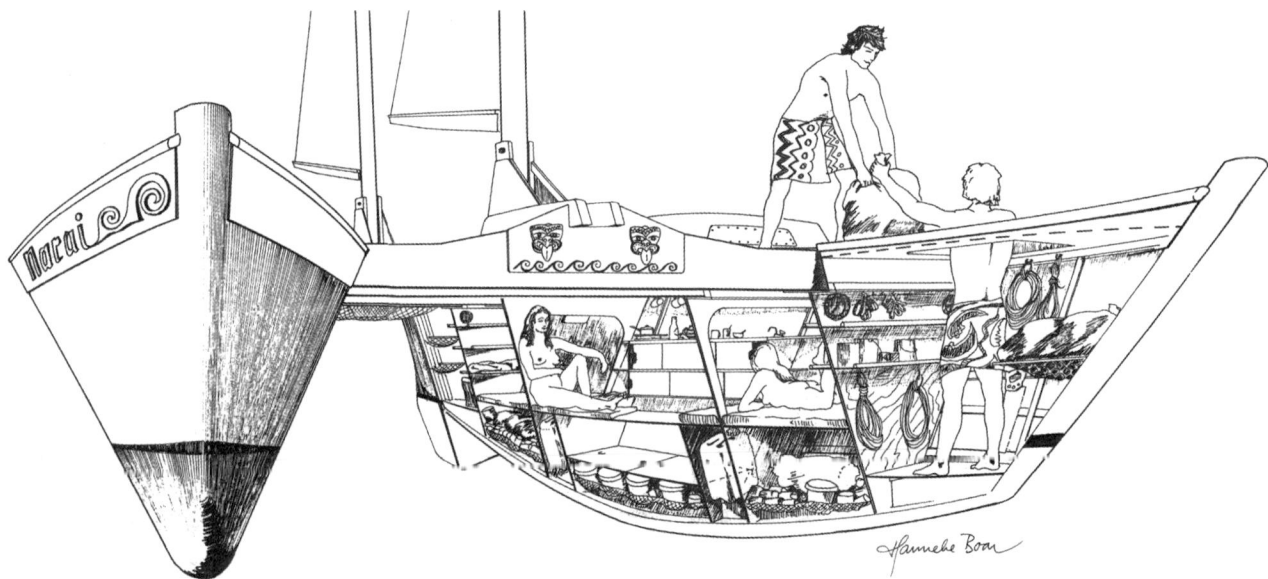

Narai Mk IV

I had been dreaming for some time of new hull shapes, going back to the Polynesian origins of the double canoe. My early studies of the drawings in *Canoes of Oceania* were still there in my mind. Seeing Herb Kane's artistic representation of the Tuamotu voyaging canoe, originally drawn with great accuracy by Admiral Paris in around 1820, made me want to design a boat based on this hull shape. Both Paris and Cook had described it as the most seaworthy of the remaining canoes in the Pacific and I knew that Éric de Bisschop's *Kaimiloa* had used a similar half-moon hull shape.

I designed a 22ft hull to build as a prototype. I called it *Areoi* after the groups of Polynesian artist-performers that voyaged the islands in their days of glory. I had read stories about these people; they were my vision of 'Sea People', whose culture had been destroyed by the missionaries.

Nuala had shown interest and aptitude in working with the new GRP materials and did research into their application techniques. We built the prototype in our Longhouse workshop in the foam sandwich method, and for the first time lashed the cross beams to the hulls in Polynesian tradition.

Hanneke spent the summer of 1972 with us and with her sailing childhood background was keen to sail our new Areoi prototype on its first trial. Admiral Paris had drawn the double canoe with a long steering oar, and this was similarly depicted on Herb Kane's art drawing. It looked exciting so I had designed the boat to be steered like this. We rigged it with the mast and spritsail rig of a 22ft Hina. The boat made good speed and was manoeuvrable, but the steering oar was difficult to handle and it was easy to lose control, so it was hauled out of the water again for further development.

Looking back in time, this 1972 prototype of the Tuamotuan hull shape was the origin of all my Pahi designs and eventually led to the Tama Moana design true Polynesian double canoe we sailed on the Lapita Voyage in 2008. But that is another story I will return to later. I did however already see a larger version in my mind's eye and described it to Hanneke, who turned my vision into an artistic sketch, which we sent out as a Christmas card in 1972.

The GRP foam sandwich building technique had been successful, so we decided to apply it to a new Classic design I had on the drawing board. This was a development of our plywood 27ft Tane. One Tane had already made the Atlantic circuit, sailed by a tough singlehander called Peter Sheard. He had used a junk rig on her, which had been a lot more successful than the one we had used on *Tehini*. The Tane had been designed for racing and so had very slim hulls and minimal accommodation. The new Tanenui had increased freeboard and slightly wider hulls, making it a nice weekend or holiday cruiser.

In January 1975, nine months after our return from sailing to the West Indies, we had our first stand at the London Boat Show. Our small but very lively spot on the upper gallery at Earl's Court attracted a lot of interest with its evocative photos of tropical sailing and beautiful boat models—made by Hanneke—as well as being staffed by a group of attractive, knowledgeable sailing women.

There were several other stands selling production catamarans: there were the Prout brothers with their 36ft 'Snowgoose', there was Reg White's Sailcraft stand selling Rod Macalpine Downie's 'Iroquois' and other designs, there was Tom Lack with the 'Catalac' designs. These were all GRP-built deck cabin catamarans, evolved round the concepts first designed by the Prouts and Bill O'Brien.

By 1976 multihulls were becoming mainstream. In America there was *Multihulls* magazine published by the Hungarian Charles Chiodi and his German wife Ava Burgess. We also had a US-Canadian agent called Pat McGrath in Toronto, Canada, who with his hard driving Australian wife Gillian joined up with Charles and Ava to organise the 'First World Multihull Symposium' to be held in Toronto. This was going to be a major event with 'all' the major multihull designers of that time taking part. It was decided that I would attend with Maggie as my PA and Hanneke as my design assistant.

It was the first time I would be face-to-face in public discussion with all these other designers, so I was determined to do my homework and know everything there was to know about them and their boats. I had been publicly caustic about some of the designers who strutted around saying 'my designs are faster'—ignoring their history of capsizes due to the high masts and large sail areas. But others had noticed and mainstream articles had been published about multihulls with worrying titles like 'Unsafe on any Sea', echoing Ralph Nader's book on modern American cars *Unsafe at Any Speed*. With Hanneke's help I prepared folders of information on the dimensions, weights and sail areas of all the current catamarans and trimarans, from which she calculated their stability.

The actual symposium was a bit of a circus, starting with all the designers lined up on the podium in alphabetical order, each one giving their history in multihull design, with one of the American ones bursting into tears at the emotional impact of it all. I played along with this when I, with the name Wharram, was the last to speak, telling them that my mother's maiden name was Cook, with the inference that Captain Cook was one of my ancestors. I was disappointed that the discussions never really touched the deeper design principles of multihulls.

The conference was a highly-charged event, with Gillian McGrath, our agent's wife, shielding the 'celebrity designers' from the 'groupies' by shepherding us into elevators and to our rooms. Fortunately for us, two of my Canadian builders brought us some incredible food baskets (of fresh fruits, salmon, sliced meats and freshly baked bread), which we ate in comfort in our hotel room.

We additionally took under our wing the English designer Rod Macalpine Downie, who we got to know better there. He was in fact one of the designers who had achieved speed with (too) large sail areas. And yes, his designs had capsized! But we found on closer acquaintance that he was a very nice man. I also started a closer friendship with trimaran designer Jim Brown and reacquainted myself with Dick Newick, whom I had last met in 1959 in St Croix. Bob Harris was also there, whom I had met in New York.

One of the major leads from this symposium was meeting the Gougeon brothers, who were just starting to spread their ideas of the use of WEST (Wood Epoxy Saturation Technique). They came armed with samples and big claims for the technique. I was somewhat sceptical and asked them 'how deep does this epoxy actually 'saturate' into the wood?' When the answer was just 1/1000 inch, I was not yet convinced this material was all it was claimed to be. But on meeting Meade Gougeon again a few years later in Holland, at a symposium on yacht design organised by the HISWA boat show, I learned their ideas had gelled into a system that looked like it could be the future of wooden yacht building, and I was ready to start using it.

The other public high point was the shocking news half way through the symposium that the 60ft trimaran *Gulfstreamer*, designed as a racing multihull by Dick Newick for Phil Weld, had capsized in the Atlantic. Hanneke and I immediately went to check our files on the stability of *Gulfstreamer* as we had calculated that this boat had high wind stability and should not have capsized. Then the news became clear that she had capsized not by wind, but by wave action.

Then 'my' young, twenty-three year old Hanneke started doing some drawings which showed that when sideways on to large waves a trimaran with low-buoyancy floats, as was then the preferred configuration, lacked beam stability! The trimaran designers were out-thought by a young, shy Dutch girl. Hanneke showed her drawings to the two trimaran designers at a cocktail party that evening. Derek Kelsall—a British trimaran designer—dismissed them and tried to convince her she was wrong with his own theory of stability. However Dick Newick, the designer of the capsized *Gulfstreamer,* quickly understood her reasoning. It took several years and an article written by me called 'The Stable Multihull', before the subject became a matter of open discussion and final acceptance. Hugo Meyers, another American designer at the symposium—designer of the 'Seabird' catamaran—later took Hanneke's theory and with complex mathematical calculations claimed it as his own. In the years after this event, trimarans were designed with much larger floats and wider overall beam, as can be seen in all the high speed racing trimarans today.

17 We move to Ireland

Milford Haven in the mid-1970s was developing into a major oil port. It was made clear that our relatively cheap rented offices and workshop would be part of new development schemes. We no longer had security of tenure in our Longhouse. We had some savings and started looking for somewhere to buy our own land base.

We wanted to buy the strip of land along the lane leading down to Sandy Haven where *Tehini* was moored. We had rented it for several years from the local farmer and had used it as a secret garden. The local industrial liaison officer was interested in our plans and helped us design a new A-frame design office, but the planning office was less keen and permission to build was not granted. We looked for other properties and pieces of land, but nothing suited.

Temptingly, across the water from Pembrokeshire lies southern Ireland. It was only a short drive to Fishguard and a ferry trip across the Irish Sea to Rosslare in County Wexford.

Ireland at that time was recovering from hundreds of years of English wars, followed by Roman Catholic Church domination. Through emigration, large agricultural areas were almost depopulated. Farm buildings, with acres of fields, could be bought for an incredibly low price. Ruth offered to go on a reconnaissance trip on her bicycle to see what might be available and suitable for our expanding design business. She returned with a short list of properties, then she departed to sail across the Tasman on a 35ft Tangaroa, whose builders had paid for Ruth to fly out to Australia to teach them to sail their boat. Ruth always loved ocean sailing and she snapped up this chance of another voyage on a Wharram catamaran. She said we could manage without her for a while.

Our first exploratory trip across the Irish Sea came to an ignominious halt before it even started. A few weeks before our planned trip our Bedford van had been in a crash and was a write-off. We bought a Commer van cheaply from a friend. Anyone remembering this vehicle from the 1970s will know it was like a tin can on a narrow wheelbase, no lining inside, just a big hollow space. I was travelling with Nuala, who was Irish, Hanneke, and my old friend from Trinidad, Denis Solomon, the man who had sailed with us on *Rongo* to the Virgin Islands in 1961, who had happened to visit and said: 'I would love to come with you.'

When going through customs at the ferry port in Fishguard we were called aside by some plain clothes Special Branch policemen; they wanted to have a closer look at our van. Several went inside searching and tapping the single sheet steel panelling, looking for what? It all seemed very inefficient. We told them if they had any worries about us, or the van, to contact the police station in Milford Haven. We had given them some old hulls to make a raft for the local raft race and they had won. The local newspaper had published a big photo of the raft, the police team and myself. Special Branch, however, dressed to intimidate in leather jackets and platform shoes, knew better.

Time was ticking by and it looked as if we would miss the ferry. They started to question me in a belligerent manner and after a while I said: ' Who do you think you are? The SS?' I don't think this went down very well and next thing I was told they were arresting us under the provisions of the 1974 Prevention of Terrorism Act. We were told to follow them to Fishguard police station. This was the time of IRA bombings in the UK, hence the Special Branch presence at the ferry port.

They took our fingerprints, then more questioning at the police station; the local Welsh police were thoroughly out of their depth, they were faced with two irate, very tall and articulate men, a Dutch woman and an Irish woman. When questioned, Denis reeled off his impressive education including University degrees at Harvard and Cambridge, with the police woman's eyes getting wider and wider. What he did not tell her was that as well as his black heritage through his father his mother was from Belfast, hence the slightly reddish hair and freckles on a brown skin. We still had no explanation as to why we had been arrested.

However they said they had the right to hold us for seventy-two hours, so were told to again drive our van to Haverfordwest police station, where there were cells. One Special Branch officer sat on the back seat to 'keep guard'. We were never searched for weapons, either in Fishguard or on arrival in Haverfordwest. I was taken to our boat, *Tehini*, as they wanted to search it. After a perfunctory search I asked

Narai Mk I, Kattegat, 1982; photog: unknown

them if they were finished. 'Yes', so I then opened the bilge and showed them the big spaces under the floor they had completely missed.

After a night in a cell Denis was getting claustrophobic. He was in the next cell to mine and we were allowed to walk in the small, gated corridor outside the cells. I tried to distract him by pretending we were on Captain Hornblower's ship striding up and down the deck.

In the morning, with no sign of Special Branch, the duty uniform policeman told us we did have the right to contact someone, so I was on the phone to Maggie, who called our friend the ex-mayor of Haverfordwest, who was now our professional boat-builder (builder of the first Tangaroa Mk IV); Denis called his father who was the Trinidadian High Commissioner in London, who contacted the UK home secretary Roy Jenkins; and Nuala phoned her father in Dublin, who contacted his friend Lord Longford, who in turn also contacted Roy Jenkins.

It was not long before we were released. A week or so later Special Branch came for a visit and apologised. We heard through our contact in the Milford police that the man in charge was put back on the beat. The photograph of the raft team on the wall of Milford police station got the caption: 'James Wharram and his gun running team.'

When we finally did travel across to Ireland, we bought the first property on Ruth's list, which we instantly fell in love with. It was in county Wexford not far from the ferry port and situated on the River Barrow, down river from the town of New Ross. This wide navigable river runs into the sea near the town of Waterford. There was a sheltered estuary for test-sailing boats. We were able to buy a ten-acre site, with two basic undeveloped cottages and a quay to moor our *Tehini* to. The nearest fresh water supply was in a spring across a field, there were no sewage facilities and no electricity; but to pioneering sea people it seemed spacious and beautiful, with lots of potential. The main cottage overlooked the River Barrow and behind it was a field surrounded by huge beech trees and enormous granite boulders. It had an ancient Neolithic feel; it was these trees and boulders that made us decide to buy it. We bought it at a ridiculously low price.

From Milford Haven to New Ross was a 70nm voyage across the Irish Sea. In three or four trips on *Tehini* we transported all our possessions across and towed the 21ft Areoi prototype to 'our quay' on the river Barrow. This whole episode, from my now older more sensible perspective, was an incredible—some might say

hare-brained—undertaking. But with the backing of five women made tough, physically and mentally, by an active sea-life, it just seemed the logical thing to do. In fact, in my mind there seemed nothing I could *not* do. By the ancient Greeks we are told 'Whom the gods would destroy they first make mad'. But I was not aware of this when we moved to Ireland and started a new life on the land.

The 1978 Round Britain Race was on the horizon; after three failed attempts I still had not learned my lesson. This time I would use my new design ideas and building techniques to ensure I would have a chance. With my then total arrogance, five hard-working women and the dream of what I could achieve, I planned to build *two* multihulls.

The first design was to be a 35ft catamaran, using the Tuamotu rockered hull shape we had built as a 21ft prototype in 1972. She would again be constructed in GRP foam sandwich, which allowed us to have gently curving V-shaped hulls. I had already designed this boat back in Milford Haven; Hanneke had made a beautiful model of her, which we had exhibited at the 1975 London Boat Show and taken to Toronto. It is still in our design studio today. We had transported the pre-fabricated parts to make the mould across the Irish Sea on *Tehini*.

How sails work, and how to sail close to the wind, are subjects which have preoccupied many sailors and yacht designers over the years, and my own library holds many of their books. In the 1970s data and concepts from the development of fixed wing aeronautics started to filter into modern sail design. A leader in these concepts was Professor Tony Marchaj from Southampton University; the essence of his advice was that you had to reduce the turbulence caused by the mast in the airflow over the leading edge of the sail, and to control twist and camber in the sail. Many designers try to achieve this with wing masts and highly expensive hardware.

Following Marchaj's advise, my new catamaran rig was designed to control twist and camber and to reduce the loads in a practical and simple way. I would use a Bermudan cutter rig with a loose footed mainsail with kicked up boom and tack close to the deck, which gave the longest luff length with lowest centre of effort, i.e. greatest stability. The outhaul tension to the end of the boom controlled camber and the twin sheets gave excellent downward pull to control twist as well as precisely controlling the sail's angle to the wind.

Having realised I myself was not the best sailor for hard racing, I had arranged for two Scotsmen to be the crew of this boat. They had made an earlier RBR attempt in 1974 in my 27ft Tanenui design, but this boat had been badly built in foam sandwich by a firm in Port Talbot and literally leaked like a sieve. She had sailed fast, while the crew operated the bilge pump from their helmsman's seat, but when the deck started to lift off the bulkheads they called it a day and returned to port. They were both keen to give it another try in a well built boat, and my new *Areoi*, as she would be called, was for them to sail the race.

So confident—or arrogant—was I regarding my own abilities, I designed a second boat to enter the race. Maggie was keen to have another try at it and become a yachtswoman in her own right, and our design student Richard Woods wanted to sail as her crew. He had been racing Moth dinghies from an early age.

The fastest traditional canoe craft of the Pacific were always acknowledged to be the single outrigger proas of the Micronesian islands, with slim asymmetrical hull and outrigger float always kept to windward, which meant they tacked by reversing end for end. I designed such a proa at 31ft length, though I did not give it an asymmetrical hull, using a similar hull shape to the 35ft *Areoi*. We would build this hull out of Douglas fir plywood sheathed in fibreglass, a method used by Jim Brown in America on his trimaran designs.

Instead of the traditional Pacific triangular lateen style sail with spar top and bottom, that would need to be swung round when tacking and would be hard to handle by a two person crew, I designed a trapezoidal lugsail that could be used in two directions without needing to be swung round. She would be steered by two Viking-style side rudders, which could be easily raised out of the water when the boat changed tack.

So the Wharram Team, as well as settling into a primitive cottage life—no toilet, running water or electricity—was committed to building, in just two years, two potential racing boats for the Round Britain Race! Nuala, Lesley and Hanneke were building the new catamaran out in our open field under two plastic agricultural tunnels, which suffered from dripping condensation. I, with the help of Richard Woods and sometimes Maggie, when she was not busy in the office, was building the proa in a nearby farm shed.

Ruth, during our years in Ireland, was in her mid-fifties and deserved some time to do what she was happiest doing. She was never a supporter of my racing schemes

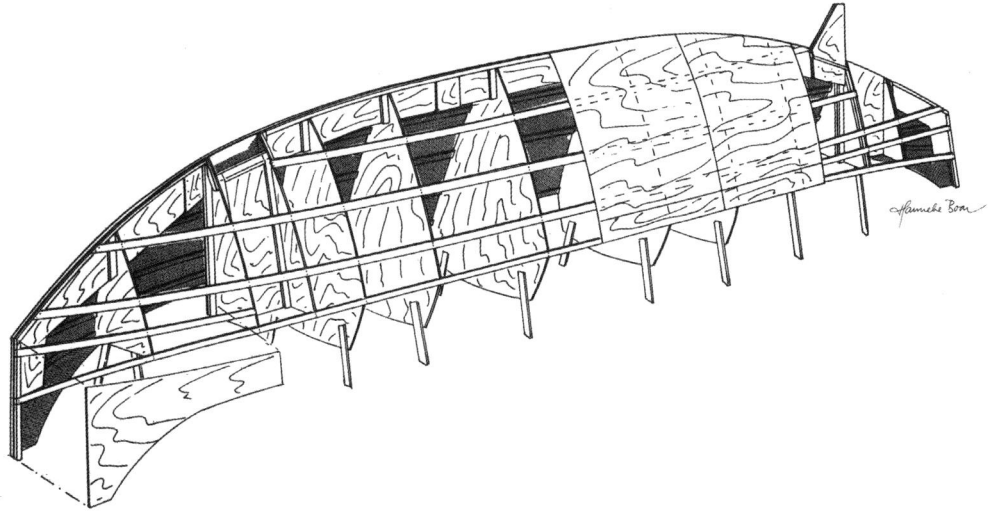

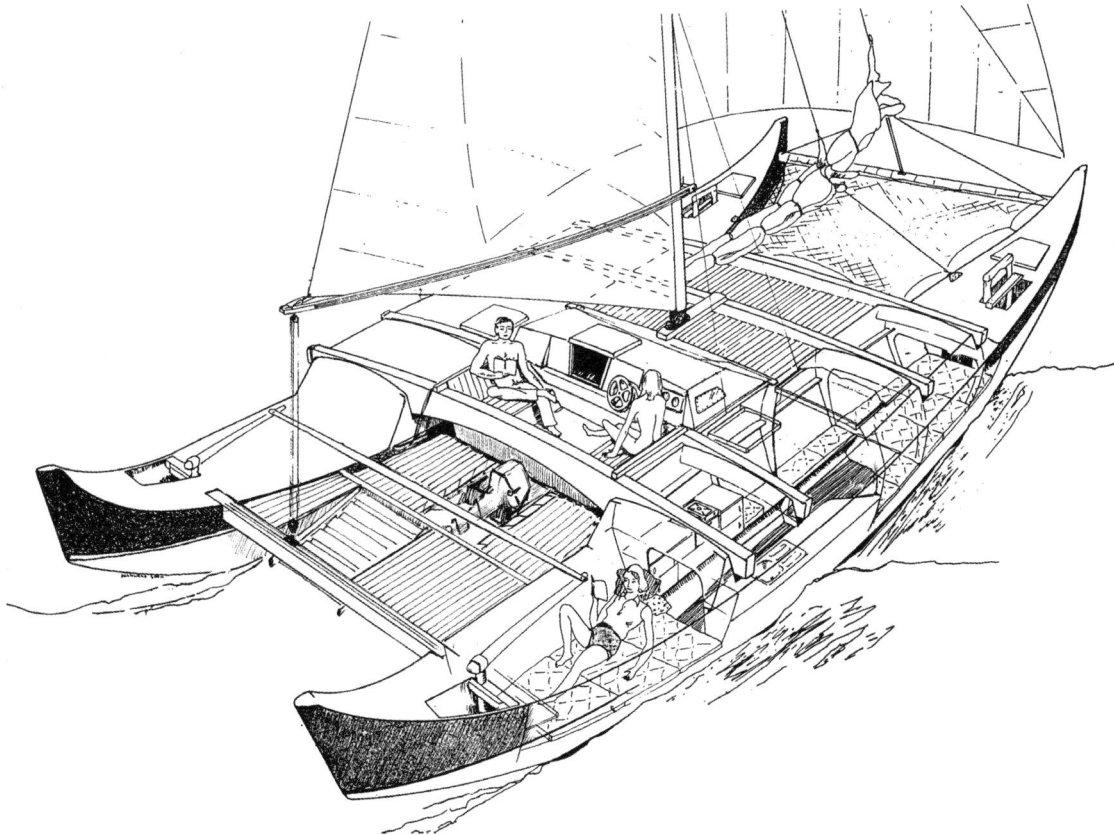

Pahi 42 'Captain Cook'

and was not really a boat builder. Due to her constant communications with Wharram builders round the world she had made many friends who invited her to come sailing on their boats. So while we were busy boatbuilding, Ruth sailed across the Atlantic in a 27ft Tanenui, *Vereo,* built by Thomas Firth Jones and his wife Carol in America, and made several voyages on George Payne's 36ft Raka. Tom Jones had a very high regard for Ruth's navigational and ocean sailing abilities and dedicated his book *Multihull Voyaging* to her.

We soon found that building a large hull in foam sandwich on a male mould had some problems, which we had not discovered when building the much smaller prototype. We produced a nicely shaped shell on the mould, but when it was lifted off and turned over for the inside to be glassed, the problems started. The hull shell of the slim slightly curved Vee'd hull was more flexible than expected, in fact, being yellow, it somewhat resembled a banana skin. We placed it in two cradles, but this was not enough support for it to keep its shape accurately, and many hours were spent in propping it up while fitting the pre-cut bulkheads. The end result was not as fair as I wanted. I was very strict in those days and insisted on constant refinishing to get the smooth outer skin that I felt could win me the race. This attitude did not improve my relations with the girls.

Both boats were finished in the spring of 1978 in time for the race, and the proa successfully completed its 200nm qualifying sail along the south coast of Ireland. Sailing this boat was a complete relearning of sail handling. Every action to tack the boat was contrary to normal sailing instinct, but we soon learned, and discovered that this proa, with its unusual trapezoidal lug rig, sailed well to windward, in fact as well as the 35ft *Areoi* with its modern cutter rig. We could even short tack her up the river. But then bad luck struck. On one of their test sails Maggie and Richard hoisted the new large light weather lugsail and sheeted it in tight. It set beautifully in a perfect aerofoil. So powerful was this sail that when a gust of wind came down the estuary, the boat flipped over and brought an end to plans to enter her into the race. Maggie was devastated, as she had dreamed of becoming a 'yachtswoman', like Clare Francis who had been making a name for herself in ocean racing.

However, the foam sandwich *Areoi* did extremely well in the Round Britain Race in spite of a navigational error on the first leg, which put her far back in the racing fleet, from which she then recovered by sailing the fastest second leg of all the fleet.

But on the last leg her major speed-producing genoa blew out, slowing her down once again, but at least she finished the race.

After the race Maggie and Richard sailed *Areoi* to 'Brighton Week' and took part in racing there, which made up somewhat for the disappointment of the capsized proa.

Subsequently *Areoi* was sold to an Irish yachtsman and farmer from Cork, who owned it for many years. In 2006 we heard she was owned by a Frenchman, photographs showing her in a setting of tropical palm trees; the structure had been made rigid and carried a deck cabin. The well-built foam sandwich glass structure did prove itself very durable. In fact the boat may still be sailing somewhere in the world.

Our sailing dreams and ambitions, which had held the group together, had started to sour through the constant stress and hard work, but after the RBR we tried to pull together and focussed on developing our land. We drew up plans to extend the cottage, get electricity, and instal a proper sewage system. We built two new wooden office buildings, one for the admin and dispatch office and the other fitted out for Hanneke and me to work on new designs.

Over the winter Hanneke had been working hard in a large caravan, which had been converted into a drawing office, creating a beautiful set of building plans for the new 31ft Areoi, our first commercial Pahi design. We had combined all we had learned from sailing the 35ft foam sandwich *Areoi* and the plywood construction of the 31ft proa hull into a new design for self-building. It had the more feminine curves of the new 'Pahi' hull shape, we used less solid timber in the keels making it lighter than my Classic Wharram designs, and with the DIY jigsaw now commonly available to self-builders, we could design new ways to construct the hulls. It was a great success with the public and we started to sell the plans.

In our newly built design office Hanneke and I started work on a larger 42ft version, the 'Captain Cook'. We also designed a new brochure for our designs, a much more visual and evocative wall poster with colour 3-D drawings. It was time to move into the modern world of multihulls.

However living in Ireland had not been a success from a business point of view. Our problem in Milford Haven had been too many visitors; in Ireland our problem was too few. The extra travel across the Irish Sea was too much for our customers. But there was worse luck to come. In February 1979 the Irish postal workers went on strike. Little did we know this strike would continue for 4½ months! For our business, which as a mail-order supplier of boat plans totally relied on postal services, this was a disaster. Maggie and I moved to Wales for a time to a friend's house to run things, but as orders came through adverts in the yachting magazines, news of the strike and our change of address were slow to reach our customers. By the time the postal strike was over and several huge sacks of post were delivered, many of the cheques were out of date.

As the final straw we ended up fighting a legal case over a land dispute with our new neighbour, a television personality who had bought the mansion at the top of our lane. He had ambitions to keep a boat on the river and unbeknown to us applied to build a pier off our land. Though in theory we were the defendants of our rights in this case, the corrupt handling of it by solicitors with political affiliations led to us having to settle out of court and paying a penalty. Ireland's politics under Prime Minister Haughey in the 1970s were not straightforward and a lot of underhand corrupt practices were later discovered.

The stresses had built up for too long. We had lost the tight bond of being a boat crew; our *Tehini*, after two years of sitting unused moored to our quay, had been sailed out to the West Indies by a new skipper and crew, with big plans to use her to make money through chartering. This project had also failed, the skipper had not been able to get his act together to organise charters out of St Lucia, then the postal strike stopped prospective guests booking berths on the return voyage to the UK.

Inevitably, these built-up stresses erupted and there was a confrontation. Ruth, my solid companion in life and oldest member of the group, and Hanneke the youngest—lover of design, boat building and sailing—stuck by me. We three went back to Milford Haven to think things over. Even with the help of our good friend Bob Evans, who tried to arbitrate, relations never improved and we split up permanently.

With hindsight I take the blame for this disastrous break-up. I was too ambitious, too hard, too unforgiving. Maggie had suffered a deep blow to her confidence with the capsize of the Proa; my bond with her had been on a strong psychic level, and what she needed was my love and emotional support, and I did not give it to her. The other two girls sided with her in her distress. People know how hard a divorce can be, but divorcing three women at once!? I was very lucky to have the continued love and support of Ruth and Hanneke, but it left deep emotional scars on all of us.

A NEW BEGINNING

Is there a ghost of an ancestral treaty

For mutual survival,

As you shared

And share

This earth's fragile hospitality?

And what explains the sense of some ancient, hidden nature

Overlapping somewhere along the line with man's…

A nature venerated in antiquity,

When this shape-shifting sea-sprite

Was Poseidon's messenger, a Gaia pilot…

A demi-god.

Heathcote Williams.
'Falling for a Dolphin'

18 The phoenix rises

I have a lifelong friend, Roger Murray, artist, raconteur, sailor and advertising executive. He once said to me: 'James, put you in the middle of the Sahara Dessert [he had motorcycled there!] and you will end up with two or more girls designing boats.' He turned out to be right.

That winter of 1979–80 was not a happy time. Ruth, Hanneke and I were able to find a temporary home with our friends Bob and Anthea Evans in Milford Haven. Our shared 'James Wharram Associates' bank account was frozen. However, we were lucky with our bank manager at the National Westminster in Milford Haven. In those days bank managers were still people with personal care for their customers. He knew us from the previous time we lived in Milford Haven. After explaining our situation to him he asked: 'Are you the owner of the copyright to your Plans?'

To which I answered: 'Yes'.

'Then start up a new business, with a new name and a new bank account. What do you want to call yourselves?'

'How about "James Wharram Designs"?'.

'OK, how much do you need to get started again? Would £1000 do?'

This was the equivalent of nearly £6000 in 2018, and got us going again.

That January we exhibited at the London Boat Show—our stand had been booked before our breakup—a stimulating place where our new design ideas on using epoxy and the 'stitch & glue' building method were discussed.

Then we had to sort out our living accommodation. We had a stroke of luck in that our *Tehini* had been sailed back from the West Indies and, for some not very clear reason, had been left at a boatyard in the Salcombe estuary in Devon. Hanneke and I moved on board in the early spring and started getting her ready to sail back to Milford Haven. After two Atlantic voyages, and no maintenance for several years, she needed some TLC.

Attracted through adverts in yachting magazines, volunteers came to help us.

Looking back I am amazed at how adventurous and free-spirited young people were in the 1980s. There were three young women, all school teachers, who without knowing us were happy to come and live and work on a very 'basic' boat—for pleasure! One of these women is still a good friend and godmother to my second son.

Meanwhile Ruth in Milford Haven kept our business running. She managed to find another office for rent in Milford Docks, smaller than our previous 'Long House', but with a workshop below and two rooms above to use as offices. As soon as she was sea-worthy, we sailed *Tehini* round Land's End to Sandy Haven to become our home again.

Hanneke and I started to draw and build our first 'stitch & glue' design, using the new WEST epoxy system. The concepts had been there in Ireland, I was now ready to start testing this new build method. We called the new design *Hitia*, which means 'Sunrise' in Polynesian—a New Beginning.

Six sheets of 4mm plywood and just 5kg of WEST epoxy produced a light and elegant car-top catamaran. The 'stitch & glue' method had been used on the famous Mirror Dinghy and 'Granta' canoes, which we had viewed at the London Show. These designs, before the age of epoxy, were all 'glued' using polyester resin and glass tape; we were going to use epoxy fillets to make the joints.

I also had to find new structural solutions to build our catamaran hulls in the new building method. We devised a way to fit a strong stem and stern post, cut from thick plywood, between the two hull sides, something no one else had ever tried. It meant we could easily incorporate the skeg as part of the sternpost. The tops of stem and stern became handles to lift the hull by. The crossbeams were lashed to the hulls, no longer using the bolts as on my other small Classic designs like the Surfcat, Hina and Hinemoa. Lashings are easier to fit when assembling the boat on a beach.

When fitting the rudders, I took one look at the standard metal gudgeons and said, 'They don't fit with the rest of the design. How about using rope?' Together with two design students who had come to help us, I tried various different ways of using rope, until we arrived at the figure-of-eight lashing that now is a standard feature on all our Tiki designs. Later I discovered that these types of hinges are often used on model aeroplanes for the wing flaps; we had re-invented the wheel.

The *Hitia* was a success, she had more hull buoyancy than my earlier 12ft Surf-cat, of which we had sold over 400 sets of plans in the previous ten years, and could therefore easily carry two, or even three people. She was lighter, more elegant and lifted over the waves. We used a sprit rig, which had always been successful on my small designs—but with a difference. The luff of the mainsail was a wide pocket that slid over the mast and became a perfect aerofoil—a very simple rig, needing little hardware, with a mast the same length as the boat for easy car top transport.

In 1981 Hanneke and I loaded our *Hitia* on the car roof and took off to Norway to a big International Multihull Meeting (IMM) in Stavern in the Oslo fjord. It was a great gathering of seventy-two multihulls, which included a number of Wharram catamarans and a large group of Wharram sailors. I still remember a wild evening party aboard a Danish 40ft Narai where I was the guest of honour. The Norwegian Wharram builders produced a special bottle of whisky for me. I knew how expensive alcohol was in Norway, so I asked, 'what are you all drinking? 'Oh, we drink our own home made spirits'. 'In that case we will share the whiskey first and we will then all drink your spirits'.

I have never been so drunk; even the next morning, when the residual alcohol was released with a cup of tea, I was still drunk. It was the day of 'the race'; Hanneke insisted we take part. I vaguely remember lying flat on my back on the platform while Hanneke sailed the boat. There was hardly any wind, so what the hell.

This visit to Norway turned into a tour of Europe with us driving to Denmark (where we visited the Roskilde Viking Ship Museum), Germany, France and back via Cornwall to Wales.

I have always been an ocean sailor, and on my boats we would live naked when possible, it just seemed the natural thing to do. With Ruth and Jutta being German, I knew about the naturist movement in Germany in the 1930s. After our first voyages across the Atlantic, Ruth produced a small story booklet about them called *People of the Sea* with many photos of us sailing naked, which was published by the German Naturist Federation (FKK), and also in English in the UK. Otherwise we had never been part of the 'naturist scene.'

When planning our tour of Europe I said to Hanneke 'why don't we try to find naturist campsites?' So we joined the British Naturist Federation and got all their information on campsites in Europe. It was a revelation—crawling out of a small tent first thing in the morning, without first wriggling into some modesty clothes gives one an enormous sense of freedom. So does sharing showers in the open. The people in these campsites were like a family, giving a sense of safety and security.

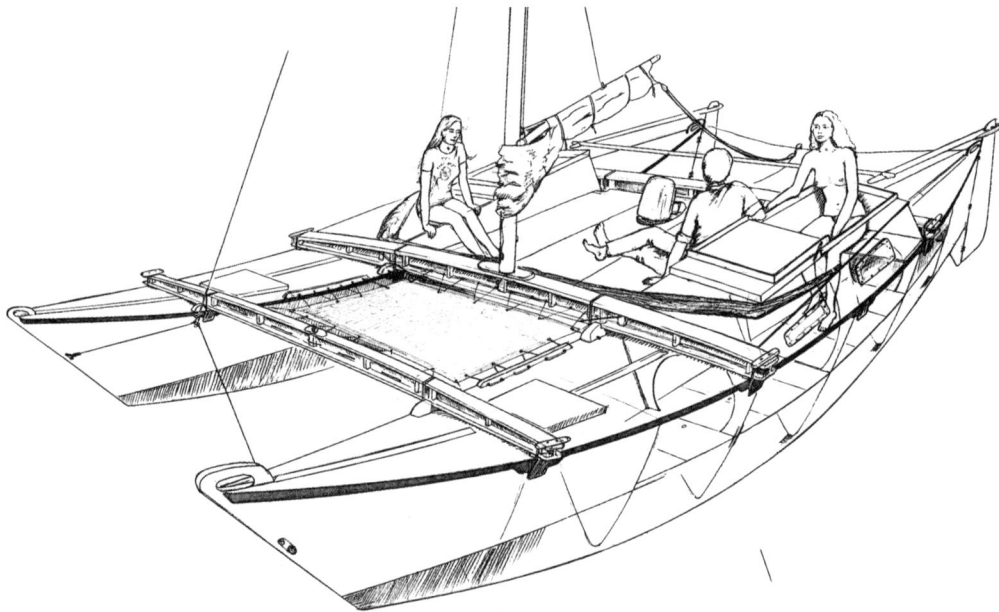

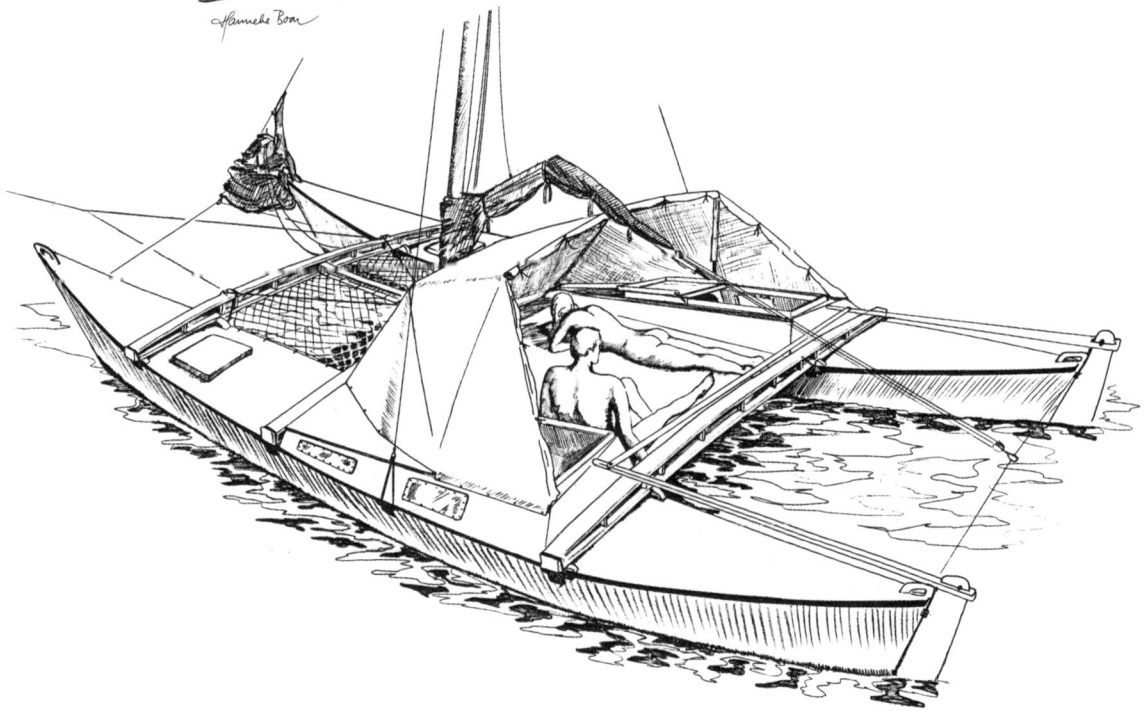

Tiki 21

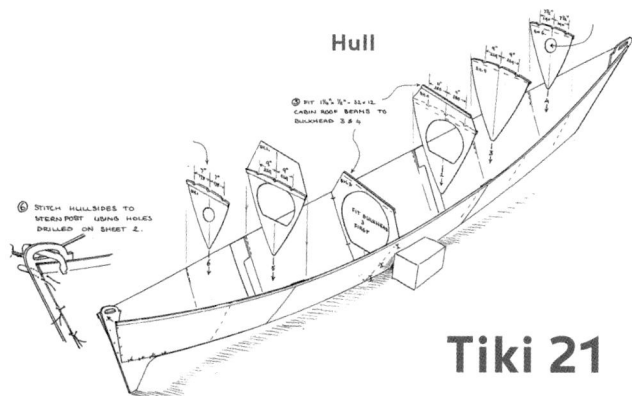

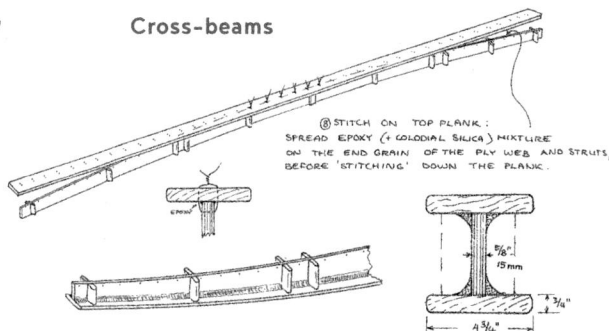

Hull

Cross-beams

Tiki 21

Hull annotations:
- FIT 1¾" × ⅜"–22×12 CABIN ROOF BEAMS TO BULKHEAD 3 & 4
- STITCH HULLSIDES TO STERN POST USING HOLES DRILLED ON SHEET 2.

Cross-beams annotations:
- STITCH ON TOP PLANK: SPREAD EPOXY (+ COLODIAL SILICA) MIXTURE ON THE END GRAIN OF THE PLY WEB AND STRUTS, BEFORE 'STITCHING' DOWN THE PLANK.
- EPOXY
- ⅝" 15mm
- ¾"
- 4¾"

Hollow mast construction – Stitch & Glue method throughout

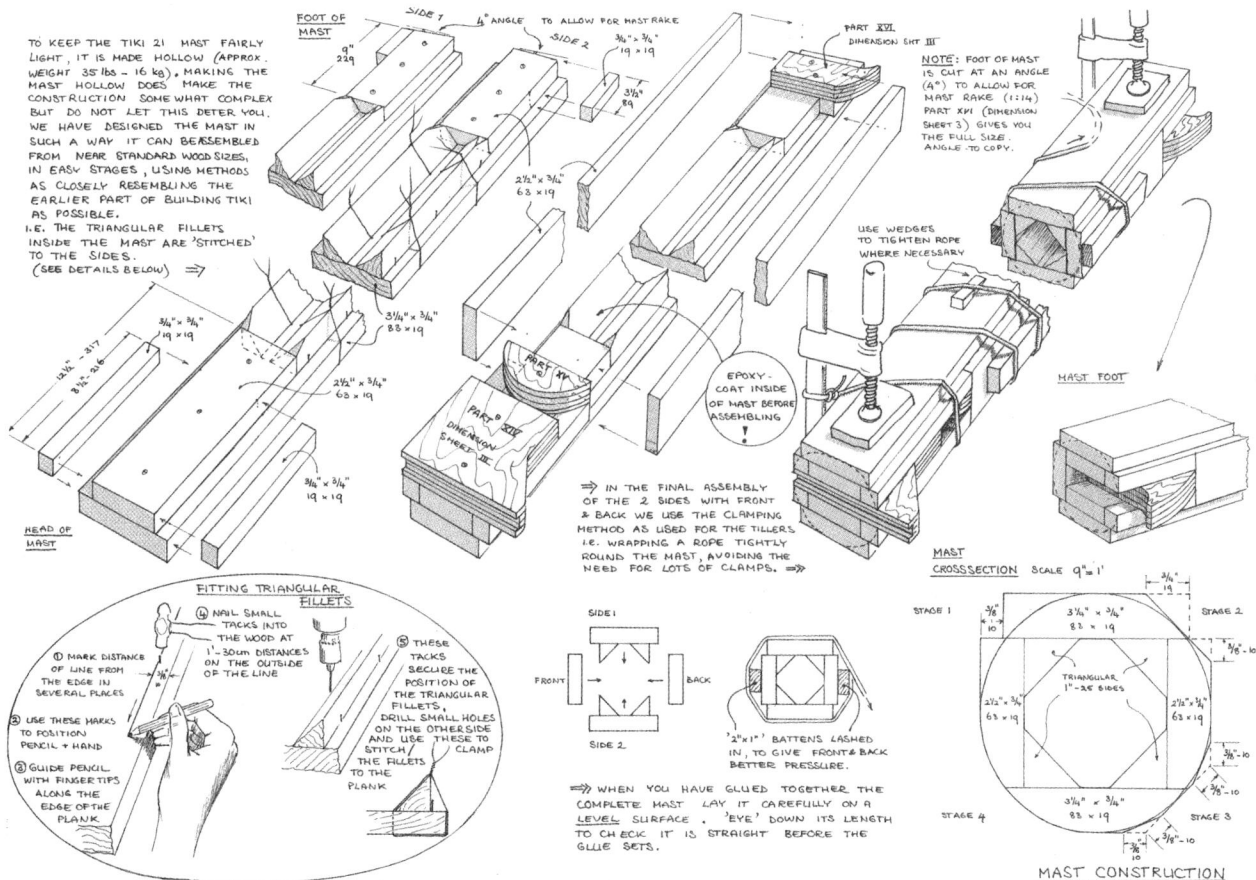

TO KEEP THE TIKI 21 MAST FAIRLY LIGHT, IT IS MADE HOLLOW (APPROX. WEIGHT 35 lbs – 16 kg). MAKING THE MAST HOLLOW DOES MAKE THE CONSTRUCTION SOMEWHAT COMPLEX BUT DO NOT LET THIS DETER YOU. WE HAVE DESIGNED THE MAST IN SUCH A WAY IT CAN BE ASSEMBLED FROM NEAR STANDARD WOOD SIZES, IN EASY STAGES, USING METHODS AS CLOSELY RESEMBLING THE EARLIER PART OF BUILDING TIKI AS POSSIBLE.
I.E. THE TRIANGULAR FILLETS INSIDE THE MAST ARE 'STITCHED' TO THE SIDES.
(SEE DETAILS BELOW) ⇒

FOOT OF MAST — 9" 229
SIDE 1
SIDE 2
4° ANGLE TO ALLOW FOR MAST RAKE
¾" × ¾" 19 × 19
3½" 89
2½" × ¾" 63 × 19

PART XVI DIMENSION SHT III
NOTE: FOOT OF MAST IS CUT AT AN ANGLE (4°) TO ALLOW FOR MAST RAKE (1:14) PART XVI (DIMENSION SHEET 3) GIVES YOU THE FULL SIZE ANGLE TO COPY.

¾" × ¾" 19 × 19
8½" – 216
3¼" × ¾" 83 × 19
2½" × ¾" 63 × 19
PART XV
PART XVI DIMENSION SHEET III
HEAD OF MAST
¾" × ¾" 19 × 19

USE WEDGES TO TIGHTEN ROPE WHERE NECESSARY

EPOXY-COAT INSIDE OF MAST BEFORE ASSEMBLING

⇒ IN THE FINAL ASSEMBLY OF THE 2 SIDES WITH FRONT & BACK WE USE THE CLAMPING METHOD AS USED FOR THE TILLERS I.E. WRAPPING A ROPE TIGHTLY ROUND THE MAST, AVOIDING THE NEED FOR LOTS OF CLAMPS. ⇒

MAST FOOT

MAST CROSSSECTION SCALE 9"=1'

FITTING TRIANGULAR FILLETS

① MARK DISTANCE OF LINE FROM THE EDGE IN SEVERAL PLACES
④ NAIL SMALL TACKS INTO THE WOOD AT 1'–30cm DISTANCES ON THE OUTSIDE OF THE LINE
⑤ THESE TACKS SECURE THE POSITION OF THE TRIANGULAR FILLETS, DRILL SMALL HOLES ON THE OTHER SIDE AND USE THESE TO STITCH/CLAMP THE FILLETS TO THE PLANK
③ USE THESE MARKS TO POSITION PENCIL + HAND
② GUIDE PENCIL WITH FINGER TIPS ALONG THE EDGE OF THE PLANK

SIDE 1
FRONT
BACK
SIDE 2
2"×1" BATTENS LASHED IN, TO GIVE FRONT & BACK BETTER PRESSURE.

⇒ WHEN YOU HAVE GLUED TOGETHER THE COMPLETE MAST LAY IT CAREFULLY ON A LEVEL SURFACE, 'EYE' DOWN ITS LENGTH TO CHECK IT IS STRAIGHT BEFORE THE GLUE SETS.

STAGE 1
STAGE 2
3¼" × ¾" 83 × 19
⅜"–10
TRIANGULAR 1"–25 SIDES
2½" × ¾" 63 × 19
2½" × ¾" 63 × 19
⅜"–10
3¼" × ¾" 83 × 19
STAGE 4
STAGE 3
⅜"–10

MAST CONSTRUCTION

Tiki 21 construction

We found wonderful campsites all over Europe; the last one in Brittany was close to a naturist beach where we launched *Hitia* and sailed her through the gentle surf. When returning on the ferry to Cornwall we stayed at a standard, but beautiful, campsite, very close to where we now live. We fell in love with the area and with the sheltered waters of Carrick Roads, where we again launched our *Hitia*.

To finish our naturist tour we wanted to visit a British naturist site for comparison. With the rather prudish attitude to nakedness in Britain, these sites tended to be hidden 'clubs', but with the help of our book we found one in the middle of Wales. As we were pitching our tent, our naked next-door neighbour walked out of his caravan and showed a great interest in the little catamaran on our car roof. He had heard of Wharram and wanted to know all about the boat. It turned out John had worked for Marcos the designer of plywood racing cars in the 1960s. He now worked in town planning as a civil engineer.

John and his wife Pam became good friends and soon they came to visit us in Sandy Haven to sail on *Hitia*. Hanneke and John went sailing in the estuary on a windy day with large swell and rollers coming in from the Irish Sea. They returned sopping wet and totally exhilarated. John was hooked. He then came to me quietly and said, 'Can I make a model of the *Hitia*?' I said, 'No, if you want to make a model, please make one of the new design that I have in my head'. That is how the Tiki 21 design came to life.

Making a model is a very good way to work out details of a new design. It is visual and three-dimensional. In this present age of computer modelling I still find it a much more friendly and tactile way to design. And I am lucky that Hanneke is an excellent model maker.

John was also a good model maker and with his help we developed all the details of this new design. We used the same build method as the Hitia, but exploited 'stitch & glue' to the full. My goal was to design a boat that would be simple to construct for total beginners, who would have limited skill with sharp-edged tools like chisels or planes. I wanted every step in the build to have the same skill level. Hence the crossbeams, which I designed as a plywood webbed I-beam, were assembled using wire stitches. The hollow wooden mast used wire stitches and rope wrapping for assembly, as most builders would not have a large collection of clamps. I also saw that if a man/woman team could work together the boat would be built quicker. The making of epoxy fillets and the applying of glass cloth were skills women were often more adept in.

I realised that as well as simplicity in construction, the design drawings had to give the beginner builder the confidence that he or she could do it. Most first time builders are not used to reading technical drawings. This is where Hanneke's drawing skills came in. Instead of the two-dimensional construction drawings that were the norm and how my earlier plans had been presented, I suggested she made more sketch drawings of the build method and sequence. We separated the technical dimension drawings from the construction sequence, which became a sketchbook full of 3-D sketches with clear written instructions.

Finally the rig. Throughout my design career I have been looking for rigs with a low centre of effort for greatest stability, and that are easy to handle and can be lowered in a following gale. My pioneering ocean voyages had taught me a great respect for what the weather gods can throw at me and I always wanted to be prepared for the worst. Yet I also wanted rigs that sailed well to windward. I had experimented with the sprit rig, with the Chinese junk rig, with a loose-footed cocked-up boom Bermudan rig on the *Areoi* and with a lug rig on the proa.

I had learned from Professor Marchaj, at a sail symposium in Bristol, that you had to reduce the turbulence of the airflow over the leading edge of the sail created by the mast, and to control twist. He had also pointed out that the ideal sail shape was semi-elliptical like a Spitfire wing, but that the more square-tipped Messerschmitt wing was also very effective.

Hanneke and I had also some experience of the wrap-around sail designed by Gary Hoyt for his Freedom 40 design. We had sailed on one in Salcombe in 1980 as the owner wanted our opinion on how best to handle it. The Gary Hoyt sail is made of double cloth and wraps round the unstayed mast, the clew is held out with a wishbone. It has the shape of a Bermudan sail and as a result it proved very hard to lower, particularly when wet, when it would stick to the mast.

Contemplating Marchaj's ideal elliptical sailshape I realised that its closest equivalent was the high aspect ratio Dutch gaff sail as used on traditional 'platbodems'. In order to reduce mast turbulence I combined this high aspect ratio gaff sail with the wrap-around-the-mast idea, by adding a wide luff pocket, as already tried on the Hitia sprit sail, eliminating the need for mast track and expensive sliders.

It was so simple; it needed minimum hardware, the gaff was simply made from

HOISTING & HANDLING THE WINGSAIL

① THE GAFF IS ALWAYS HOISTED HORIZONTALLY SO THE SAIL POCKET STAYS SLACK, USING BOTH HALYARDS.

IT IS NOT NECESSARY TO HEAD TO WIND TO HOIST THE SAIL, IT CAN EVEN BE HOISTED WITH THE WIND DEAD BEHIND. IT WILL ALSO DROP IN SECONDS IF LOWERED IN A FOLLOWING WIND.

② ONCE HOISTED TO THE CORRECT HEIGHT THE PEAK HALYARD IS TIGHTENED UNTIL ALL CREASES DISAPPEAR

LEE SHROUD

A VANG TO THE PEAK OF THE GAFF IS PRIMARILY USED WHILE HOISTING SAIL WITH A FOLLOWING WIND, TO HOLD THE GAFF OFF THE 'LEE SHROUD.

(THE VANG CAN BE SET TO WINDWARD GUNNEL TO REDUCE TWIST, BUT IT IS GENERALLY FOUND THAT INCREASING TENSION BETWEEN PEAK HALYARD AND SHEET WILL REDUCE TWIST EFFECTIVELY)

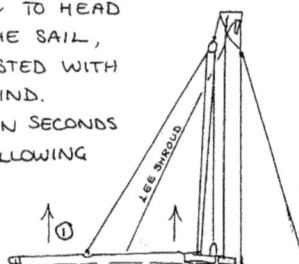

SAIL POCKET IS SLACK WHILE SAIL IS HOISTED

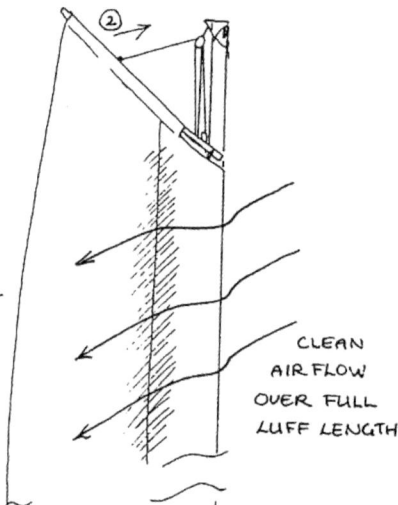

CLEAN AIR FLOW OVER FULL LUFF LENGTH

DOWN HAUL

PEAK & THROAT HALYARDS

ON A WIDE BEAMED MULTI HULL THERE IS NO NEED FOR A BOOM

THE HALYARDS ARE INSIDE THE LUFF POCKET CAUSING NO TURBULENCE

③ THE DOWNHAUL IS TIGHTENED UNTIL THE LUFF IS SMOOTH.

④ & ⑤ THE SHEET AND TRAVELLER CONTROLS ADJUST THE ANGLE OF THE SAIL TO THE WIND.

The Wharram Wingsail

wood. With its two halyards—peak and throat, which were led down the luff pocket, reducing turbulence even more—the tensions in the four-cornered sail could be carefully controlled. It needed no boom due to the width of the catamaran, just a rope traveller across the sterns.

In practice we found it did not have the sticking problems of the Freedom rig because the short gaff, when scandalised (dropping the peak) took all the pressure out of the luff pocket and its weight brought the sail down. In fact it can be lowered even in a following gale, because there are no sliding cars to jam in a mast track. We called this sail the 'Wharram Wingsail'.

The Tiki 21 became a seminal design of which nearly 1000 plans have been sold to date. A year after her debut she won the Cruising World Design Competition for a 'Trailable Gunkholer', And many were already being built around the world. Ten years later in the 1990s Rory McDougall sailed his Tiki 21 *Cooking Fat* around the world, the smallest catamaran to do so. She was never designed for that purpose, but this showed the inherent strength and safety of the design.

Over the next two decades we produced more Tiki designs, slowly working larger to 26ft, a 31ft workboat, then back to a 17ft Hitia, as well as a 26ft stitch & glue Pahi. These were followed by bigger ocean going designs, the Tiki 30, Tiki 38 and Tiki 46. All these designs were drawn with the Wharram Wingsail rig, the larger ones with two masts to keep sail areas smaller and easier to handle. In the development of the Wingsail rig we worked in cooperation with Jeckells of Wroxham, the old sail-making firm, who had been in business for a hundred years and had made many of my earlier sails. I had known three generations of Jeckells and Chris Jeckells, the youngest, was keenly interested in our rig and worked out the best ways to construct it. After many years he told me they never had a customer who had bought a Wingsail Rig come back and ask for a Bermudan replacement.

19 Dolphin encounters

Our smaller office on the docks in Milford Haven was not ideal; like the Longhouse previously the rental agreement was insecure, and the building old and draughty. We again went searching for a site to build our own offices, but again could not find anywhere suitable or cheap enough in Pembrokeshire.

After our camping visit, we decided Cornwall would be a much better place for us to settle. Its sheltered south coast is the jumping off point for many ocean voyages. We ourselves had left from Falmouth on *Tangaroa* in 1955. Based here, we would not need to negotiate the difficult strong tidal crossing of the Bristol Channel or the hazardous rounding of Land's End, as we had done so many times from Milford Haven.

Hanneke and I went in search of a low priced piece of land. We entered into negotiations with the planning department for a site on some wasteland just outside the town of Truro. Ruth, not liking the proposed site, took her bicycle on the train to Cornwall and found at the top end of Restronguet Creek, in the quiet village of Devoran, a ¾ acre site for sale, including a small bungalow and planning permission for a workshop. With its waterfront access, at high tide it gave us a direct sea route to the sheltered Falmouth estuary, leading into the Bay of Biscay and the oceans of the world.

Devoran had been a busy port for the tin trade. The village was still populated by the descendants of Cornish tin miners, boat builders and sailors. It had memories of being a boisterous seaport with three pubs and, so I was told, a brothel. There were men in the village whose families had built many of the trading and fishing boats that had made Devoran a maritime centre for centuries. After sailing our *Tehini* up the creek we were soon accepted by this group.

The simplicity of our new base—the small bungalow style building, built as a doctor's surgery, as our office—with our ocean-going *Tehini* moored on the creek behind, meant that we did not sink into becoming a land-centred business. Consciousness of the ocean reached us with each incoming tide, opening a new aspect of our sea lives.

A few people in the early 1970s, living close to the sea, began to see whales and dolphins not as lumps of meat, containing valuable oils, but as sentient beings. In New Zealand our friend Wade Doak was using one of our 36ft Raka designs as a human base for interaction with wild dolphins. Ruth had been corresponding with him since the early '70s and had visited him in 1976 on arrival in New Zealand after crossing the Tasman Sea. Wade had set up 'Project Interlock' to study the interaction of people swimming with friendly wild dolphins, and had been gathering data on many significant encounters.

I had first heard of human-dolphin contact when meeting Dr John Lilly in the Caribbean in 1959 on our voyage from Trinidad to New York. The American Government was financing him in his work, obviously, to me, for military purposes; when I questioned him on this, Lilly had said 'classified'. Later in his quest to open his mind to possible dolphin/human communication, he took LSD, which eventually destroyed him. At the end of our first North Atlantic crossing on *Rongo* we had had a very special encounter ourselves with a large pod of pilot whales, which had left a deep impression on us.

In Britain, we had our own dolphin/human relationships exploration. A Dr Horace Dobbs had in the mid-1970s encountered a lone friendly bottlenose dolphin in the Irish Sea off the Isle of Man and built up, through many hours swimming together, a close relationship with him. The local people gave him the name 'Donald'. The dolphin then migrated south to Pembrokeshire and finally Cornwall, where he was given the name 'Beaky'. Horace Dobbs wrote a book about these encounters called *Swimming with a Wild Dolphin*.

One day in our 'Longhouse' office in the mid 1970s a very excited diver friend had rushed in and told us how he had just been swimming with this very friendly dolphin in Broadhaven on the coast of Pembrokeshire. Ruth, Nuala and Hanneke quickly found wet suits and drove off to Broadhaven and managed to have a short swim in the company of this large and boisterous dolphin, which we later found out was 'Donald'. It left a deep impression on them.

In 1980 we met Horace Dobbs at the London Boat Show where he gave us a copy of his book. We became friends and when in 1983 Horace was in negotiations about making a television film in Brittany about another female bottlenose dolphin, he contacted us with the suggestion: 'Can you sail your *Tehini* over to the Bay de Tré-passer as a base for our film operation?'

This sounded like an exciting project, though rather daunting when we checked the location of the Bay de Trépasser ('Bay of the Departed', as this is where drowned sailors often wash ashore). It is at the very tip of Brittany exposed to the might of the open Atlantic, with fierce tidal currents round the rocky headlands. It would only be possible to anchor *Tehini* in this bay in the most settled weather conditions. Still, full of enthusiasm, I said yes and with a mixed crew of English, German, Dutch, & Irish enthusiasts we sailed *Tehini* into these perilous waters. We were lucky—the weather was settled during the week in August when the film was made.

We learned a lot about film-making, particularly the over-exacting requirements of cameramen, soundmen and directors. While the film team were busy making end-less preparations on the centre platform of *Tehini*, we would watch the dolphin swimming close round the boat. Then when they were finally ready to film, the dolphin would have lost interest and swum off, not to be found. They would speed off in the rubber dinghy in search of her. Then in the quiet of the evening, with the film team in their hotel ashore, we would slip overboard and gently swim with this sensuous female dolphin, who loved to slide her body in a slow spiral round our anchor warp, or quietly play with a piece of seaweed. At night we would sometimes hear the distinctive 'puh-huw' of her breathing close to the boat.

On the way back from the Bay de Trépasser the weather was not gentle sailing winds, but winds of force 5 gusting 6. *Tehini* rode the waves as she had done for fourteen years, but as her builder I knew she was tired and had had enough of riding hard seas. On inspection we found trouble with the glue of her joints. We discovered that the urea-formaldehyde glue I had used in building her had a limited lifespan. In particular where the wood was slightly damp the glue started to flake and fall out of the joint. This led to leaks and more moisture and more glue failure. This did not look like something we could cure and I knew this would be the end of *Tehini*'s sailing days.

Later that summer we once more took *Tehini* out to sea when pilot whales were spotted close inshore near some rocks called 'the Manacles' in Falmouth Bay and Hanneke was able to be towed between the hulls observing a small family group of pilot whales for many miles as they accompanied *Tehini* out to the open ocean, a unique farewell from the ocean to this special ship. *Tehini* was used as guest accommodation for many more years and finally was given a Viking funeral.

The same year we sailed to France, another lone friendly bottlenose dolphin was seen off the north coast of Cornwall. As payment for our participation in the TV film, we had been given the rubber dinghy and 30hp outboard motor the film company had bought for their work. Now, on a clear November day, we took this dinghy to the rocky coast near Godrevy lighthouse and launched it. We were strong in those days and had the help of an American girl artist who was staying with us.

We were lucky and met up with the dolphin in the strong tidal passage between the rocks and had a memorable swimming encounter. It is amazing how in the company of this intelligent wild sea creature you lose your fear of the turbulent cold water and start to feel at home in the sea.

The next summer—1984—this dolphin, now given the name Percy by the locals, was frequently seen along the north coast of Cornwall. One local diver befriended him and often swam with him from his rubber dinghy. We had bought one of the first Tiki 21s, built in Cornwall; we trailed it to Portreath on the north coast and launched it there. Our crew were summer volunteers with an interest in dolphins and boat work.

Percy seemed to love the catamaran and would swim to meet us and dance under the speeding bows. We would then anchor and through swimming and diving with him he became bolder and started to nudge our swim fins, which eventually led to being able to stroke and touch his velvety skin. We always allowed the dolphin to take the initiative, never pushing our wishes on him.

I particularly remember one night when I slept on the boat: I could hear him breathing, then gently bumping the side of the boat until I came on deck and said hello. He spluttered and splashed, looking at me, showing keen awareness, and then swam off; he probably wanted me to come for a midnight swim. Sadly his fame led to him being mobbed by tourists and at the end of the summer he disappeared. I had one final swim with him, when he determinedly kept swimming out to sea, as if to say 'come with me, let's find somewhere quieter to live'.

I will side track a little here and discuss a theory about human evolution. In 1930, Sir Alister Hardy, a marine biologist, was reading the book *Man's Place among the Mammals*, by the British observational naturalist, embryologist, anatomist and anthropologist Frederic Wood Jones. This book included the question of why humans, unlike all other land mammals, had fat attached to their skin. Hardy realized that this trait sounded like the blubber of marine mammals and began to suspect that humans had ancestors that were more aquatic than previously imagined.

He then evolved the theory that millions of years ago a branch of apes was forced by competition over terrestrial habitats to hunt for food such as shellfish on the sea shore and sea bed, leading to adaptations that explained characteristics such as man's functional hairlessness, subcutaneous fat, and bipedalism. Fearing a backlash against such a radical idea, he kept it secret until 1960, by which time he had achieved an academic reputation and had received his knighthood. His theory became known as the 'Aquatic Ape Hypothesis' in academic circles.

Sir Alister Hardy's hypothesis gained a wider audience when Elaine Morgan, a well known Welsh author and scriptwriter, published her book *The Descent of Woman* as a counter to Desmond Morris's male-orientated book *The Naked Ape*. In this book Elaine not only started with the premise that 'woman' was as important in the evolution of 'man', but also explained Hardy's aquatic hypothesis in laymen's terms.

The Descent of Woman was published in 1972 and I borrowed it from Milford Haven library soon afterwards. It made a deep impression on me, making so much sense, I having spent a large part of my life on and in the sea. I borrowed it for such a long time that I have to own up that it remains on my bookshelves to this day. Elaine Morgan made further studies on early woman's origins during the rest of her life.

In the absence of fossil proof the Aquatic Ape Hypothesis has stayed controversial, but in 2016 it achieved a measure of acceptance and serious scrutiny when Sir David Attenborough, in a pair of radio programmes entitled *The Waterside Ape*, discussed the recent discovery of growths in the ear in hominid fossils, which are today found in diving cultures and some surfers.

Elaine Morgan's second book *The Aquatic Ape,* which went deeper and more scientifically into the subject, was published in 1982, just before we started our swimming with dolphins. Its publication renewed our interest, Hanneke, Ruth and I felt it made so much sense, it explained why people spend their holidays on the seaside, why water sports like diving, surfing and sailing are so popular, why we felt to be 'sea people'. This affinity with water must be somewhere in our ancient DNA. Our swimming with dolphins gave us a very close connection to this aquatic heritage.

In 1984, the summer we were swimming with Percy, Hanneke made it clear she was ready to have a baby and she decided this baby should be born underwater like a dolphin. Besides Elaine Morgan's books we had also read *Water Babies* by Eric Siedenbladh about the Russian water birth pioneer Igor Charkovsky and about the water births carried out in France by Michel Odent. So when Hanneke became pregnant in the autumn, we went looking for a doctor or midwife who could help us with a water birth.

In 1985 there had been few water births in the UK, none in the South West, so Hanneke was a pioneer in this concept. Our NHS doctor shuddered at the thought, but did give us the name of a homeopathic doctor in Penzance, Roger Lichy, who apparently had conducted many home births. We visited him and he became enthusiastic about trying a water birth. He asked us for all the documentation we had collected and it was up to us to organise a suitable birthing tub.

In our research into dolphins we had learned that with their sonar they can 'see' pregnancy, and in their group behaviour will protect pregnant females. We wanted to find out if they would also act protectively towards a pregnant human by introducing a pregnant Hanneke into a group of dolphins.

From Horace Dobbs we had heard that a group of approachable dolphins lived close to the Rock of Gibraltar where the seas are warm. As I don't drive cars, only boats, six-months-pregnant Hanneke drove our car with Tiki 21 in tow across Spain to Gibraltar. Ruth and several volunteer dolphin enthusiasts joined us there and together we launched *Tiki* and sailed out to find the dolphins.

We had some lovely sails and the dolphins would swim under *Tiki*'s bows, but when Hanneke entered the water wearing her extended wetsuit the dolphins shied away. So we never discovered if dolphin behaviour showed signs of recognising pregnancy.

The water birth in July 1985 was a great success. In just six hours Jamie Wharram, a big baby, was born with Hanneke suffering little pain and no tearing, due to the soothing warm water. The doctor was impressed and went on to conduct around seventy more water births using our tub, which he would transport around Cornwall on top of his VW Beetle. This pioneering water birth led to the hospitals in Cornwall installing birthing tubs, and this method of giving birth becoming an acceptable alternative.

Hanneke's plan was to make Jamie into a proper little 'aquatic ape'. Following the teachings of Igor Charkovsky she had the courage to dunk her little baby under the water at just three weeks old and soon found out he loved it. With her guidance he grew to be happy underwater and later would dive to the bottom of the swimming pool on her back, picking up objects over her shoulder. We were members of the local naturist club at this time, so took Jamie regularly to a swimming pool where we were surrounded and accepted by our 'family' of fellow naturists.

With Jamie three months old we again trailed our Tiki 21 to Gibraltar, this time with the hope we could actually swim with Jamie in the warm sea with dolphins. Again things did not work out, we heard the dolphins had been harassed by tourist boats and would not come near us. He did swim daily in the pool at the Spanish naturist resort and loved the water. He still is a remarkable underwater swimmer and free diver; as a boy of eleven he was able to impress young Polynesian men in the Pacific as their diving equal.

20 Spirit of Gaia

Shortly before Jamie's birth an eccentric American explorer called Gene Savoy contacted us. He was an 'Indiana Jones' type character who had been discovering ancient cities in the Peruvian jungle. He had also made a double canoe out of bundles of reeds and made an experimental sailing voyage up the western coast of Peru to Central America. He wrote that he had found some ancient petroglyphs in the Peruvian jungle that would indicate there had been double canoes in South America. Could we design him such a double canoe?

Gene had discovered me through a prize-winning article I had written in 1979 for the American magazine *WoodenBoat*, the subject 'a waterborne community'. I suspect I was given the prize, not for my words, but for the superb drawings by young Hanneke which illustrated my concepts. They featured romantic images of a large Polynesian style double canoe with palm leaf deck hut and crab-claw sails, and a fleet of accompanying smaller double canoes.

Gene gave us little detail of any original Peruvian design, so I designed him a pair of 63ft Polynesian style hulls on which he planned a bamboo platform and reed hut. He would rig the craft with a large square sail as used on the Peruvian balsa rafts and steer it with steering paddles.

With Hanneke having just given birth and preoccupied with her baby, we brought in a designer friend who drew an artist's impression of this craft, which Gene approved. We then had a volunteer architect student help us draw up construction drawings for the hulls.

I became fascinated by these big slim hulls and could see them as a large ocean-going catamaran with which we could study dolphins out in the open ocean for long periods. We would no longer have the interference of shore people upsetting the delicate interaction with the creatures, as had spoiled our contacts with Percy and the dolphin pod in Gibraltar.

Tehini was no longer fit for ocean sailing, so I put the idea of building such

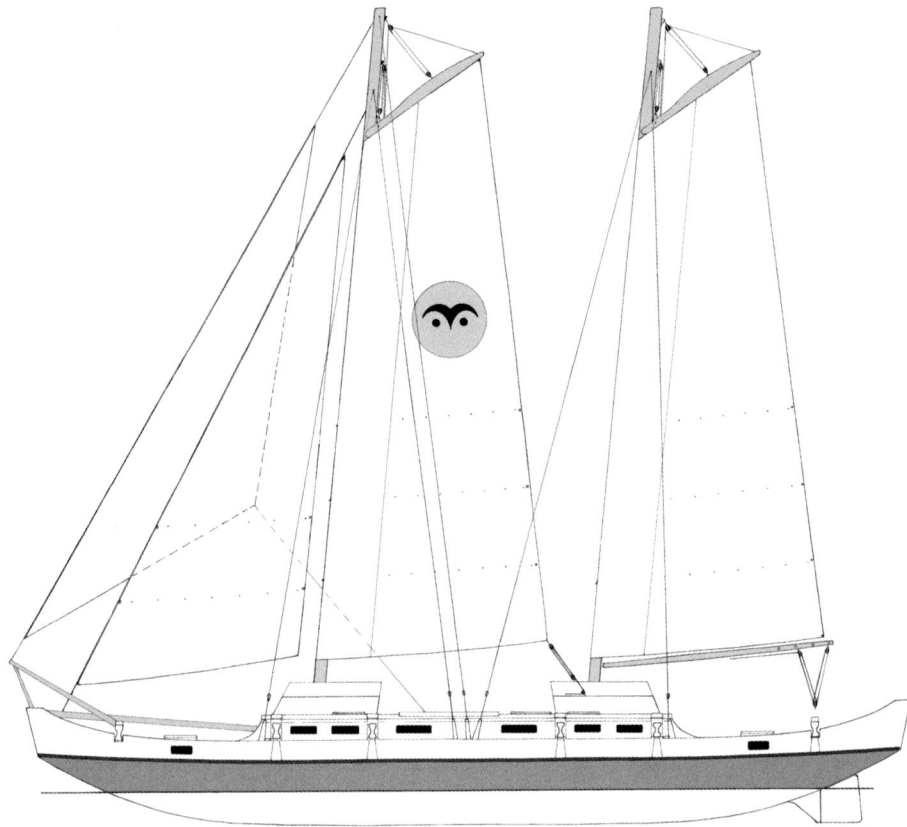

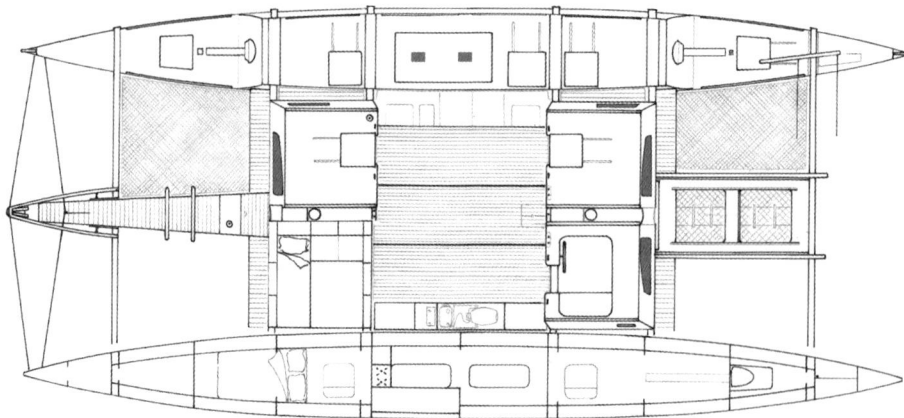

Pahi 63 profile and deck plan

a catamaran to Ruth and Hanneke and was able to persuade them this was a good idea. We did need another ocean voyaging boat or, as the French sailing hero Bernard Moitessier had told me so many years ago, 'we would rot on the land'.

Our new site in Devoran had come with outline planning permission for a workshop, and we would need one to build our Pahi 63 dolphin expedition ship. With the help of our friend André Viljoen, a newly qualified Irish architect, we drew up a design for a 75ft by 25ft workshop. Now thirty-five years later André is a professor of architecture at the university of Brighton. With his help we piloted through the planning/building regulations with ease. My mother had died the previous year and with our share from the sale of her house we were able to get our new workshop built. It had, and still has, the feel of a Viking hall.

In our new Viking hall we started to build our new ship, not a Viking ship, but a design of the people frequently referred to as the 'Vikings of the Pacific'.

'Lofting the lines' for a new boat has the same sensuous involvement as an intense love affair. You mark out full size the measurements from your preliminary lines drawing on to a large floor. First the full-size profile, followed by the cross sections and plan view, then using long flexible battens you connect up the marked points into flowing lines, constantly cross-referencing measurements between the three. It is like a dance, with a small adjustment here and another there, until the whole has fair curves in every direction. Adjustments of the flowing lines are like the physical caresses of human love.

I have seen the birth of my son. To see the birth of a hull shape that could ride the seas in a storm, or ghost quietly along without a ripple in a light wind or calm, is... I will not make comparisons that could be misinterpreted; all I can write is that the birth of a new boat design is similar, emotionally, to the birth of a child.

Whereas creating a baby takes nine months, building our 63ft catamaran, to be called *Spirit of Gaia,* took us five years. At the start of the build we were joined long term by another Dutch girl, Joke (pronounced Yoka). She visited as a friend of a friend and discovered she really enjoyed boatbuilding. Hanneke, Joke and I became the chief builders throughout the five years of building *Gaia*.

After articles about the design were published in several yachting magazines people became interested in our project and came offering to help. An American wrote to us, wanting to come for a prolonged period as he wanted to build a Pahi 63 himself and wanted to learn. We were cautious, telling him he should come for a two-week trial period. Then one day a tall blond man with big rucksack stood on our doorstep, saying 'Hi, I'm Bill, I've come to help you build your boat'.

Bill turned out to be a friendly giant, had worked for Caterpillar in Chicago and was an inventive expert in using electric tools. He stayed a whole year till both hulls were built and turned over. After six months he suggested his wife should join him. Again we hesitated, not sure if an American woman would be able to adapt to our simple lifestyle. Again she turned out a treasure and a good boat builder. They had their sleeping quarters on our old *Tehini*, along with various other volunteers who came and went. During the day we cooked and ate together as a community.

Looking back on this period of immense creativity in my life, I can draw parallels between the community of people building our boat and the communities of the Arts and Crafts movement of the late nineteenth century. We practised the same approach to design, hand crafting every part, to create a unity between function and beauty.

The volunteers came from far and wide. There was Dave, an Australian hitch-hiker who stayed for a couple of months and helped with the glassing of the hulls. In the evenings he would entertain our two-year-old Jamie with stories of 'Jack the rabbit'. There was Nick Webb, a scientific instrument designer who had spent time swimming and interacting with 'Donald' the dolphin in Falmouth and now wanted to help us build our dolphin research vessel. There was Avril, a retired head teacher, who added her motherly care, as well as giving foot massages; John Barker, a builder and designer of hovercraft; Selina a teenage girl mad about dolphins. A man from Ghana who wanted to build Wharram kits came a short while to help us fit the hardwood gunnels; Vilhelm, a Danish woodworker added his skills and there were others whose names I have forgotten. The many volunteers who came and helped all added their 'Mana' (Polynesian for spirit) in her structure. People who now sail on *Spirit of Gaia* feel this accumulated 'Mana'. It has made her a very special ship.

And Ruth? Ruth was never a boatbuilder, but without her there would be no *Gaia*. It was she, helped by two other ladies in her office, who kept our boat plan business running, who communicated with all our builders round the world, who kept the finances in order and made sure there was money to buy materials.

We designed *Spirit of Gaia* as we built her. Her hull lines were drawn and basic structure designed in advance, but many of the details were worked out on the job.

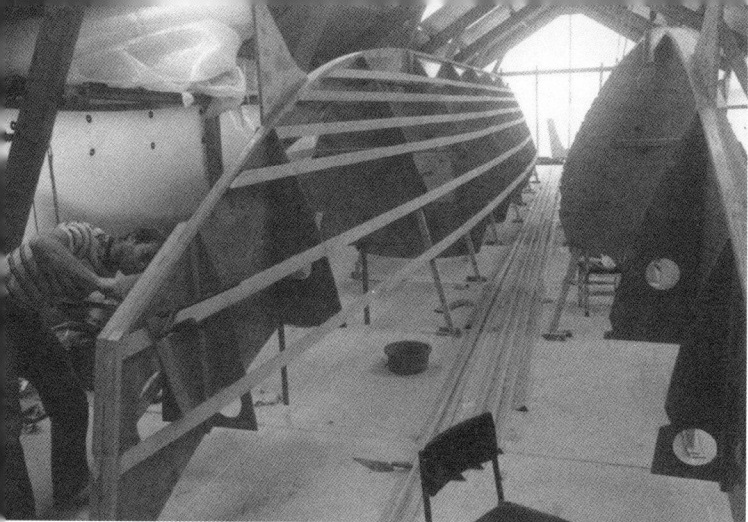

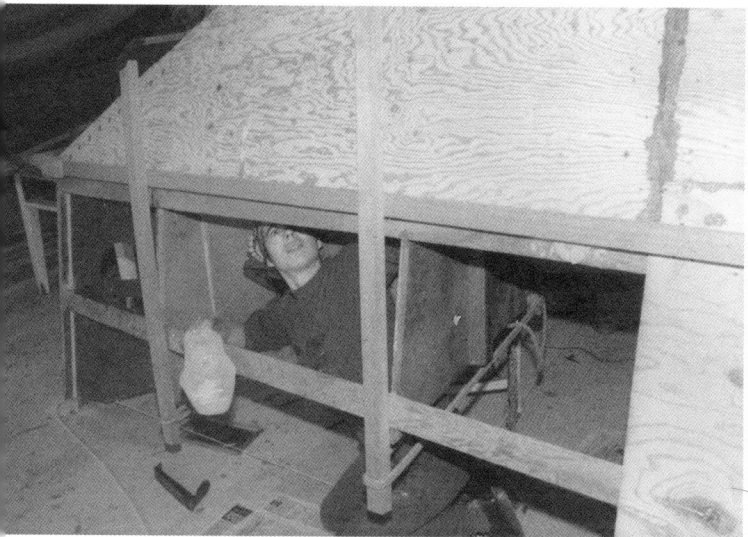

This is an excellent way of hands-on designing for people like us, who have boatbuilding experience combined with memories of ocean voyaging. I would not advise this method to anyone without prior designing or sailing experience.

For building materials I wanted to use only renewable, temperate-climate wood species—softwood plywood, Douglas fir timber for stringers and crossbeams, and northern hardwoods for hatch coamings. I had used Douglas fir plywood for building my double outrigger *Tikiroa* and also to build *Tehini* in the 1960s. When I built those boats its quality was excellent, with all knots made good with veneer inserts. The Douglas fir plywood available in 1987 was of lesser quality with only 'one side good' and sold as 'shuttering ply', but I still believed it would make a good boatbuilding plywood.

I had seen rough Douglas fir plywood used for concrete formers in my early years working as a builder's labourer and knew how tough and durable it was. As all the wood and plywood would be coated or glassed with epoxy, this would ensure its durability. We would put the 'good' side of the plywood facing the interior and the side with the knots on the outside. These knots were filled with any left-over epoxy glue as we were planking the hulls. The glass sheathing on all the outside surfaces would ensure a stable, durable and low-maintenance surface.

Gaia's hulls are designed with the principles of 'flexispace'. This means each hull has simple horizontal levels fitted as structural members, which can be used in multiple ways. This makes the structure very simple. Most parts of the hull have a dual purpose—structural strength member and furniture—floor, seat, bunk, shelf etc.,—this makes a hull much lighter, as we are not adding extra furniture or linings. Pre-coating every part with epoxy meant the interior was finished, requiring no further painting.

Wherever possible we would combine functionality with beauty by shaping the parts to resonate with the Jungian archetypal subconscious. We added curved plywood knees to the ends of shelves that resembled the iconic Cretan Double Axe. Curved openings in bulkheads were carefully shaped to give a womblike feeling. Handholds cut into knees add beauty as well as practicality. The stem heads were shaped in the tradition of Mediterranean boats, resembling the male phallus; the sternposts a more feminine shape; their practical function was as samson posts for mooring lines. All these parts were hand crafted in the spirit of the Arts & Crafts movement.

We made the decks of a plywood and foam sandwich. Our boat would be sailing in the warmer waters of the world, hence insulating the decks against heat was more important than insulating the hull sides against cold water. The deck edges were given a slight overhang, which would cast a shadow and add definition to the sheer.

The crossbeams that would join the hulls were built in a new method, using a thick vertical plywood web cut to a gentle curve, with laminated solid timber flanges, making it an I-beam. This method is approximately one third lighter than the solid laminated beams I had used on all my Classic designs. It is a method to construct beautiful curved beams without the need for a building jig and lots of clamps—the ply web is the jig. The beam's hourglass cross section also allows more twist under torsion loading when sailing through big waves than a solid or box beam. Many designers use box beams for lightness, but I have always shied away from these as the hollow space within is an ideal place for rot to develop. Our new I-beams had no such hidden spaces.

The beams were lashed to the hulls with synthetic rope, as I had started to do on my smaller Pahi designs. Beam lashings are like the shock absorbers in a car. When a big catamaran rides over large ocean waves the stresses are enormous and continuous. Allowing the structure to flex improves its strength and durability. Beam lashings can be replaced whereas stress fractures, as often occur on the large rigidly joined catamarans, are extremely hard to repair.

We tried to eliminate metal hardware wherever we could. Hence our 'chain plates' were made of hardwood glued to the sloping cabin sides in line with the shroud angles. These have slots through which the lanyard is threaded. All stresses act in shear over the large gluing area, rather than being point-loaded on bolts like traditional metal chain plates. To match them we spliced beautiful hand carved deadeyes, made by Hanneke, on the end of the shrouds, triangular shaped with five holes to match the slots in the chainplates.

During the five years of building *Spirit of Gaia* with our group of volunteers, we also initiated a professional boatbuilding firm, Wharram Built Ltd. We designed and started to professionally build a Tiki 28, a coastal cruising design with a low fixed central pod cabin. Four boatbuilders worked on these boats for customers. Andy Smith, under our supervision, became their manager; many years later he became our Wharram builder in the Philippines. During five years they built four Tiki 28s and two Tiki 36 designs, as well as a Pahi 42 in another workshop nearby. Our place in Devoran was a hive of industry.

There were times during the build of *Gaia* when there was a need to make better progress, so when finances allowed we employed our professional boatbuilders to assist in a particular job. This is how the beautiful hollow masts were built using the 'bird's mouth' technique, out of Alaskan yellow cedar. Making such masts requires professional tooling and a large team to apply glue quickly and assemble the many parts accurately. We designed the masts like giant bamboos, adding internal webs every six feet to prevent the possibility of buckling.

Early in 1992, after five years of building our dolphin ship, I was invited to speak at an International Whale and Dolphin conference in Kona, Hawaii. I gave a paper there about the building of our *Spirit of Gaia* and how we planned to use her as our dolphin research vessel. I did not like the big hotel where the conference was held; it gave me very bad vibes. I discovered I was not the only one feeling this. Talking to an Australian Aborigine speaker, who I had befriended, he explained to me the hotel had been built on an old sacred Hawaiian site and the spirits had not been asked permission. Billy planned an Aboriginal dance to exorcize the bad vibrations and asked me to take part. This dance was an incredibly powerful spiritual experience for me.

Fortunately I had friend living in Hawaii, Kiko Johnson. Kiko was a Wharram catamaran enthusiast and keenly interested in Hawaiian sailing canoes. He had been working on some old Hawaiian canoe hulls, restoring them and rigging them with crabclaw sails. Kiko rescued me from the bad atmosphere of the hotel and took me home. Whilst with him I realised it was time to set a deadline to get our *Spirit of Gaia* finished and afloat. I suggested May as a good time for the launching and invited Kiko and two other friends to come over and help us arrange a proper Hawaiian ceremony for our boat.

Back home we set a date of Saturday 16 May, the day of the full moon with a high spring tide in the late afternoon, perfect for a launching on Devoran village quay. It was also the day after my sixty-fourth birthday. We had still a lot of boatbuilding to complete, but with a date set we got moving.

Launching a 63ft catamaran is no mean task. Many of our friends and building volunteers came to help, from Holland, Germany, France, Denmark, Australia, America, Hawaii. We had a team of around twenty people. I still remember us all gathered in our small living room, with everyone arguing over how to do it. Young Kiko came up with some way-out suggestions, then my old friend Ernald Pearson, sailor of many of my designs, said: 'look sonny, this is how we will do it'. I knew Ernald's experience in leading building teams on jobs in Saudi Arabia and decided he would be the man in charge of moving the ship.

We had to transport the two hulls through our village to the quay where there was space to assemble the whole boat on the beach. Each hull was held upright in a cradle; we attached small wheels to these cradles and could manhandle and push them down the road. Jamie's school class of seven year olds came to help. Crossbeams and platforms were transported on a trailer. A whole day was spent lashing the crossbeams in place. It was an incredible work of cooperation, expertly led by Ernald.

Launch day arrived. In the morning a team of women were making Hawaiian *leis* from big colourful flowers picked in a friend's garden. The Hawaiians were making a modern version of an 'earth oven' to slow-cook haunches of pork and breadfruits brought from London by our friend André Viljoen. Raw fish salad and other exotic Polynesian dishes were being prepared. We would have a Hawaiian feast in the Village Hall in the evening with around seventy people invited. The hall was prepared with tables at floor level decorated with flowers.

News of the big launching spread, other people wanted to be part of this very special event. The local gig club brought their boats to add Cornish nautical flavour; the local 'black sheep' Morris dancers came to entertain the waiting crowd with their rude pagan-style dancing, brandishing their sticks like large phalluses.

I had visualised the powerful experience of the boat sliding into the water and had asked for two kettledrums and large round pebbles for all the spectators to click together in unison. This created a problem: where would we find a large load of suitable pebbles? None of the beaches had stones that were suitable. In the end a local man suggested we ask the Water Board office in Redruth if we could borrow the pebbles from their water feature. He had worked there and knew people. We were given permission to collect a small trailer load of pebbles, 'So long as you bring them back!'

Dressed in blue robes and adorned with sacred *ti* leaves Kiko stood on the wooden pulpit eight feet above the crowd and chanted the Hawaiian words specially composed for *Spirit of Gaia,* or *Makua Hine Honua,* her name in the Hawaiian language. The deep monotone of traditional Hawaiian chanting is powerful and stirred up archaic

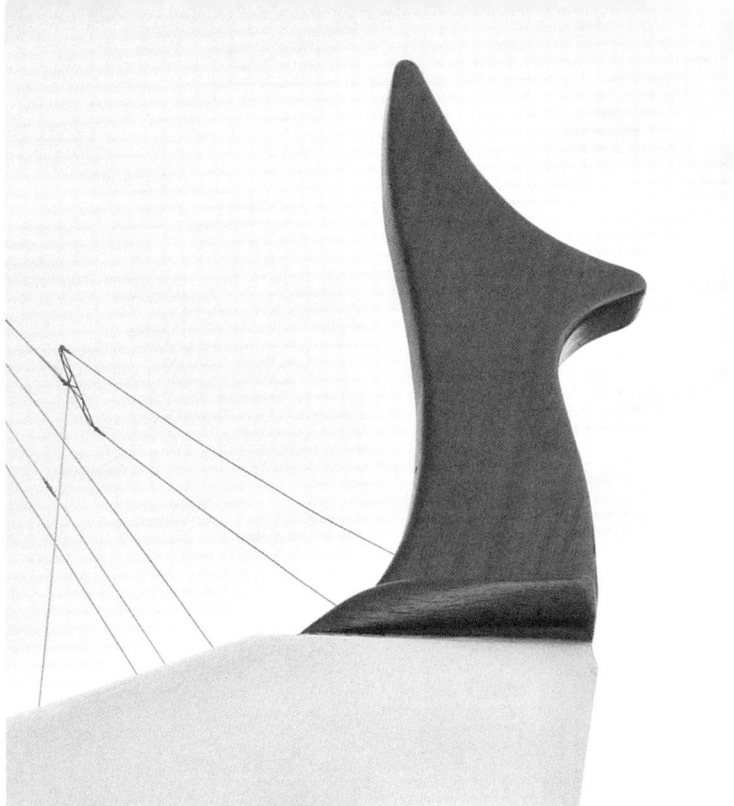

emotions; the large crowd was spellbound. The Hawaiian chant was followed by the same words translated into the old Cornish Celtic language, delivered by George Ansell, the Grand Bard of Cornwall. Then Michael Palmer, the vicar of Devoran, who was a sailor, came to give his blessing, dressed in a long white robe and carrying a large silver bowl for the holy water. Finally two fresh coconuts, brought from Hawaii, were sliced open and the water poured over the twin bows.

The tide had risen and it was time for the big push. *Makua Hine Honua's* keels sat on rows of greased logs ready to slide into the rising tide. The kettledrums went 'Boom, Boom', the hundreds of stones went 'Click, click'. Then under the Hawaiian ritual chant of 'E-ola' people pushed, and pushed again. She would not move. I walked over to the bow and rested my hand to help the effort and suddenly—she shivered and slid into the sea. A conch shell was blown and everyone cheered. Later I heard from two separate psychic friends who had been in the crowd that they had observed a blue aura round the bows of our *Spirit of Gaia*.

With no deck cabins or masts the boat floated high. Hanneke, Ruth and I stood on the beach and hugged each other. We had done it!

The strong warm easterly wind that had been blowing all afternoon eased, and *Spirit of Gaia* was towed by the gigs to the back of our property, steered—one on each tiller—by Aubrey and Norman Ferris, twin brothers of an old Devoran boatbuilding family.

That evening invited people gathered in the Village Hall for the Hawaiian feast. People sat on the wooden floor Polynesian fashion, but we had prepared one high table and chairs for the elderly Cornish locals. When they saw how everyone else was sitting on the floor, they wanted to join them; they even wanted to try the outlandish raw fish salad and breadfruit.

At the end of the wonderful meal the Cornish *grand dame* of the village, Betty Phillips, took charge of the kitchen and regimented a group of guests to help with the washing up; she was magnificent and terrifying. More than twenty years later people come to me and say: 'I still remember the launching of *Spirit of Gaia*, it was the greatest day in my memory of Devoran.'

PEOPLE OF THE SEA AGAIN

Join us

We offer to you freely

Our strength

Our vision

Our wisdom

To finish this canoe

To sail this canoe

To return this canoe

From distant realms

From nearby shores

To the river Fal

The land is free

The sea is free

The heavens are free

Hannah Kihalani Springer
Spirit of Gaia launching chant

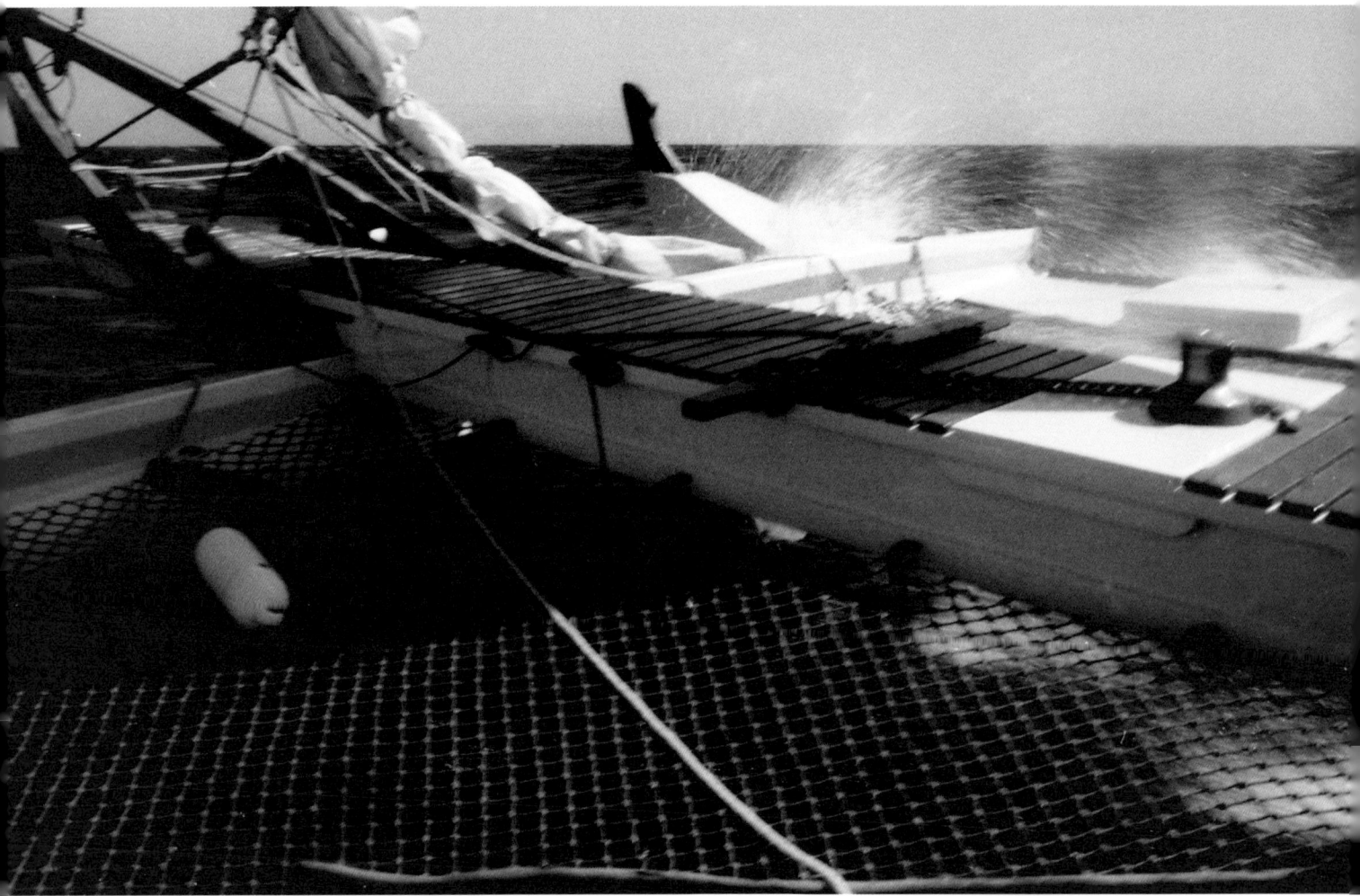

21   Testing voyages

Launching your boat is a great event, but it doesn't mean you have a sailing ship yet. There was a lot more work to do before *Spirit of Gaia* was ready to sail. We manhandled the four deckpods on board; these are also the strong mast supports that spread the loads over a wide area. We raised the two masts—by hand, without the use of a crane, just a sheer pole and lots of pulleys, and people. Dane, one of the Hawaiians, stayed on and helped us fit the two outboard motors and together with Hanneke made the beautiful wooden steering wheel. By the middle of summer it was time for her first sail.

We motored down Restronguet creek, I steered carefully through the many moored boats at the entrance; with a 28ft beam it is not easy to find a passage wide enough. Out in Carrick Roads we hoisted our new wingsails; *Gaia* picked up speed fast and was soon heading out to sea. On board were various friends and helpers, including our friend Dave Greenwell, who at that time was boat tester for *Practical Boat Owner* magazine. Dave had been part of the launching crew and was keen to experience how she would sail.

Outside in the open sea the wind blew stronger, *Gaia* speeded up, 7, 8, 9 then 10 knots, the rigging took up the strain and the new lanyards creaked, the waves hissed along the sleek hulls; I felt elated. I then looked down from my position at the helm and saw Hanneke crouched in the corner of the cockpit. My brave sailor girl looked terrified; Dave knelt down beside her and soothed her with the words, 'She will be alright, *Gaia* is a strong boat, don't worry'. Hanneke had been responsible for all the calculations of the crossbeams, masts and rigging and now, feeling, hearing and experiencing this huge boat take off at speed overwhelmed her.

After several more trial sails, with masts and rigging holding up, we soon gained confidence. Hanneke adjusted sails and sheet angles until she was happy. We had just one problem: how to sheet the foresail. Gaia has a wingsail schooner rig with two equal-sized masts and a same-sized wingsail on each mast. We had made a traveller for the foresheet from a stainless steel tube across the top of the aft deckpods, similar to the traveller on a traditional sailing ship. The ends of the tube were lashed into hardwood sockets, which were glued and bolted to the pod roof.

On one of the trial sails we had Gene Savoy on board. Yes, the Gene Savoy who had asked us to design this boat for him. He had still not built his ethnic version of the design and came over from the USA with some colleagues to see how our boat sailed, so he could decide how he would build his own. He proudly stood at the helm as *Gaia* sped along when suddenly… BANG… the tube traveller, including a chunk of deck in front of the steering wheel, flew off into the air. Fortunately no one was hurt, but it showed what great forces were on this sheet. What was interesting is that the deck tore, but the thin rope lashings holding the tube did not. It confirmed our faith in the strength of lashings.

With a new double sheet arrangement attached to aft mast and crossbeam the problem was solved. We concentrated on making *Gaia* fit for ocean sailing. All hatches were fitted with rubber seals and secured with lanyards; stores and tools were put aboard. Then on 8 September we were ready to set sail south, to Spain, Portugal and… Beyond.

It was thirty-seven years since Ruth, Jutta and I had sailed out of Falmouth on our little 23ft 6in *Tangaroa,* on a boat type that had not been used since Western missionaries destroyed the Polynesian sailing culture. Now I was at the helm of a beautiful big Polynesian double canoe, ready to sail the world's oceans. As we approached the Lizard in the early evening a pod of dolphins joined us swimming under our bows; the perfect start to an ocean voyage on our new dolphin ship. Ruth stood with young Jamie on the foredeck with a beaming smile on her face, watching the dolphins; after years in the office she was an ocean sailor again.

Our voyage south was not as easy as we'd hoped. The weather forecast got it wrong and we were getting headwinds. Instead of fighting them we coast-hopped round to the south of Brittany from where we got a light favourable wind for northern Spain. We were a crew of six: besides myself, Ruth, Hanneke and young Jamie, there was Joke, who had spent five years helping us build *Gaia,* and Ernald who had organised her launching and was a very experienced ocean sailor. We saw many dolphins and pilot whales and often slowed down to try to interact.

Half way across Biscay the wind again turned against us and became squally, and we had to learn how to handle this large double canoe in these conditions, beating to windward in steep rough seas under reefed sails. We had made a simple improvised firebox in the centre of the platform out of half an oil drum. Suddenly a wave hit the firebox from below and knocked it loose; it disappeared down into the ocean and left a four-foot-square hole in the deck. It was very scary to see the churning waves through this big hole. We quickly improvised a grid over it from logs, oars and lashings.

We also had some trouble with the aft crossbeam. It was not secured well enough and started to tilt in its lashings under the weight of the aft ramp and dinghy. We needed to stop and do repairs. Ribadeo, our old home port, beckoned us. As soon as we laid a course *Gaia* took off, the wind turned more favourable, and we sped for the coast. Our log records a boat speed of 13½ knots.

In sailing into Ribadeo, *Spirit of Gaia* joined up my early voyaging life chapters. Ribadeo and the Sela family had been a part of all my previous boats. Each had made the pilgrimage there, first *Tangaroa*, then *Rongo, Tehini* and now *Spirit of Gaia*. The Sela family were all still there, the three older sisters, my dear friend Pepe, his wife Marichu, all older, but little changed, the magnificent old house still the same.

I soon discovered that Pepe was not well—he was suffering from depression. I now believe that like my Jutta he suffered from delayed post-traumatic stress, from his terrible experiences during the Spanish Civil War. I like to think that with our visit and seeing his old friend James again he started on his way to recovery.

With repairs completed we left Ribadeo and followed the coast of Portugal south, and had an exquisite encounter with dolphins at Christmas in the middle of the night, their phosphorescent trails clearly outlining the torpedo shapes of their speeding bodies under the black and starry sky. This is an experience one never forgets. It blotted out some horrible previous days of pouring rain and headwinds, when we had to turn back to the nearest port for shelter, sailing back 60nm in just six hours.

From Portugal we sailed down to the Canary Islands, where we swam with pilot whales off Tenerife. Jamie, aged seven, was a competent swimmer and diver and followed his mother as she swam with a small family group of the whales. Not many young boys get this as part of their education.

In March we also nearly lost our *Gaia* at Tenerife. We had taken shelter in an unfinished marina on the south-east corner of the island, just a harbour wall made of large boulders giving shelter from an impending strong southerly gale. We spent three days in there as the weather worsened and waves started to break over the wall. On day two the friendly owner of the marina took us by car to Los Christianos, where we saw huge waves breaking inside the harbour; we were very glad we were not moored there. An old Tehini that had been left at anchor without crew got wrecked in that surf, with just chunks of wreckage strewn on the beach to show it had existed.

On the third day the wind shifted to the south-east to blow straight onto the wall, more and more waves washing over the wall taking boulders with them. In the dark of the evening we could hear the boulders rolling. We started our outboard motors as the anchors were beginning to drag; a single rock was just behind our sterns and we did not want to hit it. For several hours we were all on watch, anxiously adjusting the speed of the outboards in tune with the surging wind. We did hit the rock just once, a sharp blow to the back of the rudder; it felt like a blow to my own body.

Our main anchor was no longer effective as the wind direction had shifted. The slack loop of the warp got caught in one of the propellers and was cut. We lay to two secondary anchors with slightly short scope, facing the wall, which slowly transformed itself into a reef as more and more boulders rolled into the harbour. White surging water surrounded the ship.

Eventually the wind eased a little. Two of our crew, our very strong surfer friend Sergio and Justus, an Austrian Wharram builder, rowed out in the dinghy to recover the main anchor, which fortunately was buoyed. They then had to reset it to windward close to the destroyed wall. We arranged signalling with a torch to give directions and Sergio rowed hard into the gale with Justus in the stern to drop the anchor. When we flashed the torch to signal the place to drop nothing happened for quite a while; we could see Sergio rowing vigorously, but Justus did not drop. It was some weeks later when Sergio explained what had happened. Unbeknown to Sergio Justus was deaf and had not understood the arranged signalling, he also did not hear Sergio shouting at him to drop the anchor. In the end it was a kick up the backside that got the anchor dropped.

Throughout that night of worry I was remembering the words of the Hawaiian launching chant that called on the Polynesian gods to protect the ship. They heard me.

Sailing in the Canary Islands is a good testing for any boat. The high volcanic islands that lie in a generally strong northerly airflow create wind acceleration zones, where the wind speed will increase by about two forces. So a force 6 wind will become a force 8 in the zone. Sailing out from the lee of an island one was soon in the full

strength of a force 8, with fully-reefed sails. I still remember one crossing from Tenerife to Gran Canaria with a large crew of Sergio and his Spanish friends sailing under just foresail and staysail. *Gaia* leapt over the waves at speeds of around 16 knots with sheets of fine spray shooting over the foredecks and rooster tails at the sterns.

From the Canaries we headed back to the Mediterranean; it was May and the winds were light when we left Gran Canaria bound for Madeira. There were just three of us on board, Hanneke, our Canary island surfing friend Sergio and myself. Ruth and Jamie were back in the UK for work and school.

Sergio was an early pioneer of 'big wave' surfing; as a teenager he had surfed in Bali and Hawaii. He had also spent three years in a Moroccan jail for trying to smuggle marijuana out of Morocco on his own small sailing boat when he was just eighteen years old. In jail he had practised yoga to keep his sanity. Later he lived alone in a Guancho cave* for a year on Grand Canaria.

The voyage from Grand Canaria to Madeira was magical. At times we ghosted at 3–4 knots close-hauled in very light north-east winds, just *Gaia*, the wide gently undulating ocean, and us. Other times the wind increased and we picked up speed to 7–10 knots. With three people aboard the decks were empty; the boat often steered herself.

On arrival in Madeira we spoke to the crew of a replica of *Joshua*, the heavy steel monohull that Bernard Moitessier sailed single handed round the world in the 1968 Golden Globe race. They had left Gomera at around the same time as us, but had motored nearly all the way, claiming there was not enough wind to sail. They had almost run out of diesel. This showed us what a good sailing boat *Spirit of Gaia* was; we never needed to use a motor, except for entering harbour.

Our sail from Madeira to Portugal started as a roller coaster ride. In an area with normally N to NE winds we got a strong south-westerly that propelled us in a direct line for southern Portugal. For forty-eight hours we averaged 8½ knots, covering more than 400nm. The wind got lighter as we approached Portugal. Suddenly in the middle of the night a low flying aeroplane swooped over us and zapped us with a searchlight; it then returned for a second pass and was gone. Before dawn we could smell the strong pine scent of land on the offshore wind. As it got light many ships in a naval exercise with helicopters overhead were on the horizon.

---

*   The Guanches were the aboriginal inhabitants of the Canary Islands, of North African descent.

That summer with Ruth and Jamie back on board we explored the western Mediterranean, sailing to the Balearic islands and far up the east coast of Spain, with the plan to go to the Golfe du Lyon where a friend was engaging with dolphins. However the weather in the gulf is notorious for very strong Mistral winds and the forecast was bad and stayed bad as we waited in Cadaqués. We decided to give the dolphins a miss this time.

We had our first 'workshop' on board organised by Sergio, sailing back down to the Balearics and Alicante with a group of Catalan ladies that practiced 'Re-birthing', a method of self discovery through breathing exercises that take one back to the traumas of birth and early life. Sailing with a group of strangers emphasised the special qualities of *Spirit of Gaia*.

Spirit of Gaia, at 63ft in length, is what I call a 'tribal boat', a boat designed for a group of people to sail together. The hulls of *Gaia* are divided into several separate spaces by watertight bulkheads. Each space is a simple private cabin for two people with its own hatch entrance. When sailing for long periods with a larger crew 'privacy' is an important element of harmonious living.

Between the hulls are two low deckpods, each of these doubling as a strong mast case for her wingsail schooner rig. The front deckpod houses two more private single cabins, the aft one my skipper's cabin and a sheltered cockpit with an off-watch bunk for me to sleep in in bad weather, close at hand for whomever is at the helm.

The cabins circling the open centre deck are like a 'village'. The slatted central platform is the 'village square'; it has a 'hearth'—a fire box around which we can gather at night—and with a hatch in the platform it also has a 'well'. The private cabins, with their own entry hatches, are the 'cottages' surrounding the 'square'. The galley and chartroom on each side of the central square are the communal areas where people work together to prepare food, or to sit and converse. Washing up is done communally on deck, using seawater raised by bucket from the 'well'. On a ship with a large crew sailing in warm waters this is preferable to a cramped little sink in the galley. This simple hatch in the platform, with rope hinges, has become the boat's most admired feature. As well as a safe area to raise a bucket of seawater—even when sailing at 9 knots!—it is also a place to clean fresh caught fish, or more prosaically a sea toilet, or somewhere to be sea sick in safety.

Sailing with our group of Re-birthers we were a 'waterborne community'.

Everyone felt at home. They felt no need to go ashore, preferring to spend an evening at anchor.

I remember a night in a quiet Mallorca anchorage, sitting on deck with our mixed crew of Canary Islander Sergio, our Japanese friend Shige, and the four exotic Catalan women, the fire flickering in the central fire-pit, stars overhead. The crew began to beat drums, tap together pieces of fire log, and click stones in a hypnotic rhythm. Someone began to blow a conch shell. From the aft deckpod the call was chanted into the night: 'Makua Hine Honua'. Shige began to dance a primitive Okinawan dance. Then one of the Catalan women, dressed only in a sarong, stood up and also began to dance. Her long dark hair swaying in a cloud around her, she approached me and drew me into her dance.

Living on *Gaia* with her strong 'Mana' infused by all the people that built her and sailed her has a special effect on visitors.

That summer came to an end back in south Portugal. We left *Gaia* in the guardianship of several Portuguese divers who owned Wharram catamarans, while we went home for the winter to work on new designs.

22 Three expeditions

Our Portuguese guardians had formed an organisation called GEO—Grupo Estudio Oceanis; like us they wanted to study dolphins in the wild, and as divers to study underwater life and archaeology. In return for them looking after our ship, we arranged to sail an expedition with them the next summer to Madeira, Desertas and Selvagem islands, finishing in the Canaries. In the Canaries we would carry on with another expedition, negotiated by Sergio, with a group of Eco Warriors called 'El Guincho' who wanted to charter our ship for one month for a publicity campaign to draw attention to pollution in the harbours and excess water usage by hotels and tourism. This expedition would be called 'Revivir el Mar'.

Expedition sailing was a new experience, sailing with a large group of people with their own agenda is different from me and my close friends making decisions on where to sail and when. The GEO expedition was well organised by Alberto Machado with welcoming meetings for the crew with the mayors of Porto Santo and Funchal, and getting a permit to moor off Isla Desertas, which is a restricted nature reserve. Jamie, now nine years old, got his first experience of scuba diving under the tutelage of Alberto.

Having a group of seven people and all their heavy scuba diving gear on deck made me realize the extra stresses put on a boat by expedition sailing. When we were asked to anchor off the very rough and exposed rocky island of Selvagem, I, as captain, had to put my foot down and limited our stay to just a few hours, while they went for a dive. I was not prepared to risk our ship by spending the night at anchor there.

The El Guincho expedition was tougher still. It was August, the hottest and windiest month of the year in the Canaries. They had gathered a large crew of around ten to eleven people, each with a dedicated task on board—cameraman, dolphin expert, PA to the leader, dinghy handler, etc.,—who had been 'trained' in a shore camp in La Graciosa, the small island that lies off the north tip of Lanzarote. There was also a shore team that would travel overland and by ferry to prepare the reception of the ship in all the harbours. As well as the El Guincho crew there was our own core crew of me, Ruth, Hanneke, Jamie and Sergio. The 'flexispace' lay-out of *Gaia* worked well, with two or even three people in each cabin, with us keeping our own private spaces.

The schedule of this expedition was harsh: we were to visit every island in the Canaries, sailing from La Graciosa to Lanzarote, down to Fuerta Ventura, then a long night crossing to the capital Las Palmas and circling Gran Canaria, another tough crossing to Santa Cruz Tenerife, down to La Gomera, across to La Palma and finally the western outpost of El Hierro. The whole programme was finely timed with welcoming parties of fishermen in many of the ports. With the strong winds it was possible to plan each journey with precision, adjusting our departure times to our known sailing speed.

Most of the crew were smokers, spoke little English, and their Spanish was the Canary Island variety that I could not understand. Half the crew also had little appreciation of the ship, having no interest in handling sails. Fortunately there were two divers on board, a gardener and a truck driver in normal life, who were strong and together with Sergio quickly learned to handle the sails. In the very strong winds in the wind acceleration zones we were frequently reefing, and with brief commands in my basic Spanish, 'dos rizos', 'tres rizos' 'quatro rizos', kept the boat going.

Food was another problem. Normally when sailing with a large crew we take turns in the galley, with others helping with the preparations. The El Guincho command told us that they had a dedicated cook who would prepare all the meals. He was a Brazilian and a vegan, though he was prepared to cook non-vegan dishes. He started off well with interesting wholesome food during the first week, but soon he started to flag, cooking for around fourteen people three times a day whilst sailing in rough seas was just too much.

By the time we reached the port of Santa Cruz de la Palma and were offered a dish of just plain wholemeal pasta, with on my insistence a sprinkling of cheese, we were all desperate for a 'proper' meal. Sergio and Hanneke went to the wonderful Spanish food market in the town and came back with meat and fresh vegetables. Soon smells of cooking meat rose out of the open galley hatch where a row of crew gathered, sniffing deeply and sighing 'Carne, carne' (meat, meat). From then on we took turns cooking and with the competition each meal got better.

Our roughest passage was sailing down the coast of la Palma, the wind accelerating stronger and stronger with our instruments recording wind speeds over 40 knots. After taking in reef after reef we ended up sailing at 9 knots under bare poles. Then as we rounded the bottom corner of the island the wind dropped from 34 knots to calm within two minutes.

After four weeks of hard expedition sailing we arrived in the barren windblown harbour of Restinga on El Hierro. The El Guincho crew packed up their gear, including extra dinghy, two outboard motors and heavy diving bottles, and departed on the ferry. *Spirit of Gaia*'s spirit rose with her waterline as around two tons of weight was taken off. She had been tested, sailing to a tight schedule, in very strong winds.

❧

Resting in Los Christianos after the El Guincho expedition, I was enjoying a quiet reflective moment in a bar, when I was approached by a tall, slim, vivacious German woman called Martina. Martina had heard about me and had been trying to meet us. Sitting in the bar she explained to me the theories of the German Dieter Duhm, who argued that Western sexual concepts, one man, one woman, one relationship, limited much of the human psyche.

Dieter Duhm and his followers had formed a community called 'Zegg' near Berlin. Martina and five others—three men and three women—had left the community to set up a similar one on board a 70ft Turkish *Gulet* sailing workboat, *Kairos*, built for them in Turkey. On *Kairos* they took groups of like-minded Germans out of Los Christianos, sailing, swimming, and singing with the resident pods of pilot whales, whilst running workshops and practicing the sexual philosophies of Dieter Duhm.

Visiting *Kairos* and talking to the crew I soon realised it is one thing running a commune on land, but on a sailing ship there is much greater need for regular care, duties, planning and thinking ahead. Already two of the men had not been able to cope and left the ship, and now Martina, as the strongest of the four that were left, was asking me for advice to help her organise their ship.

To learn more about sailing Martina joined us on a rough sixty-mile trip on *Spirit of Gaia,* crossing the 'wind zones' from Tenerife to Gran Canaria. This was our toughest sail yet. Our wind meter registered a steady 32–38 knots, increasing in squalls to 42–45 knots, gusting 48. *Spirit of Gaia* was magnificent, she was riding the big seas in great sheets of spray, the Vee'd hulls leaping off the crests and slicing gently, not banging, down into the troughs. How she seemed to feel her way through the waves was inspiring. Martina and Hanneke got highly charged with the energy that flowed around the ship. They were like naked goddesses with wild blond hair in the gale force wind.

Watching these two beautiful naked women on our magnificent Polynesian double canoe, I was reminded of the scenes described by Captain Cook and French Admiral Bougainville when they arrived in Tahiti at the end of the eighteenth century. The free and open sexual customs in the Polynesian islands at that time had been a total revelation to the European sailors, brought up on strict Christian morals. In Polynesian society female nakedness was not a sin. These explorers returned with descriptions of having discovered 'Natural Man' living in a Golden Age, which had a strong social impact on European society.

Nearly 200 years later when Thor Heyerdahl sailed his *Kon-Tiki* across the Pacific, the aspects of sexual freedom in Polynesian society still had a social impact. After the voyage, Bengt Danielsson, Swedish crewmember on *Kon-Tiki*, spent many years exploring the social and sexual customs in the Pacific islands. His book *Love in the South Seas* published in English in 1956 (the year I first crossed the Atlantic on *Tangaroa*) described the open sexual customs in the Polynesian islands in detail. It was a 'best seller' and was an important stimulus for the Western sexual revolution of the 1960s.

Talking to Martina about these Polynesian sexual customs it was clear that Dieter Duhm's theories followed the same theme. It was also clear that my group's lifestyle had parallels with the Dieter Duhm philosophy.

In the light of our similar attitudes to sexuality, Martina suggested we could run a workshop together with the two boats. They had too many people booked for their 'Die Welt ist Klang' (the world is sound) workshop in November, so we agreed we would join them and take eight people on board *Spirit of Gaia*.

The sailing with *Kairos* was a total contrast to the two previous expeditions. Whereas the others had been hard sailing with practical objectives, this voyage was one of sensuousness and mental connection. We would sail out to sea in the shelter of Tenerife and connect with the pods of pilot whales. When contact was made, our group

REVIVIR EL MAR

naturally would go quiet, their sensitive minds reaching out to the whales, not screaming in excitement, like so many of the tourist groups do.

The Germans on our ship had 'chosen' to sail on *Gaia* rather than on *Kairos*, being subconsciously attracted to her beauty and 'Mana'. Even though none had met before, through their like-minded philosophy they quickly bonded with us into a sensual, cohesive crew.

With me as leaders were Hanneke and Joke—who had returned to us after some time in Holland—while Ruth and Jamie had gone back to the UK for work and school. I decided to organise our eight guests into two groups of four, each led by one of the girls. One day one group would be in charge of all the boat handling, the other all the household tasks, the next day they would swap.

This was a very successful arrangement; every evening the 'boat' crew after anchoring and tidying the ship would light the fire, while the 'household' group prepared a meal. Our crew naturally bonded round the fire and opened their minds in discussion, whereas on the *Kairos* things were more regimented with daily, organised group discussions. No one on our ship was pressed into acting out the theories of Dieter Duhm, but many flowed naturally into sensuous connections with others. There was an unforced beauty in this that I had never experienced before and have never experienced since.

It soon became apparent that *Spirit of Gaia* was a much faster ship than the heavy cumbersome *Kairos*, and soon our crew started to want to experience her sailing qualities, rather than tamely drift in the company of the slower vessel. So after some days we decided to each go our own way for a few days with *Gaia* making a fast crossing to the next island of La Palma. I still remember with delight the trip we made into the island's interior in two hire cars. We all gathered high on the mountain and stood there in total sensual harmony looking down into the deep and beautiful caldera.

Our time together with this wonderful crew led to deep friendships that have lasted to this day. The two couples in the crew each joined us later on our ocean voyages and another man sailed with us across the Indian Ocean and still returns with his new partner to sail on *Gaia* today.

At the end of the *Kairos* expedition our future plans took a decisive turn. Since *Gaia*'s launching we had been dreaming of sailing into the Pacific, to *Makua Hine Honua's* Polynesian homelands. This had been our dream in 1961 when Ruth, Jutta, Hannes and I set off on our world voyage on *Rongo*. Jutta's death had put a halt to this. Now thirty-three years later we had the perfect ship to do it.

One plan was to visit the Bonin islands to the south of Japan where we were told were many dolphins. Our contact with Japan was Shigefumi Nakamura, a shy young architect I had met there after my visit to Hawaii. Shige had sailed with us in the Mediterranean the previous year and joined us again in the Canaries after the El Guincho expedition. He urged us to come to his beautiful tropical islands to meet the dolphins.

That summer, with burgeoning plans to sail to the Pacific, I had started a correspondence with Herb Kane, the inspirational artist in Hawaii who had painted those evocative scenes of Polynesian canoes, and I suggested to him that we might visit Hawaii. I had sadly missed meeting him on my visit there in 1992, but he had heard about me. Herb Kane had been the designer of the double canoe *Hokule'a* and initiator of the Polynesian Voyaging Society we had first heard about in 1974 in Antigua, though he had retired from any involvement many years back.

With my first letter to Herb Kane I sent a copy of an article I had just written about the performance of *Spirit of Gaia* as a modern version of the traditional Polynesian double canoe. Later I wrote to him about our experiences with the El Guincho group and how *Gaia* had performed in the strong wind zones. In his letters Herb told us the background to the designing of *Hokule'a* and the second Hawaiian canoe *Hawaiiloa*. He also informed us that there was going to be a gathering of Polynesian replica canoes in Raiatea in March 1995.

I had also sent my article about *Spirit of Gaia* to a young man called Karim Cowan in Tahiti, whom I had read about in a French multihull magazine. This young enthusiast in the revival of Polynesian double canoe sailing responded with a phone call received by Ruth in our office in England at the time we were sailing with our *Kairos* crew. He told her about the 'Great Gathering of the Canoes' in Raiatea and asked us if we would join them.

When Ruth returned to *Gaia* she told us we should telephone Karim. I still remember crowding into a small telephone box with Ruth and Hanneke. In that phone call an enthusiastic Karim gave us the official invitation to attend the Great Gathering of the Canoes with our double canoe *Spirit of Gaia* and told us the government was thrilled at having a double canoe coming from England. The Gathering would start on 16 March in Huahine, near Tahiti. Confident in the seaworthiness of *Gaia* after our tough expeditions, I said: 'Yes we will come.'

Putting the phone down I asked Ruth 'How far is it to Huahine?' Back on board she measured it on the chart and told me that it was roughly 4000nm to the Panama Canal, and then 4500nm to Huahine, a total of 8500 sailing miles. With some quick calculations we worked out it could be done, but we would have to depart soon.

23   From Atlantic to Pacific

A long ocean voyage needs preparation. With 8500nm to sail we would need some form of self-steering. We had used an electric autopilot in our first years of sailing, but we did not like it, it used too much electricity and made too much noise. We wanted a 'wind vane' steering system.

To get some ideas we studied a number of wind-controlled self-steering systems on yachts anchored in our Grand Canaria homeport of Arguineguín and applied that knowledge to design our own. In tune with our philosophy, we designed a system that we could build ourselves out of wood, with a minimum of hardware and fittings. The hardest part of the design was to construct a separate 'amplification paddle' that was strong enough to withstand the forces of sailing at 9–10 knots. This paddle is steered by the windvane and its water-driven power is used to move the tillers.

Our system was a success, though the paddle did need some modifications and strengthening after the first trials, but by the time we reached the Caribbean Sea it worked and has worked throughout all our voyaging ever since.

Next was food and water. We have always kept our *Gaia* simple; the fewer 'systems' you have, the less there is to maintain and repair, and the less electricity you need. We sail without a fridge or water maker. We store our water in 25-litre (5-gallon) jerry cans, which fit under the bunks in the cabins. The advantage is that you can see how much water is used (we used one can every two days with seven crew); and you can label each can's contents with date and origin. When filling up at a water source that doesn't taste very nice, you do not spoil your whole water supply, as can happen with large fitted tanks. Also it is easy to take some cans in a dinghy and fill them at the nearest tap.

To supplement our water supply we had designed a built-in rainwater catchment system in our deckpod roofs. One hour of heavy rain fills three to four 25-litre cans. On a voyage we always wash dishes in seawater. We also wash our bodies and hair with seawater and use about a cup of fresh water to rinse salt out of our hair. These practices reduce one's fresh water needs enormously.

We keep our dry stores in large plastic tubs, and tinned stores fit neatly in the Vee-shaped epoxy-coated dry bilges. Fresh fruit and vegetables are stored in shallow wooden fruit trays, which can be stacked. To prevent sprouting, potatoes are stored in a dark cardboard box. With our many separate cabins, we were able to dedicate one whole cabin as the fresh food store.

Crew was not a problem. Apart from my core crew of Ruth, Hanneke and Jamie, Joke also wanted to sail with us. In addition, for the Atlantic crossing, we would be joined by a young German couple and Avril the English retired head teacher who had helped us during the building of *Gaia*. In Antigua they would leave the ship.

Our excitement at sailing into the Pacific communicated itself to Udo and Rosmarie, who had been part of the *Kairos* cruise. They were a sweet quiet couple in their early forties who had first met only that summer. On hearing our plans, Udo asked us shyly whether they could sail with us. As he first had work to do in Germany, he suggested he and Rosmarie could join us in the West Indies. It was agreed that they would fly out to St Maarten and join us there.

On 18 December 1994 we left Arguineguín and sailed to Gomera to stock up on drinking water. The water in Gran Canaria is desalinated seawater and doesn't taste good. In Gomera I fell ill with tonsillitis, so we delayed our departure for another four days for me to get better, which gave the crew time to calibrate our log and get the last fresh food on board.

I have crossed the Atlantic on the southern trade wind route five times, each time with a bigger boat, and each time the voyage was easier. Our crossing on *Spirit of Gaia* was straightforward; the large slim hulls sailed fast and rode the big trade wind waves with ease. Our crew of eight meant we could have three-hour night watches of two people and get plenty of sleep. The food was good and we even caught several fish. We reached Antigua after twenty days easy sailing having averaged 134nm a day.

Arrival in Antigua on 11 January was a window into the past. Though English Harbour was now a mass of anchored yachts and the old warehouses were converted into luxury accommodation, many of our friends from our last *Tehini* visit, twenty years earlier, were still there. Jol Byerley was still running a charter business with his family. Jol was the man who had taken me to meet Edward Dodd in 1974, who had given us our first introduction to the *Hokule'a* project and the Polynesian Voyaging Society, which we were now sailing out to meet.

With our very tight schedule we could afford to stay only three days in Antigua, then we sailed another 100nm to St Maarten to pick up Udo and Rosmarie, our new German crew. Full crew of seven on board, we sailed the next 1000nm to Puerto Colón at the entrance of the Panama Canal. This voyage of seven days across the empty Caribbean Sea culminated in two days of gale force trade winds of 28–35 knots.

It was extremely hot and humid, the sky a clear blue, and below it the big tumbling white capped following seas, which we judged to be around six metres high, with *Gaia* surfing under a reefed staysail, and as the wind increased just bare poles. We took off the self-steering paddle and hand steered at 7–8 knots. At one time *Gaia* took off at 11 knots surfing down a set of even bigger waves.

As the wind increased and waves became bigger, I noticed Udo getting anxious and took him on top of one of the deckpods to show him how *Gaia* would ride easily down each sea, how the slim canoe sterns would gently lift and split the chasing waves. The occasional wave would break under the boat and we watched the white crest harmlessly foaming up through the slatted centre deck. Sitting there watching these forces of nature was inspiring.

On the seventh day, with the wind gone down, dozens of anchored ships filled the horizon, all waiting to transit the Panama Canal.

Puerto Colón was an introduction to the worst of Third World cities; it could literally be called the 'Arse End' port. The streets smelled of sewage, and there were guards armed with machine guns at the shop doors. When approaching the meat counter in the back of a supermarket we quickly decided we would forego the fresh meat as the smell hit our nostrils.

We anchored outside the town off the Yacht Club in heavy humid heat, and arranged our transit of the canal for 3 February. This gave us a few days to restock the boat for the long voyage ahead, which we would most likely make non-stop. We were planning to sail straight out into the Pacific and not stop in Balboa.

After our experience in the supermarket and a worse one in the chaotic, and to Udo very frightening, local market, I suggested to Joke she should approach the Chinese owner of a better looking shop we had noticed in town, and ask him to get all our fresh foodstuffs delivered to our boat. This was a great success. The fresh vegetables and fruit were all of excellent quality and lasted for weeks. In fact we still had our last orange and tomato on the last day of our thirty-three-day non-stop voyage.

Many other sailors have written about transiting the Panama Canal, so I will only mention the near disaster that struck in the last of the locks. On the descent to the Pacific we had to go through three locks. In each of these we were directed by our pilots to moor alongside a US landing craft manned by a crew of soldiers. This landing craft either did not have suitable mooring cleats, or the crew did not know how to use them, for in every lock they messed about getting us tied up. We tried to climb aboard and do it ourselves, but were told to 'keep off' as it was 'US territory'.

In the third and last lock they once more were incapable of tying us up quickly. A big ship entered after us and created a strong displacement current. Our stern line, which should have held us close to the landing craft, was again not cleated off and *Gaia*'s stern started to swing out with the strong current. By the time they had the line fixed, *Gaia* was lying at 45 degrees under terrific strain. Our end of the mooring line was attached to a temporary crossbar lashed across our stern netting beams; it suddenly gave way with a terrific bang. The line with crossbar and me holding on to it went overboard. I was swimming in the roiling waters of the lock—I could have drowned—but fiercely clung on to the rope and was hauled in by the US army crew. I stood bleeding on the 'forbidden' deck and gave them a 'bollocking' my father would have been proud of, the words of which are better not written down, but which began with references to the 'Boston Tea Party'.

Meantime *Gaia* had swung at right angles to the lock and shot bows first into the granite wall. She then swung further round and ended up lying stern-first alongside the wall. Hanneke, shaking with shock, ran to the bows to see how much damage had been done, but discovered that due to the high water in the lock, the stem had hit the rounded granite edge low down where it is incredibly strong and she could only see a small dent in the thick fibreglass.

After a holdup while *Gaia* was turned around we finally exited the Canal and moored on one of the buoys off Balboa Yacht Club where we took stock of the situation. The pilots told us we could lodge a complaint and we should get compensation, but this meant we had to stay in the Canal Zone until things were sorted out; this could take a week or two, which we did not have.

We assessed the damage to the stern netting beam, which in fact was not structural to the boat, and decided we could tie our ladder across temporarily and 'get sailing'. At six the next morning we were on our way out into the wide Pacific.

Ahead of us lay 4500nm of ocean to the French Society Islands. Most sailors making this passage will try to stop in the Galápagos and the Marquesas islands, but we had a deadline of 16 March, the starting day of the Great Gathering of the Canoes in Huahine. We had to sail non-stop.

Winds in the first part of the voyage were light, becoming lighter still near the equator. We were making little progress for nearly one week, ghosting in terrific heat. In the middle of the day when heat was greatest we sometimes motored for a few hours, but as our petrol supplies were minimal, all this achieved was some cooling breeze across the deck. We rigged an awning to give us some shade, we swam in the crystal clear warm sea, and worried if we would ever be able to get to Huahine in time. We saw one cargo ship which passed fairly close and we joked about asking them for a tow. In the end we just spoke to them on the VHF and they passed on a message to the organisers in Tahiti.

Our son Jamie, now nine years old, was pressed into doing his schoolwork under the supervision of Rosmarie, who had been a schoolteacher in Austria, but it was hard to get him active in the gruelling heat. He preferred to sit in a tub of water on deck.

Meals were the highlights of the day, with fresh fruit and vegetables from the excellent store provided by the Chinese shopkeeper. If vegetables have not been refrigerated in the shop, they keep much better in the heat. During the first week a portion of the fruit and veg starts to go bad, with cucumbers becoming 'sea cucumbers', but then the hardy ones survive and keep surviving. Every day the cook would check over the stores and pick out what needed eating and design a meal around them, combining the fresh food with our tinned and dry stores.

The clear tropical starlit nights were the best part. When seeing that huge dome of dark sky filled with bright stars and no land lights to spoil the vision, one can easily understand how the Polynesians developed their superb star navigation methods. That night sky, also when ashore on their islands, was to them like their bedroom ceiling; they knew it like you or I would know every crack and blemish in ours. It is an ever-moving map that one can watch and study and remember. Ruth, and Hanneke who had now taken over as navigator since the introduction of GPS, spent their night watches studying the stars and trying to memorise their names and locations.

During this long voyage I started to think about the meeting ahead. In the 1970s I had read all the reports in *National Geographic* magazine of *Hokule'a*, about her building and voyage to Tahiti, several written by my friend Herb Kane. Herb had designed *Hokule'a* and had been the initiator of the Polynesian Voyaging Society with his vision of reviving the old sailing culture in Hawaii, where it had been badly eroded by the islands becoming a state of the USA (in 1954) and becoming highly Americanised in their culture.

In 1976 Dr David Lewis, a New Zealander who had been co-navigating *Hokule'a* under the chief Micronesian navigator Mau Piailug, wrote a long report in *National Geographic* of the voyage from Hawaii to Tahiti. It described how they navigated by the stars and how they ate original Polynesian foodstuffs, which were cooked on a firebox on deck. It described the hardships of being constantly wet whilst beating into rough seas, how they had to cope with long spells of no wind in the doldrums.

It was also clear in this article that around half of the seventeen crew—all men, selected for their prowess as 'watermen', men who were experts at paddling canoes in the surf, but had no deep-sea experience—were not prepared to adapt themselves to the Polynesian sea lifestyle planned for the voyage. They started to object to eating the traditional Polynesian food and demanded Western foods from the accompanying escort boat, a large sturdy sailing ketch, fully equipped with modern instrumentation. It was also discovered that they had smuggled a small transistor radio on board on which they could listen to the Hawaiian news, which reported on the voyage progress via radio link with the escort boat. This could have seriously compromised the 'Polynesian Navigation' experiment of the voyage.

The articles in *National Geographic* had painted a wonderful, romantic picture. We were now sailing to meet *Hokule'a* and its newer sistership *Hawaiiloa*. We were looking forward to comparing our *Spirit of Gaia* with these two similar-sized double canoes, sailing together and comparing notes with the crews.

Our 4500nm voyage across the vast empty Pacific was fairly uneventful. After the first ten slow days we picked up the south-east trades below the equator and progress suddenly improved dramatically. Apart from occasional squalls we experienced no gales or bad weather. We had three weeks of daily runs from 130 to as much as 220nm, which made possible our goal of reaching Huahine in time for the meeting.

24   The Great Gathering of the Canoes

After thirty-three days at sea the mountains of Huahine became visible on the horizon. It was 9 March. We were on time; we had averaged 140nm per day on this long voyage.

We started our outboard motors and made our first careful entrance through a Pacific coral reef pass. Inside the reef there were no signs of any other double canoes, so we searched for the best place to anchor. The clear water by the village of Fare looked inviting, but it soon became clear it was bad holding ground, so we nosed into a sheltered more muddy inlet where we dropped our anchor and went ashore to clear customs and immigration. Through our contacts with Karim Cowan we were classed as part of the 'Gathering' and could stay in the French islands without paying a bond of £1000, as was normally required.

We then went looking for anyone who was part of the organisation of the Gathering and eventually found a quiet French official connected to the tourist office, who told us that the Hawaiian canoes had arrived in Tahiti and would come to Huahine in a few days.

In anticipation we started to prepare *Spirit of Gaia* for the meeting. We needed an awning to shield us from the strong tropical sun. We only had a cheap blue plastic tarp for this, which we found looked rather ugly and un-Polynesian. So we asked our contact where we could cut some coconut palm fronds and find bamboo for a frame. He was helpful, supplied us with coconut fronds and showed us how in Huahine they used the fa'au tree, a tree hibiscus, for lightweight structures. With these materials we plaited coconut leaf screens, as I had done many years ago in Trinidad, and made a Polynesian-looking roof over our centre platform. It cast dappled shade over the deck, the loose fronds along the edges rustled in the breeze, and it looked beautiful.

Soon after our arrival Udo got a message from his office that he was urgently needed back in Germany. He and Rosmarie, who had been excellent crew on our long voyage, had to leave us. But not before Chris and Evelyn, who had also been crew on our *Kairos* expedition, joined us. As an adjunct to a business trip to Malaysia, they came with their young son for a month's holiday.

A day later the *Takitumu,* a canoe from the Cook Islands, arrived. She was a reduced size replica of a Fijian Drua—a double canoe with two uneven sized hulls and rigged like a proa with the mast on the larger hull. She had been built out of plywood for the Pacific Cultural Festival held in Rarotonga in 1992. She joined us in our sheltered anchorage and her crew told us they had lost their anchor, so we lent them one of ours. They were a friendly bunch of men, who got inspired by our sunroof and decided they should make one too.

One morning we looked out towards the reef and spotted the distinctive masts of two canoes moving towards the pass. We recognised them as *Hokule'a* and *Hawaiiloa* and tracked their slow entrance into the lagoon with binoculars. They were each being towed by a sturdy monohull yacht. They tried to anchor by the village as we had done and like us discovered it was bad anchoring ground, so eventually they joined us in our sheltered inlet. We watched them drop anchor and gave them twenty minutes to sort themselves out before rowing over to say hello.

To our consternation we found both canoes had been abandoned; the crews had gone ashore to the Bali Hai hotel. They had made no attempt to greet us or show any interest. We rowed round both canoes and were rather appalled to find large quantities of heavy white nylon rope used for lashings and rigging. *Hawaiiloa*, according to the reports in *National Geographic*, was to have been built using only natural materials and matting sails.

The next day was the official welcoming party for the canoes. The New Zealand canoe, *Te Aurere*, arrived—she had been shipped from New Zealand to Tahiti. We were told that there would be a reception in the grounds of the Bali Hai hotel to which we were invited, where there would be drinks and snacks. There we discovered a special feast was prepared for the canoe crews, but that we did not qualify, so would have to make do with snacks in company with the crews of the escort boats and local guests. Talking to these escort crews—experienced 'white' yachtsmen who knew me as a designer and were pleased to meet us—we started to discover an almost racist segregation between 'Polynesian' crews and 'White' crews. None of us were happy about this. None of the crew or organisers of the Hawaiian boats had approached us.

The programme was that all the canoes would leave Huahine at four the next morning and sail the 18nm to Raiatea, to the Teavamoa pass near the sacred Marae Taputapuātea (a complex of religious sites at Opua in Taputapuātea) where the canoes would enter in procession led by the New Zealand canoe. We were told to enter last. It was a beautiful dawn as we sailed across with the full moon in the sky above Raiatea. Indeed we did sail, and were disappointed to see that all the other canoes were being towed. The only canoe to hoist sail for a while was *Takitumu*.

Next day was the official ceremony on the Marae, to lift the 'tapu' (taboo) that we were told had been laid on it around 1350. This ceremony was taken very seriously and we, as Europeans, could not be part of it, so could only watch together with the hundreds of other visitors. It was a very colourful occasion with singing, drumming and dancing. It reminded me of a Welsh Eisteddfod, only more colourful.

These first days of the 'Great Gathering' were to be a foretaste of the following weeks. We were always left on the outside of any planned events, having to resort to news from the escort boat crews to discover the day's programme. It became clear that some people of the Polynesian Voyaging Society in Hawaii, who were the unseen guiding force behind the whole event, found us a political embarrassment and would have been happier if we had never come.

We would have accepted being classed as different, but would have enjoyed sailing together with the various canoes and comparing notes, but to our disappointment none of the canoes ever sailed throughout the four weeks we spent in company. During the beautiful day sail inside the lagoon of Raiatea on our way north to the next event in Taha'a, in a light favourable trade wind, all the canoes were towed, while we sailed in their wake. We were always to be the last in any procession, so when *Gaia* at her natural sailing speed overtook the towed canoes we had to do a loop back, to stay in place.

It was amusing, watching the serious faces of the dignitaries sitting on the next canoe, while my crew of beautiful women, dressed in pareos (wraparound skirts) and flower leis, beat drums together with two handsome heavily tattooed local Polynesian men to whom we gave a lift on our boat, as no other transport was available to them.

At other times we observed the rivalry between the Tahitians and Hawaiians. Only much later did I become fully aware of the political undercurrents. The French government under Jacques Chirac was planning more atom bomb testing at the atoll of Mururoa in the Tuamotu islands in the coming months. This display of Tahitian

Polynesian prowess was a good distraction from an approaching political stress point.

The Hawaiians had their own political stresses. The canoes of the Polynesian Voyaging Society were a symbol of the cultural prowess of the oppressed minority Polynesians in Hawaii, where they had to assert themselves against the Haoles (white Americans) and dominating American culture. This could explain their antipathy towards me and my crew of white Europeans, who in their eyes were upstaging them.

On the next leg, the 100nm to Tahiti against the south-east trades, the other canoes were again being towed, so we stayed an extra day in the beautiful lagoon of Taha'a for a break from the emotionally stressful atmosphere. Just as well, as the weather turned unstable and we had some severe thunderstorms.

When we arrived in Papeete, we found *Te Ao O Tonga,* the new 70ft Cook Islands canoe, moored by the town quay. She had arrived under tow, with a broken mast sustained in the rough seas. She had come too late for the ceremony at Tapuapuatea. We were able to study her build and design.

Sir Thomas Davis, governor of the Cook Islands, had designed her, based on a sketch drawing of a Tahitian canoe by Captain Cook. She was built in plywood and epoxy, and we recognised many similar construction details to my designs. The broken mast lying on the quayside was a wooden box construction, glued and nailed with galvanised nails; it reminded me of an early hollow mast design for my Classic designs. The hulls were multi-chined and quite elegant with high sterns and low bows, but the whole was spoiled by a huge square deckhouse with full standing headroom. Inside one of the hulls was a large Volvo diesel engine.

In Papeete we finally met Karim Cowan, the young man who had invited us to the 'Great Gathering'. Karim was the nephew of Francis Cowan, who had been a friend of Éric de Bisschop and sailed on his raft voyages in 1956–57 in an attempt to reach South America and return by bamboo raft.

In the early 1980s Francis Cowan, together with Greg Matahi Brightwell, a New Zealand Maori, had built a beautiful, genuine double canoe called *Havaiki Nui.* She had been carved out of full-length logs, with raised topsides lashed-on in traditional Polynesian method, using sennit rope. Francis and Greg sailed *Havaiki Nui* to New Zealand using Polynesian navigation methods, without escort boat or radio. Sadly their arrival in New Zealand in 1985 was overshadowed by the arrival of *Hokule'a*, which got all the limelight in *National Geographic* magazine and the local press. *Havaiki Nui* was later shipped back to Tahiti to be displayed in the museum in Papeete.

At the museum *Havaiki Nui* had been kept outside in the tropical sun and rain, where she started to deteriorate. When the Great Gathering of the Canoes was on the horizon it was decided that Tahiti needed a new big canoe to represent the island. *Havaiki Nui* was no longer fit, there was little time to build a big canoe, and so the dreadful decision was made that the dugout hulls of *Havaiki Nui* should be used as the base for building a new canoe.

We had seen the new big canoe, called *Tahiti Nui*, in Raiatea where it was towed like all the others. It gave the impression of a Hollywood film prop rather than a genuine sea-going canoe. The topsides carried elaborate carvings, which looked more like Egyptian hieroglyphics than Polynesian decorations. It had an enormous steering oar and two small sails, hoisted for display while she was towed around, that were smaller than her enormous Tahitian flag.

Tahiti Nui was now moored near Papeete at a boatyard where Karim was working on his own canoe. He told us the sad story of how the government had pressed him into building this new canoe, with the cannibalised dugout hulls of his uncle's beautiful *Havaiki Nui*. As a result Karim's own canoe was not finished in time for the Gathering.

Then, a week late, another Hawaiian canoe entered Papeete harbour. This was *Makali'i*, a canoe built by an independent group separate from the Polynesian Voyaging Society. It was the nicest looking canoe of them all and the crew were friendly.

In Papeete we attended a skipper's meeting where the next stage of a scheduled voyage to Hawaii was discussed. Our plan had been to sail with the fleet to Hawaii, but we were beginning to have doubts, for the next leg was a windward voyage, 750 miles to the north-east, to the Marquesas. The canoes in the fleet were all going to be towed, the reason given that they were running behind schedule, but for us it would be a hard reach against south-east trades which can tend more easterly.

We were then told by the organisers that the ceremonies in the Marquesas would again be 'for Polynesians only'. To which I replied in a last attempt at humour: 'how much Polynesian blood do you need in your veins to be classed as Polynesian?', they told me 'one sixteenth', to which I quipped 'How about me having a blood transfusion?'

Back on board *Gaia* we considered the situation and made the decision to sail to

New Zealand where there would be a friendly welcome. Our agent in Auckland, Don Brazier, had offered us a free mooring in the creek behind his house, as well as two crew members who could fly out to Rarotonga to sail with us.

Our final meeting with all the canoes was in Tautira, a village at the eastern end of Tahiti where *Hokule'a* had visited on previous voyages. Our two 9.9hp Yamaha outboard motors had been giving us trouble since the Panama Canal. Chris, our German friend, a born engineer with a high-placed job in an electrical windings company, had been taking them apart and trying to find the trouble throughout his stay with us. In the end he had to give up and concluded it was an electrical problem he could not repair. On our sail to Tautira both engines again adamantly refused to start, which meant we would have to sail without them until we could find a qualified Yamaha repair shop.

In Tautira, where no official ceremonies were planned, we were given a more friendly welcome and talked to many of the boat crews. We also finally had the chance to go on board *Hokule'a* and *Hawaiiloa* and study both canoes close up. They both had built-up structures surrounding the solid plank centre decking, which had silicone rubber sealing in the joints to stop waves coming up through the deck. There was a mass of rope rigging, all thick white polyester or nylon; it gave the impression of the deck of a square rigger rather than the open elegance of a lightly built Polynesian ethnic vessel. The spars were also heavy and rigid, not built to flex, which traditional ethnic spars and rigs normally do. I regretted that we had not been able to see these canoes sail. To me it seemed clear that the people who had rigged these canoes had not studied traditional canoes and their rigs in Indonesia or the Philippines, where many canoe craft are still sailing.

We also met Ben Finney, an anthropologist, who together with Herb Kane had originated the idea of building *Hokule'a* back in the mid 1970s. He seemed a disappointed man and spent three long hours telling me about the twisted politics around the canoe revival in Hawaii. After sailing on the first *Hokule'a* voyage from Hawaii to Tahiti he had been pushed to the sidelines, but unlike Herb Kane, who withdrew and focussed on his paintings, had tried to keep involved.

Earlier in Raiatea I had had the honour of meeting Mau Piailug, the Micronesian navigator on the first voyage of the *Hokule'a*. A quiet man with little English, he had looked over *Spirit of Gaia* and expressed his approval of the vessel, saying: 'this is how it should be done'. Many years later I was approached by Mau (through an intermediary) about the possibility of building a Pahi 63 for use in Micronesia for fishing. As they wanted to be able to carry four one-ton fish freezers aboard, we designed him the 65ft Islander, which has the carrying capacity he was looking for. Sadly finances never materialised for this vessel and Mau died before an Islander 65 was built.

In Tautira I also had a brief meeting with Nainoa Thomson, the son of a Hawaiian senator, who after being the pupil of Mau Piailug, had been elevated to chief navigator of the Polynesian Voyaging Society. He was clearly wary of me and had avoided contact. He was regarded with almost 'sacred awe' by the canoe crews, but must have been aware I could see the political aspects of his position.

The time had come for us to leave and head west towards the Cook Islands, thence to New Zealand. We were anchored inside the fringe lagoon and had to pass through a narrow reef pass to reach the open sea. With both our motors out of action, we left in the style of the other canoes—towed out by *Hokule'a*'s escort boat—and waved goodbye.

25   Voyage to New Zealand

As we sailed round the south-east corner of Tahiti and headed west to sail the 500nm to Rarotonga in the Cook Islands the weather was unsettled and the seas big and lumpy. Over the next few days we had heavy thunderstorms and changing winds.

With all our German friends gone, my physically strong crew members were Hanneke and Joke, with Ruth and Jamie too old or too young to help with the sails, though Ruth was always there to run her watch or work in the galley. Between us we reefed, lowered sails, hoisted sails and reefed again several times a day; it was exhausting.

After five days we reached Rarotonga, the biggest of the Cook Islands. We studied the northern shoreline through binoculars and tried to contact the harbourmaster via VHF, getting no answer. Finally our call was answered by the crew on a moored cargo ship, who told us where to find the harbour entrance. Since our pilot book was written a new harbour had been built, which was much more suitable than the old one. We sailed in under reduced sail and dropped an anchor, then, as there was little room to swing, took lines ashore.

We spent two weeks in Rarotonga, getting to know the harbourmaster, Don Silk, who had been a shipping agent in the Pacific for many years and told us stories of past heroic voyages and amusing incidents. We also met Nancy Griffith, the American woman skipper of an island trading vessel. She and her husband had been ocean sailing for twenty years, including three round the world voyages. In 1963 during a storm they hit a reef off Vahanga Island and their boat was wrecked. The Griffiths spent sixty-seven days marooned on this small speck of uninhabited land in the middle of the South Pacific. In 1967 they were the first to complete an east-to-west passage south of all continents on their self-built 52ft ferro-cement yacht. Since her husband's death Nancy had been running sailing trading vessels, but at the time we met her, she was in charge of a small motor cargo ship, the *Avatapu*.

We watched the cargo being craned aboard, all sorts of equipment from washing machines to building materials and foodstuffs, destined for the small remote islands that were totally reliant on these ships bringing them necessities.

Another ship that came in was *Rainbow Warrior II,* the new three-masted Greenpeace ship that had been built after *Rainbow Warrior I* had been blown up and sunk in the port of Auckland, New Zealand in an act of sabotage by the French. Greenpeace had been involved in the political stress over the use of the French atoll of Mururoa as a nuclear testing site in previous years. Later that year *Rainbow Warrior II* would again head out to Mururoa with a fleet of protestors, including a Wharram catamaran, to try to halt further nuclear testing.

The highlight of our stay on Rarotonga was attending the annual dancing competition of young Cook Islanders. To fast high-pitched hypnotic drumming on wooden 'slit drums', the young girls, dressed in sinuous grass skirts, would swing their hips at phenomenal speed, while the boys danced with vigorous sexually explicit movements.

This was the type of dancing commented on by the first explorers of the western Pacific, Cook and Bougainville, and later depicted in beautiful drawings by Erik Hesselberg in his *Kon-Tiki and I* sketch book, and described by Bengt Danielsson in his book *Love in the South Seas.* Both these men had been members of Thor Heyerdahl's *Kon-Tiki* crew who had been captivated by the people of Polynesia and their customs. The dancing went on for hours—it was absolutely spellbinding.

With two extra New Zealand crew members, Rob and Ross, we left Rarotonga and set sail for Tongatapu, the chief Tongan island with its capital Nukualofa where the king of Tonga lives. Without motors we could not be too ambitious about visiting more challenging islands, and Nukualofa was the town where we would need to clear customs. The 500nm voyage was rough at first, but I still remember beautiful starlit nights, where I felt like a small speck on the surface of a vast ocean in an enormous universe.

The eastern entrance through the surrounding reefs of Tongatapu was a long funnel-shaped passage with a dogleg at its narrow western end. We planned to sail in with the following south-east tradewind, but had to delay to wait for daylight. At sunrise the wind was from the south-west, against us. There was no way we could safely tack up the narrow reef-lined passage, so we decided on a long detour round to the more open northern reef entrance. It took us all day tacking through the reef-strewn lagoon, with Hanneke taking frequent hand bearing compass sights for navigation to reach Nukualofa.

Amongst the reefs one cannot rely on GPS for navigation; most charts of the Pacific were drawn in the late 1800s and though updated, they frequently did not quite correspond with GPS data.

We were within sight of the town as night started to fall, and with it the wind dropped completely. We needed to get closer to find a place to anchor, so we lowered our stern ramp with rubber dinghy and started the small old Seagull outboard motor on its transom. After the inertia of our twelve-ton, 63ft double canoe was overcome, we gently slid closer inshore and came to anchor.

Nukualova was a great disappointment; it was a flat expanse of streets and houses with churches of every Christian denomination as well as many unusual graveyards. These were incredible, with elaborate graves, some in colourful draperies and one completely covered in upturned beer bottles. Was its owner fond of his beer? Otherwise the town looked a bit shabby, with tired looking shops.

Here in Tonga we saw the evidence of the missionaries at their worst. The traditional Tongan dress had been a mat round the waist. Wearing such a mat showed respect for their ancestors. The missionaries introduced Victorian long black dresses, which are worn by all the women with their traditional mat over the top; a cumbersome hot outfit totally unsuitable to the climate. We saw young women swimming in their long black dresses; to us it was appalling.

The final leg to New Zealand was about 1200nm south, following the Tonga trench, sailing out of the trade wind belt into more unpredictable weather. Rob, one of our New Zealand crew, had to head back to work and left us in Tonga, but Ross was able to stay. He owned his own Wharram catamaran and was a capable, strong crew member.

On the route south our course ran close to 'Ata island (also known as Pylstaart). It is a small uninhabited rocky island on the Tonga plate, in the middle of an empty ocean. We had heard about this infamous little island because some years before one of our 40ft Narai designs was wrecked on those rocks. The boat had drifted too close in little wind, and without a functioning motor the German couple sailing her were incapable of getting away from the shore and its surging swell. Their boat was wrecked and they were lucky to get ashore by climbing the rocks. They were there for some time before any rescue reached them. And then some of the rescue party also got stuck ashore as well, proving how inaccessible this island is.

We spotted the island in the night, dead ahead, but with careful navigation were able to keep at least 5nm off. It seemed to be a magnet to sailing boats.

After 'Ata Island the winds became changeable and there was a lot of cloud. After the tropical trade winds it was like sailing back into northern European weather. We spotted New Zealand by its famous 'Long White Cloud'; its Maori name 'Aotearoa' being 'land of the long white cloud'. Then the clouds came down and we approached the Bay of Islands in dense fog. GPS is a godsend in such conditions. With a following wind we sailed in, scanning ahead for the beacons marking the channel to Opua. The fog was so dense that we could only just make out one set at a time.

With a borrowed outboard motor from Ross's Wharram catamaran we sailed to Auckland where Don Brazier, our New Zealand agent, had arranged for us to spend some time moored in the centre of the city at the new Hobson's Wharf Maritime Museum as a 'living exhibit'.

As we tied up, Peter McCurdy, the museum curator, came out to give us a friendly welcome. He invited me to give talks at the Museum. A large group of sailors came to hear about my design philosophy and sailing adventures. Later I gave another more scientific lecture to a group of specialists, organised by the museum's archaeologist Hans-Dieter Bader.

Hobson's Wharf Maritime Museum, with its collection of Pacific canoes, was inspiring. Dominating one hall was the large Kiribati canoe *Taratai*. This 76ft outrigger canoe had been built in 1975–6 in Abaiang in the Gilbert Islands (now called Kiribati) using traditional materials and building methods. Its large main hull was made of planks lashed together with hand-made coconut fibre rope. All its parts were lashed, no metal being used anywhere.

James Siers, a New Zealander, had conceived the project to build this canoe and sail it on a voyage to windward through the Polynesian islands, to prove Thor Heyerdahl's east-to-west Polynesian migration theory wrong by showing how a genuine, original outrigger canoe could sail to windward, as he believed the original Polynesians had done.

James Siers' urge was like mine had been in the 1950s when I set out to prove Heyerdahl wrong and Éric de Bisschop right with my pioneering catamaran voyages in the Atlantic.

Taratai was sailed 1000nm to windward from northern Kiribati to Fiji in 1976, the same year as *Hokule'a* made its first voyage from Hawaii to Tahiti. The *Taratai* crew were mainly Polynesian and they sailed without escort ship, motor or radio. It was a tough voyage and the canoe, due to its large size, proved to be not strong enough, so the further voyage which was planned to Samoa, Tonga and the Marquesas was never made. *Taratai* was shipped to New Zealand where she is now preserved in the Museum.

I spent time in the museum library where I made an important discovery. Nosing round the shelves I spotted a small book. It was *The Raft Book* by Harold Gatty. I knew about this famous book, but did not have it in my own library, but I did have a copy of its excellent attached star chart, which Ruth and Hanneke had been using to identify navigational stars. This book, published in 1943, was carried by all Pacific pilots during the World War II. It described to downed airmen how they could navigate their raft without instruments. Its back cover carried this encouragement:

> The Polynesians, greatest navigators of all time, made voyages back and forth in the Pacific between small islands thousands of miles apart. The knowledge of how they did this, without instruments and without charts, has never before been explained. After years of research, Harold Gatty, the navigator of the Post-Gatty 'Round the World Flight' in 1931, has completely solved the question and presents in this book the simple and effective methods of the Polynesians for the use and benefit of those who need to find their way at sea.

Harold Gatty, born in Tasmania in 1903, was a navigator from an early age, first on ships in the Australian Navy during the Great War, later in the merchant navy, where he became an expert in celestial navigation. In 1928 he moved into aviation. In 1931 Gatty flew with Whiley Post on their record breaking fastest round-the-world flight. Charles Lindbergh called Gatty the 'Prince of Navigators'.

During his travels in the Pacific Gatty had spent time with old Polynesian navigators, learning their skills. Before his death in 1957 he wrote a second book, *Nature is Your Guide*, in which he expanded on his knowledge of Polynesian instrument-free navigation. Its foreword is by the famous American WWII Lieutenant General James Doolittle, which shows how highly this book with its useful knowledge was regarded.

The Raft Book and *Nature is your Guide* were inspirational to Dr David Lewis's studies of Polynesian navigation and he made references to them in his early books. Gatty's books pre-dated the revival of Polynesian navigation (as preached by Nainoa Thompson of the Polynesian Voyaging Society of Hawaii) by more than twenty years, but Harold Gatty's work has been deliberately downplayed by the Hawaiian Polynesian revivalists.

On a visit to the War Memorial Museum in Auckland we made another discovery. In the canoe hall Hanneke and I spotted a craft that was to have a major influence on our future life.

There, surrounded by a mixed assortment of canoes, was a beautiful nine metre outrigger canoe. It caught our eye instantly because of its distinctive Vee'd hull shape, the same V as my catamaran designs. In years past I had often been accused of falsely claiming that ocean-going Polynesian canoes had V shaped hulls (Éric de Bisschop's double canoe had Vee'd hulls). Most more recent Polynesian canoe hulls, like the paddling canoes of Hawaii, have semi circular hulls. *Hokulea*'s hulls had a deep rounded shape. People claimed that was the only shape possible when carving dug-out canoes out of tree trunks. Here was proof that one could carve a Vee'd hull, in fact an exquisitely shaped Vee'd hull, with a subtle hollow along its keel line, which I instantly knew should make it sail well to windward.

The label by this canoe told us it was a 'Sacred Tikopian Canoe', donated to the Museum in 1916. This sacred canoe, 'Vaka Tapu', according to the label in the museum, 'had spirit guardians' and 'seasonal canoe rituals were performed to protect the fishermen and to ensure a successful harvest'. With the adoption of Christianity the canoe lost its religious purpose and instead of being destroyed it was donated to the Bishop of Auckland, who passed it on to the museum.

We were given permission to measure the canoe and with these measurements Hanneke was able to draw her 'lines'. We compared these with those of *Spirit of Gaia* and discovered the close similarity, which proved that this canoe would have been very capable of sailing to windward. Here was further proof that the original Polynesian canoes could have made the windward voyages needed to discover the remote Pacific islands.

After a time moored by the museum we moved *Gaia* to her winter mooring by the house of Don Brazier, in a sheltered tidal creek in a suburb of Auckland, where she joined Don's own beautifully built 40ft Wharram Narai Mk IV catamaran. Ruth, Hanneke, Jamie and I were ready to go home and pick up our design life for the next eight months and digest the experiences of our voyages. Joke, who had done so much work in building *Gaia,* decided she did not really like long ocean voyaging and left to take up a new stage of her life back in her native Holland.

26 Vaka Moana

Hanneke and I returned to New Zealand the next February and spent a month on much-needed maintenance of the boat. We repaired the damage done in the Panama Canal. Our outboard motors were taken to a qualified Yamaha dealer in Auckland, who discovered the source of our trouble was the stator heads, both of which had failed.

With work done we moved *Gaia* back to Hobson's Wharf Maritime Museum in anticipation of a week's UNESCO-sponsored conference on the ships of the Pacific, the 'Vaka Moana Symposium'. Ruth and Jamie flew out to join us there.

The week-long conference was organised by Hans Bader, Peter McCurdy and other people of the museum, stimulated by our visit the previous year and our news of the Great Gathering of the Canoes.

People who had attended the Great Gathering were invited as speakers, including Sir Thomas Davies, Governor of the Cook Islands and designer of the Cook Island canoes, as well as Nainoa Thompson, the Polynesian Voyaging Society chief navigator from Hawaii, who to my disappointment did not turn up. Then there was Maori Hector Busby, designer and builder of the New Zealand double canoe *Te Aurere*.

Also invited was Greg Matahi Brightwell, the New Zealand Maori who in 1985, together with Tahitian Francis Cowan, built the totally traditional double canoe *Havaiki Nui* and sailed her to New Zealand without radio or escort boat. It took some persuasion (by me) to get him to attend, as he was still bitter about the treatment he had received during the building of *Havaiki Nui* from the New Zealand Government, who stressed he would 'embarrass the Maori Race by attempting the crossing'. Even here in New Zealand there were political problems around being Polynesian.

Dr David Lewis, now aged seventy-nine, who had sailed and shared the navigation with Mau Piailug on the first voyage of *Hokule'a* in 1976, came to speak about Polynesian navigation. He was living on his small, rather shabby monohull in the museum dock, on which he was planning to sail to Rarotonga. I passed on greetings to him from Priscilla Cairns, his crew on the voyage on *Rehu Moana* in 1965, when he navigated his 40ft catamaran from Tahiti to New Zealand using Polynesian techniques. As a mathematician she had kept track of their course using Western navigational methods. Priscilla was a neighbour and friend of ours in Cornwall. David Lewis, like me, has preferred female crew—he sailed round the world with his wife Fiona, two small daughters and Priscilla—and even at an advanced age had an attractive lady friend, a potter, who was planning to sail with him.

The conference was well organised and some very interesting papers were given, including one on the canoe craft still in use in Vanuatu. There was also a long voyage account by Rory McDougall who, at that point, had sailed his Wharram Tiki 21 *Cooking Fat* (Cockney rhyming slang for cat) from the UK to New Zealand. That same year he departed New Zealand for Australia and continued round the world, his boat becoming the smallest catamaran to do so.

Naturally I was asked to speak about my own catamarans, but also to give an introduction to the work done by the Roskilde Viking Ship Museum in Denmark, on the replica-building programme for five original Viking ships.

I had been closely following the work at Roskilde since Hanneke and I first visited there in 1981 on our European tour with *Hitia*. This museum was set up after five Viking-era wrecks were discovered in Roskilde Fjord in the late 1950s. The wrecks were recovered and preserved under guidance of Ole Crumlin-Pederson, an engineer rather than an archaeologist, but a man with a vision. The preserved wrecks were housed in a custom-built museum, but Ole did not leave it at that. During the 1980s he set up a programme to start building accurate replicas of the Viking ships.

These replicas were built after careful study of the wreck remains, particularly the woods used and the tool marks, so the same tools and techniques could be used for the rebuild. Many enthusiastic volunteers were involved in this process. Their first replica was one of the smaller ships they called *Roar Ege* and taught them a great deal about the process of building an original Viking ship, as well as how to rig it and sail it. From there till the present day they have rebuilt every Viking ship find, including *Ottar* a 50ft large-volume trading ship type called a knarr, and the largest of them all, *Havhingsten fra Glendalough* a 90ft Longship, of which they discovered through dendrochronology that the original was built in Ireland, hence its name.

In 1996, at the time of the Vaka Moana Symposium, only two of the ships had been built, but all their research was published in a regular magazine, which detailed precisely all discoveries that were made regarding the materials, building techniques, and sailing abilities of the ships. This was a valuable source of practical information. It was the type of information I had hoped to discover when sailing together with the Polynesian replica ships the previous year, to be bitterly disappointed when finding absolutely no cooperation or interest amongst the canoe crews. I hoped with presenting this Viking ship revival programme that maybe the Polynesian replica builders might also get inspired to do more practical research.

Since 2000 we have visited Denmark and the Viking Ship Museum many more times and I became close friends with Ole Crumlin-Pederson, who I discovered had also been interested in my work. His approach and mentality has been an inspiration to me and has guided us in our own research into canoe craft of the Pacific and Indian Oceans.

Another encounter at the Vaka Moana Symposium was with Bob Hobman. In 1985 Bob and crew had sailed a genuine double outrigger canoe replica, built in the Philippines, across the Indian Ocean from Bali to Madagascar, to show how the early inhabitants of that island could have done so, as their genetic origins lie in Indonesia. This voyage was made without escort boat, without modern instruments, and eating only original foodstuffs, cooked on a wood fire. It had been a tough voyage, but successful. We had seen the TV film of it and had corresponded with Bob, and we were keen to finally meet him. Bob was building a double outrigger canoe in northern Sulawesi and was planning further replica voyages into the Pacific, which he presented in his paper.

One lunchtime we gathered at a noodle house with Bob Hobman, Peter McCurdy, Paul Clark the director of Darwin museum, and some others. Our discussions were on the significance of the 'Wallace Line'. We had just been listening to a paper by archaeologist Roger Greene about 'The Archaeology of the Pacific', in which he mentioned the gap of deep water that separates South East Asia from the continental mass of Australia and New Guinea. This deep-water gap, too wide to swim by any land mammals, is the reason only marsupial animals were living in Australia until man managed to cross the gap around 60,000 years ago. Man could only have done so using some form of watercraft. Alfred Russel Wallace, the nineteenth century naturalist who spent many years in south-east Asia, was the first to draw attention to this difference in animal life between the two continents and its cause, hence the name 'Wallace Line'. Alfred Wallace also developed the same theories of evolution as Darwin, but Wallace allowed Darwin to publish first.

Our discussions got quite lively and then the idea was born to build a raft in Indonesia and sail it across the 'Wallace Line' to Australia! I will come back to this later.

27 In search of canoes

For many round-the-world ocean sailors New Zealand is the land of temptation. The country has beautiful weather, superb sailing waters abounding with dolphins, the people an interesting mix of Europeans—the majority Celtic Scottish, exiled from their homes during the Highland clearances—and proud independent Polynesians. Polynesians who gave Captain Cook, its first European discoverer, a 'fighting welcome'.

We had received a 'friendly welcome' by the museum and by the builders and sailors of my catamarans. Our agent and friend, Don Brazier, had organised a memorable meeting with many of them at his house. But after the Vaka Moana Symposium and our canoe studies in the museums we had a new aim.

Spirit of Gaia was built with the vision of using her as a dolphin research vessel. In the Canary islands, where we had been interacting with pilot whales, plans were made with our Japanese friend Shige to sail to Okinawa and the tropical Bonin Islands to the south of Japan, to study dolphins. This plan had been overtaken by the Great Gathering of the Canoes, also by a serious earthquake at Kobe in Japan. Shige, as a keen young architect, suddenly had work aplenty to help rebuild the city and no longer had the time to help us plan a dolphin expedition.

In 1961 I had set sail on *Rongo* with Ruth and Jutta with the intention to voyage to the Pacific to study the Polynesian culture and any remaining canoes. This never came to fruition, but now, thirty-five years later, I was in New Zealand, on our 63ft Polynesian double canoe.

It had become clear during our voyage through the eastern Polynesian islands that the canoe culture there had died. Except for the racing paddling canoes we saw in Papeete, many of which were built of fibreglass, there were no longer any original canoes. Everywhere the outboard motor-driven skiffs had taken over.

Through an excellent lecture by Francis Hickey at the Vaka Moana Symposium we learned that there were still canoes being used—and sailed!—in the islands of

Melanesia. We were keen to sail there and discover these canoes for ourselves, to study them and record them.

Our plan was to sail from New Zealand to Fiji and hopefully be allowed to study the sailing canoes of the eastern Lau island group. We would then sail west to Vanuatu, northwards up the island chain, and make Tikopia in the Solomons our furthest destination. We would end our six-month voyage in Australia, where we would lay up the boat to return to the UK for another spell of design work at home. I don't intend to write about every detail of this voyage, so will focus on the major events. The first of which was our worst gale ever on *Gaia*.

After preparations for the voyage and day sailing up the coast of New Zealand, we departed from Opua in the Bay of Islands on 16 May 1996, *Gaia*'s fourth birthday and the day after my sixty-eighth. The weather forecast had been favourable for our voyage to Fiji, but by the afternoon of the second day the weather rapidly deteriorated, with the wind settling in from the east, rising from 28–30 knots to the mid-30s (gale force 8) and by the second day into the top 40s (severe gale force 9). The waves increased in size with large breaking crests rolling towards the boat from the starboard beam. When a breaking crest hit the hulls, the boat shook and water would spout up through the slatted platforms.

Soon we were sailing under just a small storm jib, as close to the wind as she would go, which was about 60 degrees off the apparent wind. With this flat-cut little sail progress was poor, about 2–4 knots, just slightly better than hove to, but it gave us progress in more or less the right direction. We did not want to run off before the gale as our speed would be too great and we would be driven straight towards Australia. So we plodded on, clawing our way up north, with huge slamming waves on the beam.

On this voyage, apart from Hanneke, Ruth, Jamie and I, we had two other crew. One was Lew, an experienced ocean sailor and friend of Don Brazier, the other Freya, an eighteen-year-old Canadian girl, who one day sat on the steps at the Maritime Museum watching *Spirit of Gaia*, waiting for the arrival of *Rainbow Warrior II* on which she wanted to volunteer. Instead she ended up helping with the work on *Gaia* and then joined us as crew.

We had to hand steer during the gale, with Hanneke, Lew and I taking turns at the wheel. As we got more and more tired we could each do only half an hour at a stretch. The three of us lived in the steering cockpit for three days, with the two not steering sleeping in the cockpit bunk or resting curled up on the cockpit seat. We now had a good waterproof cover for the cockpit, made by Hanneke in New Zealand, which was a godsend, as it kept us dry and warm.

Dear Ruth, who was seventy-five years old and unsteady on her feet, was the hero in the galley where she produced hot meals, including pudding and custard, which were carried across the deck to the cockpit by agile young Freya in lidded plastic bowls. All galley hatches and vent holes had to be kept shut or waves would spout in, so it was like a sauna below. Every so often a wave would hit the side of the hull with a loud bang and shake the whole boat. Brave Ruth cooked sitting down, and as a catamaran does not roll, objects that are prevented from sliding stay put. The cooking stove had a restraining fiddle, but no gimbals.

What should be noted is that our central platform, though wet, was a very safe area to move around on. Ruth could move hand-over-hand along the deckpods, from the galley to her cabin, safe from the surrounding seas.

When Ruth was not cooking she was joined in her deckpod cabin by Jamie. They would play games of chess on a tiny travelling chess set. Jamie, aged ten, would spend hours reading books, whilst Ruth would be typing letters to be posted later.

The gale seemed never ending; on day two with the wind still increasing Lew and Hanneke crawled onto the aft netting and created a sea anchor/drogue out of three car tyres and lots of rope securely knotted. They attached our small 25lb CQR anchor to it as ballast. It took them about two hours. It was never launched as we held on to our northerly course in our attempt to reach Fiji, so we never found out if it would have slowed the boat enough on a run.

During the next night the wind reached its peak, with winds steady in the upper 40s (severe gale force 9), I was steering in the dark when suddenly I became aware of a huge white wall over to starboard. For a moment my tired brain panicked 'Oh my God, we are on a reef'. Then this enormous wave crest broke right over the boat, with water cascading over the cockpit roof, flexing its hoops and pouring in under its cover. As our cockpit is on the port side with its roof about 10ft (3m) above the sea, it gives an idea of the size of this wave crest as it crashed 20ft from the starboard gunwale right across the width of the boat. *Gaia* shook herself and carried on, with water quickly disappearing through the slatted decking. Nothing had broken, we were all safe, if a bit wet.

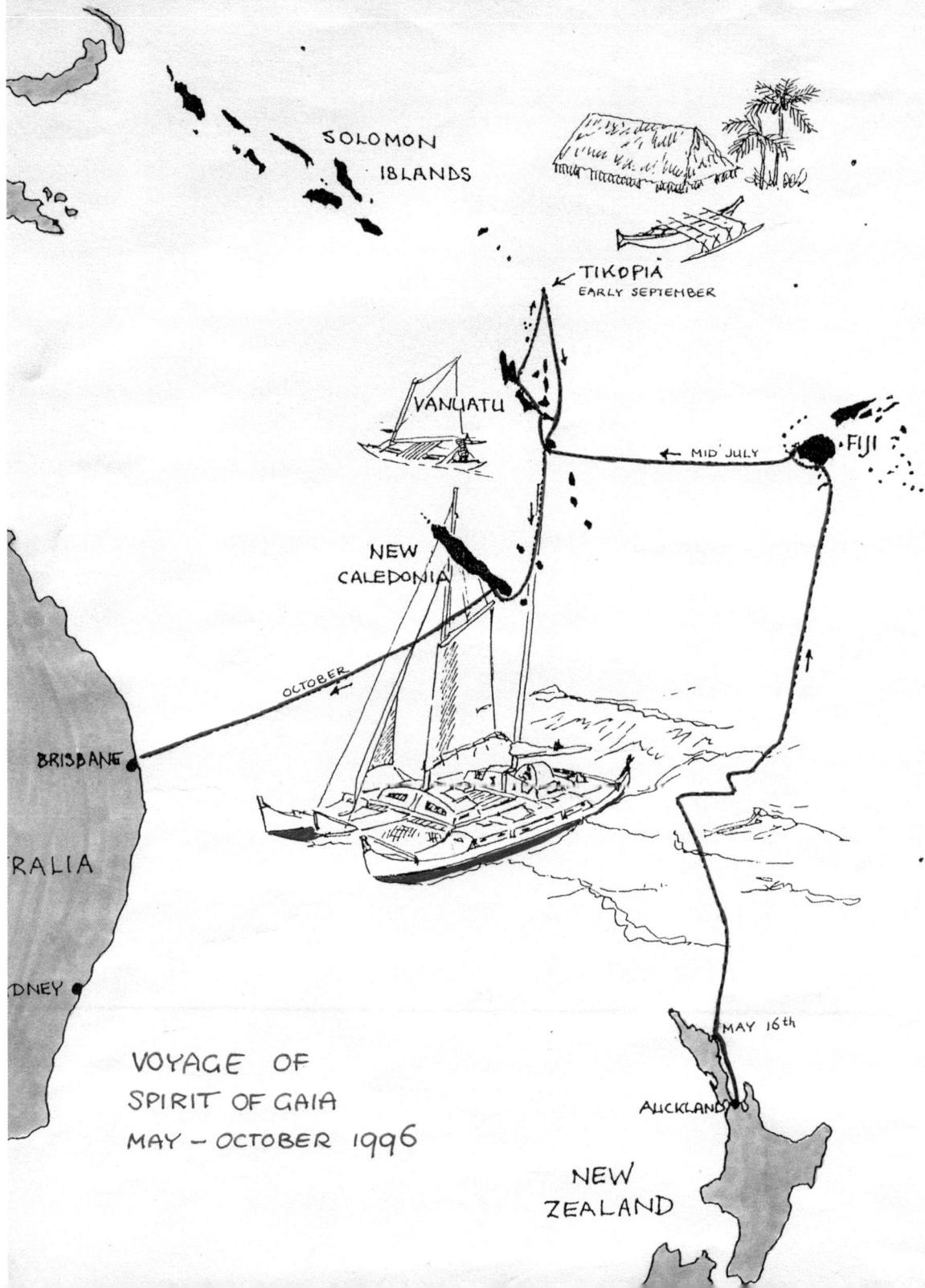

SOLOMON
ISLANDS

TIKOPIA
EARLY SEPTEMBER

VANUATU

MID JULY

FIJI

NEW
CALEDONIA

OCTOBER

BRISBANE

RALIA

DNEY

VOYAGE OF
SPIRIT OF GAIA
MAY — OCTOBER 1996

MAY 16th

AUCKLAND

NEW
ZEALAND

During the next morning the wind slowly eased. At this point 28 knots of wind (force 7) seemed almost calm. We could draw breath and feel proud to have survived without mishap. Our Polynesian double canoe, with hulls that closely resembled those of the ancient Tikopia canoe in the museum, had survived a three day long severe gale. We were never worried that the huge waves on the beam would capsize her, she would just rise up and climb over each crest. When wave crests slammed into the hull sides the rope beam-lashings could flex and take the shock loads. I was glad of our minimal freeboard and windage. What it showed was that the canoes of the ancient Polynesian voyagers would similarly have been able to survive long ocean voyages and gales.

It was six more days before we reached Suva, sometimes beating to windward, later faster with a free wind. We anchored in the muddy waters off the town and staggered ashore to clear customs. The land moved under our feet as we waited in the small office to fill out multiple forms in a country that had inherited its bureaucracy from its British colonial past.

In New Zealand I had heard that the son of the great navigator Harold Gatty, author of *The Raft Book,* was living somewhere in Fiji, so I started making enquiries. As soon as I mentioned the name Gatty in the Fiji Visitors Bureau, the man said: 'Do you mean Ron Gatty? He writes regularly for the *Fiji Times*, a very controversial, well known character! He runs a spice farm not so far away.' We soon tracked him down and he was delighted to come and meet us at the Suva Yacht Club.

Ron Gatty was a great character, about my age, tough looking with a deep scar on his cheek. Over lunch he was soon telling us about his youthful exploits in the islands, swimming with sharks with a bunch of island lads, armed only with sticks with a nail in the end. He demonstrated how you had to swim under the shark and give it a quick jab under the chin.

He also told us how he had helped his father to collect data on the ancient Pacific navigation techniques. Ron had played a part in this as he, having grown up in Fiji, spoke Polynesian fluently and could act as interpretor.

Since meeting Ron Gatty I have discovered more about his life. It is as interesting as that of his famous father, Harold Gatty, who besides the invaluable work he did as an aviator and his studies of Polynesian navigation, which I discussed earlier, had owned an island in the Fijian Lau group and set up Fiji Airways (later Pacific Airways). His death in Fiji in 1957 was honoured there by flags at half mast.

At the age of twenty, Ron had gone penniless to America, where he managed to get a scholarship and gained a professorship in botany at Cornell University. He was for a time 'Plant Explorer' for medicinal plants in the South Seas for a pharmaceutical company. He retired at the age of fifty and returned to Fiji with his French wife, a professor of history who he met at university, to became an honoured philanthropist.

Ron had made his fortune in America as a marketing consultant, and used this skill to set up a company to market spices, like vanilla and cinnamon, grown by Fijian villagers; a company in which he took no salary, corporate dividends or profits for himself. The whole concept was to help villagers make money, so they can remain in their village and improve the island's economy. Shortly before his death in 2014 Ron donated 1 million Fijian dollars to Fiji Museum to create a wing commemorating the life of his father Harold Gatty, 'Prince of Navigators'.

We visited Fiji Museum, which houses the last Fijian Drua, a relatively small 13m double canoe with uneven-sized hulls and a single triangular sail. It was constructed in 1913 by the last of the craftsmen who knew the large ocean-going Druas of the 1700s (recorded by Capt. Cook and others), which were from about 26–36m in length. The Cook Islands-built plywood Drua, *Takitumu*, which we had seen at the Great Canoe Gathering the previous year, was modelled on this boat. Other artefacts at the museum included ceremonial Kava bowls and special wooden forks for the consumption of human flesh!

We made enquiries about sailing to the Lau islands lying about 200 miles to the east of Suva. There had been recent political troubles in Fiji and as a result the Lau group had been closed to tourists. We particularly wanted to go there to study its sailing canoes. Sadly our plea fell on deaf ears; we could not be granted permission to sail there.

We did however meet up with Robert Gillette, introduced to us by Ron Gatty, who had done in-depth studies of the Lau canoes and presented us with a booklet he had co-produced for the Institute of Pacific Studies. We were sad not to have seen the southern Lau canoes for ourselves, as there are still many of them sailing, but it was not to be.

In total we spent six weeks in the Fijian islands, sailing round the south coast of Viti Levu to the many islands on its west side. We experienced a horrific night of storm force winds and heavy rain in Musket Cove, a regular stopping place for yachts. Though lying to three anchors, we still dragged on the poorly holding coral bottom and only just managed to stay clear of some large coral heads under our stern. Later we heard a yacht in another anchorage had not been so lucky and had smashed up on the rocks. Some weeks later we swam in its anchorage and saw some of the remains. The waters around Fiji make tricky sailing with many reefs. Sudden storms can blow up, often at night, leaving one fighting for survival in the pitch darkness.

Sadly, Lew, who had been a terrific crew, had to fly back to New Zealand before we departed for Vanuatu (formerly known as the New Hebrides), a voyage of some 500 miles due west.

In 1996, Vanuatu was like the Caribbean in the 1950s, with just a handful of yachts sailing up the island chain during the winter sailing season (May till October in the Southern hemisphere). As there are many islands and no proper roads, travel there is difficult. Sailing on ones own boat from island to island is the best way to visit them. Apart from the capital Vila, the islands are hardly developed. People live a largely self-sufficient life, growing their fruit and vegetables in gardens hidden in the jungle.

Vanuatu is 'the land of the canoe'. Nearly every family owns a canoe, which they use to commute to their gardens, often situated on another island. In the evening they would load up their produce and head for home. If they had a favourable wind they would create a sail out of several palm leaves stood upright. This shows how simple watercraft and the concept of sailing could have developed very early on in the life of *Homo sapiens.*

We studied many of the canoes and talked to their owners. The boats were generally from about 14ft to 18ft in length and carved out of a single log. Each village had its own style of hull shape, some very simple, others more sophisticated. In some villages there were dedicated canoe builders.

The first such builder we met in Havana Harbour, not far from our entry port of Vila. As we sailed *Gaia* towards the entrance of this large sheltered natural harbour, used by the US Navy during World War II, we were met by two small outrigger sailing canoes, each with a home made spritsail. They joined us and we logged their speed as 6 knots.

Once we were anchored the young canoe sailors came on board, admiring our big double canoe. They took us sailing on their canoes and we quickly learned how to use a steering paddle. We were invited to visit their village on Lelepa Island to meet Billy the 'canoe builder', father of one of the lads.

We met Billy on a beach covered in wood chips where he built his canoes. He told us how he could carve a 14ft canoe in one day out of a local light soft wood. He also showed us a beautiful hardwood steering paddle from a much bigger canoe. It gave us the blueprint for steering paddle design and size for our future Ethnic designs.

We took Billy and his young men for a daysail on *Gaia*. I watched Billy with his head over the bows, studying the flow of water over our hull shape. He showed a sharp intelligence and told me it gave him ideas for future canoe shaping.

On other islands people also used sails on their canoes, generally a simple sprit-sail. Sailing had been (re)introduced by aid agencies, but on Atchin Island, a small island off the north-east coast of Malekula, there was a known history of sailing canoes. I had seen a photo of the strangely shaped 'butterfly' sail of Atchin Island in the 1926 Haddon and Hornell book *Canoes of Oceania* which I had studied in my teens at Manchester Central Library.

When we anchored off Atchin Island and went ashore, we soon found ourselves seated under a palm-leaf roofed shelter on the beach talking to the 'old men'. With the aid of drawings in the sand and translation by a younger man we quickly built up a rapport through our shared sailing experience. This was very different from the days of Captain Cook, who named these islands the New Hebrides, when the people were considered particularly aggressive and warlike, and the European crews feared landing there.

After our welcome on the beach we invited the men on board. My crew made tea and served home made scones (which the visitors loved). The old men sat under the awning on the centre deck, studying our photos and drawings, the younger men helped translate. The children were told to stay on their canoes alongside and keep quiet. There was amusement when we fetched out our conch-shell horn and asked them if they knew how to sound it. Many of them tried, and some succeeded, and there was happy discussion on where to place the blow hole and how big it should be.

Later that evening the oldest man returned on his canoe. He wore thick glasses and could not speak any English, but he had proudly brought his own conch. He climbed on board and tried to blow it, but no sound came out. He then gave it a good shake, old straw and chicken shit fell out and he tried again without success. The blow hole in his conch was enormous, but maybe as a young man he had been proud of blowing it.

By island etiquette the women of the village never came on board, but Jamie was invited by the children to come and play. He would grab his paddle and get into their canoe. It was perfectly safe to let him go off on his own, the village women always knew where he was. Jamie quickly made a connection with these children without a common language, by teaching them 'noughts & crosses', scratched in the sand.

In 1980, the year Vanuatu became independent, there was a revitalising of the traditional culture after a century of colonial rule. That year the people of Atchin Island built their first seagoing 15m canoe for nearly 100 years, which they sailed to the third Pacific Arts Festival in Port Moresby, Papua New Guinea via the Solomon Islands (around 1400 nautical miles, with two 350-mile open ocean crossings). When we visited Atchin some of the people who had built and sailed this canoe were fetched from a nearby village to meet us on *Spirit of Gaia*. They were delighted to see another big voyaging canoe. Everywhere we sailed people saw our boat as a 'voyaging canoe', not a Western yacht.

Western culture has left its marks in Vanuatu. The work of missionaries for over a century has ensured most of the people practise Christianity, with the possible advantage for us that they no longer attack visitors and eat them. Independence had led to the people again practising their traditional customs (though not eating people). We heard that some inland tribes on the big island of Malekula might be giving up Christianity.

At the northernmost island of Espirito Santo we anchored off the town of Luganville. This is the only other 'town' in Vanuatu. It lacked the tourist gloss of Vila and had a more basic nature, with Chinese shops selling practical tools and household items. There was also an open air food market where locals sold their produce. The girls left me with a rucksack full of food while they went off to buy more at other stalls. I squatted down next to an old man wearing just a tiny loincloth, which is the traditional dress of the ni-Vanuatu. We nodded at each other in mutual understanding and he grinned back at me with a gap-toothed smile. When I went looking for the girls a bit later (women always take longer) they exclaimed: 'Where is the rucksack? To which I replied with a smile: 'Oh, I left it with my friend over there'.

In Espirito Santo we had to make a decision. Hanneke insisted we should sail to Tikopia, the home of the beautiful canoe in Auckland Museum. Back home she had managed to buy the book *We the Tikopia* written in the 1920s by the anthropologist Raymond Firth and had been studying it. She felt this was our one chance to see the island, its people, and its canoes.

I was not so certain. Tikopia, though a Polynesian island, is part of the Melanesian Solomon Islands. I had read in the pilot book that if we did not check in at the Solomon Islands' capital of Honiara, we could have our ship confiscated. I did not want to run this risk and there was no way we could sail more than 500 miles downwind to Honiara and return against the trade winds to Tikopia. Besides which, the weather was bad with rain and strong winds. Naturally, with two opposing strong wills, we had an argument.

Hanneke, to find a compromise, suggested she would row over to the other yachts in the anchorage and ask for a weather forecast. The first yacht she approached, *Jacaranda*, was American. By amazing coincidence they had just arrived from Tikopia on their crossing of the Pacific. Seeing our big double canoe the couple on board enthusiastically said 'You must go there, the people on Tikopia will love your boat'. They also assured her that on Tikopia the Chiefs were 'the authority', not the Solomon Islands officials. If the chiefs gave us permission to land, we would be under their protection and safe.

So the decision was made to sail to Tikopia. Ruth was also happy about this; she is not as outwardly forceful as Hanneke can be, but in her heart she really wanted to go there. When the spell of bad weather was over we left and sailed the 220 miles north-north-east to Tikopia, bypassing the remote Banks Islands. Chuck and Dianne, the American couple on *Jacaranda*, had given us a lot of advice on the protocol of meeting the chiefs and what gifts to bring—Kerosene, tobacco, tins of corned beef, rice, sugar and various other things unavailable on such a remote island that is visited by a trading ship only two or three times a year.

28 Tikopia

Tikopia is politically part of the Melanesian Solomon Islands and lies at their eastern extremity, 400nm of open ocean east of the last big Solomon island of San Christobal. The nearest small islands are the Santa Cruz (Solomons) and the Banks islands (Vanuatu), both around 120nm away and also very remote.

The Tikopia population of around 1200 people are Polynesian. The ancestors of these people had voyaged from other Polynesian islands lying to the east to settle there; precisely when is not known.

In the 1920s Raymond Firth, an early anthropologist, spent a year on Tikopia and did an in-depth study of the people and their traditional customs. Tikopia and its smaller sister island Anuta (70nm away), were first discovered by Europeans in the early nineteenth century. Soon afterward the islands were raided by 'black birders' who took many men from Tikopia as slave labour to work on sugar plantations and to collect guano, used as fertiliser.

Due to Tikopia's isolation in hundreds of square miles of open ocean her canoes always had to be seaworthy. At the time of its discovery the people of Tikopia made regular trips to the Banks islands. In 1828–9 Admiral Paris, an eminent French sea explorer, meticulously recorded some of the few surviving Polynesian canoe designs still in use in the Pacific. He recorded the Tikopian canoe hull shape in writing (Haddon & Hornell). His description closely matched the canoe we had seen in Auckland Museum. As Tikopia had hardly been touched by Western man in the 1820s, it can be true to say their canoe design was also untouched by Western influence and is therefore a unique example of a seagoing canoe hull design that has its origins maybe as far back as a millenium or more.

The first missionaries reached Tikopia only in the early twentieth century, and the island chiefs wisely made the decision to adopt the moderate Christianity of the Church of England, later renamed the Church of Melanesia. They kept most of their traditional customs, and minimal clothing. Women on Tikopia even now wear just a skirt and go topless. Children frequently are naked.

Tikopia represented for me the unspoiled island(s) I had hoped to find when I planned to sail to the Pacific in 1961. An island hardly touched by Western influences with its canoe culture still intact.

We made landfall at Tikopia before dawn and hove to till sunrise to anchor on the north-west side of the two mile long island. We had been spotted and several canoes paddled out to greet us and helped us anchor. The anchorage at Tikopia is 20m deep and surrounded by reef. We could see the white sand bottom through the crystal clear water. The south-east trade wind swept round and over the island and made the local wind come from different directions, so we had to set three anchors in order not to swing over the reef.

We were invited ashore, where a bunch of children helped us haul the dinghy up the beach, and we were led to the house of 'Chief No 1', Ariki Tafua, who is head of the village at this side of the island (there are three other Ariki on the other side of the island).

The houses on Tikopia are long and low, built on a sturdy wood frame and covered with a palm leaf thatch that reaches down to just three feet above ground level. The entrances are so low one needs to crawl through. Chuck and Dianne had warned us that one must never stand higher than the chief, so we crawled in and sat on the ground, which was covered in woven coconut palm leaf mats.

Ariki Tafua was a fine old man with long white hair and a smiling mouth, red from chewing betel nut. He was sitting crosslegged on the floor, and his son Edward told us in English we should call him 'Daddy'. We presented him with our gifts and were given coconuts to drink from.

We told them our story of finding the canoe in Auckland Museum and how we had come to study their canoes. Edward told us a lot more about the island and led us to view their oldest canoe, which lay in a clearing under some large trees. This craft had the same delicate shaping as the canoe in the museum, but looked as if it had not been used for some time.

Most of the canoes on Tikopia were small and lacked the beautifully shaped bow and stern 'beaks' of the older canoes; all had Vee'd hulls, but they were not sailed.

Hanneke measured and photographed them, while Ruth took her camera to photograph the village, houses and children.

The women make beautiful sleeping mats woven out of narrow strips of pandanus leaves, a complicated job that takes weeks. I was presented with such a mat at the end of our stay. They also make 'tapa' cloth out of the bark of the paper mulberry tree. They get one long tapering strip of cloth out of one tree. The wide bottom end is used for the traditional women's wrap-around skirt, tied round the waist with a strip of tapa dyed orange with turmeric. The long narrower upper part, which tapers to a narrow tail, is the men's wear. It is wrapped round the body a bit like an Indian dhoti, with the wide end hanging like an apron at the front.

On our first day three of the young men asked us if we had any torch batteries. They invited us to go fishing on the reef that night, but they needed batteries for their waterproof torch. We found some suitable ones in our danbuoy light and later that evening they came to take Hanneke, Freya and Jamie in our dinghy to the edge of the reef. They wore old goggles and used a simple fish harpoon held on a stick with a rubber band, to spear the fish and crayfish in the crevices in the reef wall. Hanneke and Freya stayed in the dinghy as the harpoons were swept over the side dropping fish into the dinghy bottom. They could see the young men about six to eight metres below them lit by their torch, they could also see young Jamie, naked deep underwater looking over their shoulders. The men were very impressed at his diving abilities.

Another day we were all taken on a tour of the island. On the windward side of Tikopia there is a freshwater lake, formed in the ancient crater of the dead volcano that is the base of the island. We all followed the narrow footpath through the jungle to the beach on the other side. Here were three more villages, each with its own chief. I was particularly keen to meet Chief No 3, Ariki Taumako, as it was his grandfather who had given the sacred canoe to the Bishop of Auckland. We were welcomed into his house and we presented him with a collection of gifts. He was a quiet, gentle man who spoke beautiful English. I spotted a large coil of plaited coconut fibre rope hung off the rafters and asked him about it. He told me it was a very old shark fishing line, which was very precious to him. It was the first thing he rescued when a cyclone had hit the island.

We were then taken to the edge of the lake to visit the house of the young church deacon and his wife and go for a swim. The married women on Tikopia often are bare

breasted, wearing just a cotton skirt or a pareo. Though bare breasted, it is custom for the women to keep their bottoms and thighs covered. To stay in tune with the local women, Hanneke swam in just her pareo with no top, rather than in a Western swimsuit. After the swim she changed into a dry pareo, but did not put her shirt back on as the other women were also bare breasted. We walked back to the house of Ariki Taumako and when his wife, who had looked rather dour before, saw Hanneke, her face broke into a smile.

She then took charge. We were asked to sit down again and wait while she busied herself with one of the young women. With Hanneke now like one of 'their' women she should receive an official welcome to the island. Turmeric powder (which has sacred qualities) was mixed with coconut oil and then carefully applied around Hanneke's shoulders, chest and face by the younger woman under the precise directions of the chief's wife. Freya was similarly decorated.

On our walk back to the anchorage we met many people on the footpath carrying loads on their shoulders. The trading ship that only visits maybe twice a year had arrived. Hanneke topless, painted in turmeric, drew welcoming smiles from everyone.

Our stay in Tikopia could not be long for we had a long way to sail to Brisbane in Australia, from where our flights home had already been booked. On our last evening at the house of Daddy, Ariki Tafua, by the dim light of a hurricane lamp, we were each presented with a traditional tapa cloth: skirts and belts for the three women and loincloths for Jamie and me. In return I presented Daddy with a special knife and we gave them *Spirit of Gaia* T-shirts.

The weather deteriorated and it was time to leave. Before we left, several men paddled over in their canoes and told us it was now time for 'trading'. They had brought some artefacts they wanted to trade. We exchanged a set of swimming fins, mask and snorkel for a wooden food bowl. Another man wanted a pareo in exchange for a coconut grating stool. Hanneke gave him the choice of several, but he shook his head, they were not the one he wanted. It turned out his wife coveted Hanneke's beautiful flame-red pareo and no other, but as it had been a special gift from our friends Udo and Rosmary she was not ready to part with it.

Fourteen years later, when Hanneke returned to Tikopia at the end of the 'Lapita Voyage' expedition, she still owned this same flame-red pareo and on departure presented it to the lady who had so much wanted it all those years ago.

Leaving Tikopia was difficult. To keep us clear of the reef in the gusty changing winds, I controlled the ship with the two outboard motors, while Freya and Hanneke with the help of Jamie hauled up one anchor after the other. First the two smaller anchors from the dinghy, carefully avoiding the warps getting caught on coral 'bommies'. After pulling the dinghy up the stern ramp, they brought in around 80m of heavy nylon main warp. We had no anchor winch, so with a water depth of 20m, they then had to lift the full weight of 10m of vertical chain with a 65lb anchor hanging off the end of it.

But that was not the end of it, they now had to hoist sail fast as we were immediately out in the open ocean. The two girls, naked in the tropical humid heat and hauling on halyards and sheets looked magnificent. Then they collapsed exhausted on the deck while I sailed the boat away from beautiful Tikopia.

That year, 1996, the weather in Fiji and Vanuatu had been bad, with every two weeks a front passing through, which meant strong winds, heavy cloud cover, rain and very rough seas. We have photos taken during our voyage which show the foresail with four reefs, and water spouting up through the platform slats. In New Caledonia we met up with a smart 50ft American yacht. Its owner was so disappointed with the bad sailing conditions that he was planning to ship his yacht to Australia and sell it. He had had enough.

We approached New Caledonia in one of these bad weather spells. To make landfall in the daylight we had to slow down. The wind was blowing force 7 from the north-east, driving us along at 6 knots under just staysail. As the wind increased to force 8 we lowered all sail and let the boat lie ahull with the helm lashed. We had not attempted this before and found *Gaia* lay steady, beam-on to the seas, with a much gentler motion than expected. We could go below and sleep. Our progress was a gentle 1–1½ knots downwind, in winds of 30–40 knots.

The final 780nm voyage, from Noumea to Brisbane, we sailed in 5½ days. These were the best sailing days of that season, some of the time running under genoa under a clear blue sky. Now, sitting in my studio, I look up at a large beautiful photo of *Gaia* sailing the ocean with the two bronzed naked girls, Hanneke and Freya, winching in the genoa sheet. The Polynesian sea gods would have approved.

29 New designs

Parallel to our life as 'sea people' we still had our life as 'designers'. Laying up *Gaia* at a boatyard near Brisbane, we returned to Cornwall to catch up with our ongoing design work.

Building and ocean-sailing *Spirit of Gaia* had given us a new wealth of proven data on material strength, construction details, and boat ergonomics, which we were adapting into further Tiki designs.

In 1992 we were asked to design a boat to be used for 'Sailing Safari' charters on Lake Kariba in Zimbabwe, to take guests to see the wildlife from the comfort and safety of the deck of a catamaran. For them we designed the Tiki 30.

Hanneke and I flew out to Zimbabwe to oversee the start of the building of a fleet of ten boats. We worked with the local workforce of men, many of whom had been agricultural labourers before turning to boatbuilding. What I observed was that these men had grown up in houses shaped by nature. As a result they were not used to straight lines, or perfect curves and had to be taught that these were essential in a boat acceptable to a Western yachting public. It was a delight to work with them as they were all eager to learn.

Initially the 'Sail Safaris' business was a great success, but it was later destroyed by the disastrous policies of Zimbabwe's president Robert Mugabe.

One successful design often inspires another. By 1994 there was a need for a new 'family ocean cruiser' in the Tiki concept. We had designed the Tiki 36 for professional builders, but her construction was not ideal for self builders, so we reworked the design into a new Tiki 38.

When starting a new design, Hanneke and I have lively brainstorming sessions with me describing the vision and concept I have in my head. If I am lucky Hanneke gets inspired and starts to sketch out this vision, adding ideas of her own. From these sketches new ideas flow. During this process a design takes on a life of its own, where all the elements coalesce and 'talk back' to us.

The Tiki 38 hulls are built with two tiers (like the Tiki 30 and Tiki 36), a lower hull with top strakes fitted later, with a small knuckle on the joint above the waterline, which increases interior width at bunk level.

All the Tikis so far had been designed for the 'stitch & glue' method. We had built the professional Tiki 36 hulls like this, but as the average self-builder cannot handle the large hull panels involved, we had to think up a new way of assembly for the Tiki 38.

So for ease of building we designed the lower hull on the proven 'backbone and bulkhead' principles of my Classic and Pahi designs. Working in two tiers has the advantage that the lower hull, whilst being built upside down, is low to the ground, with the keel within easy reach, so no scaffolds or ladders are needed.

Once built and epoxy/glass sheathed the long thin lower hull is turned the right way up and set into cradles. It being so low, access to the inside is easy, so floors and bunk levels are fitted before the upper part of the hull. The hull becomes very strong with each glued-in floor, bunk, and shelf adding stiffness to the structure.

The upper bulkheads are then added. They can be placed in different locations to the lower bulkheads, giving greater scope for interior layout. The bulkheads are joined up with stringers and only then are the upper plywood hull panels glued on and the hull finished with decks and hatches.

In designing we added many successful features from *Spirit of Gaia* to the centre deck structure. Deckpod, outboard motor boxes, and stern ramp were designed on the same construction principles and attached to the I-section crossbeams with the same flexible joints.

It is one thing to hack out the concept and basic details of a design, but to draw a full set of detailed building plans, which our builders have referred to a 'course in boatbuilding', is a lengthy task for Hanneke to complete to her exacting standards.

In New Zealand in 1995 we visited one of the first Tiki 38s under construction and got valuable feedback from its builders. Since then many have been built and long ocean voyages made on them. Outstanding to me is *Pilgrim* (Tiki 38 No 99) built by a Frenchman, Jacques Pierret, in New Jersey, USA and sailed across the Atlantic to his home in Marseille in the south of France at record speed. He made this voyage of

4500nm in just thirty-one days, including two short stops in the Azores and Gibraltar, averaging 150nm a day. On the last few miles into Marseille he recorded a top speed of 16.6 knots.

In 1996, after our return from studying canoes in Melanesia for six months, we had another new design project to work on. In one of the Maskelyne Islands at the southern end of the big island of Malekula, we had been in conversation with some of the village elders. Jack Enrel, their spokesman, told us that the day before our visit there had been a meeting to discuss the lack of suitable 'canoe trees' and that they should consider building canoes out of plywood.

Hearing that we were experts in plywood design, they asked for our help. We gave a lecture on the use of tools, glues and plywood building methods in their 'education centre' and offered to send them drawings of our designs. When we left I promised we would design them a simple plywood outrigger canoe out of just two sheets of plywood.

This we did, and with the help of two volunteers we built the prototype in a couple of weeks and called it the 'Melanesia'. The hull has a chined U-shaped cross section, similar to the dug-out hulls we had studied, but is built in the stitch & glue system from 6mm plywood, joined with epoxy fillets and glass tape.

Beams and spars were made from natural straight saplings, the outrigger float from a larger tree. This float is attached to the beams in the proven method used all over Melanesia, with sticks set into the solid outrigger float at opposing angles, locking them in place when crossbeams are lashed on. No need for glue, and the sticks can be easily renewed. The crabclaw sail was hand stitched out of a plastic tarp.

As well as this traditional sailing version of the Melanesia, we also designed a different outrigger float, similar to those used on the racing paddling canoes we had observed in Tahiti and New Zealand. These six- to eight-man racing canoes were very expensive, which meant that many children, keen to be involved in the canoe racing scene, got little chance to practise. This paddling Melanesia would make an ideal 'starter canoe', rather like the Optimist dinghy is for racing dinghy sailors.

We sent the Melanesia plans to the village in the Maskelynes and never heard back from them.

HULLSHELL BUILDING SEQUENCE

① MAKE BACKBONE AND
LOWER BULKHEADS
(SEE PAGES 2, 3 & 4)

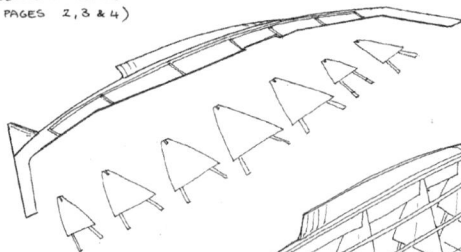

② ASSEMBLE BACKBONE & BULKHEADS
AND SQUARE THE SKELETON READY
TO TAKE STRINGERS AND
PLY HULLSIDES (SEE PAGE 5)

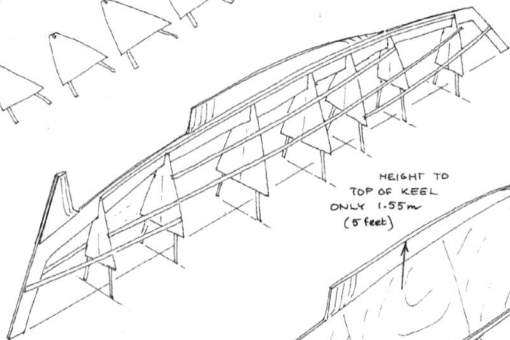

③ THE LOWERHULLSIDES ARE GLUED ON
IN EITHER ONE, TWO OR THREE
PIECES DEPENDING ON THE
NUMBER OF BUILDERS (SEE PAGE

HEIGHT TO
TOP OF KEEL
ONLY 1.55m
(5 feet)

④ THE LOWER HULLS ARE GLASSED
AND FINISHED BEFORE THEY ARE
TURNED OVER AND WHILE ALL
PARTS OF THE HULL ARE WITHIN
EASY REACH. (SEE PAGE

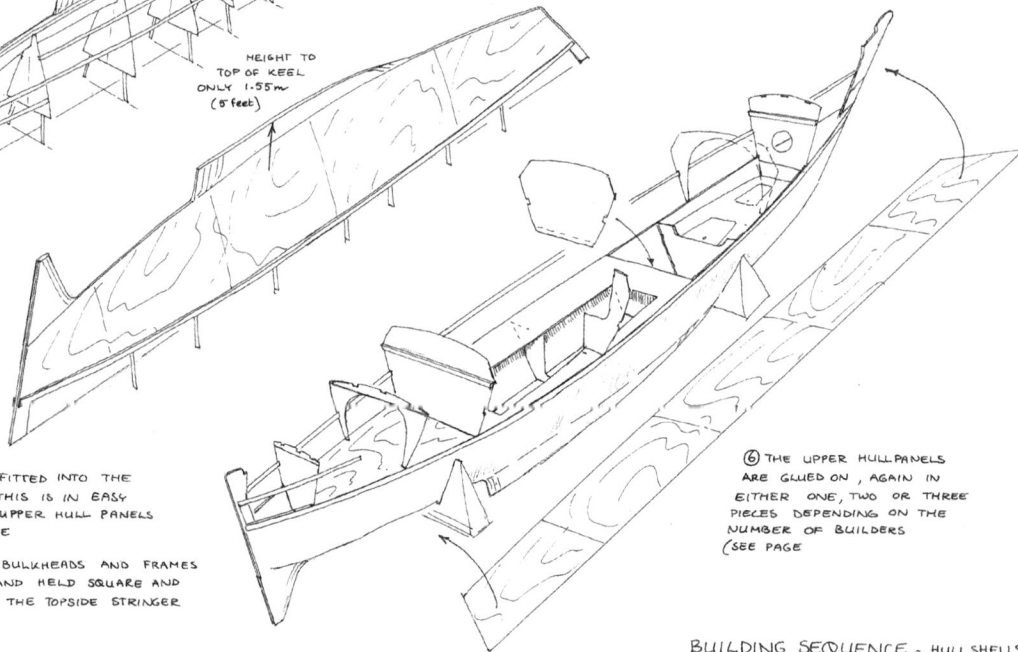

⑤ ALL FURNITURE IS FITTED INTO THE
LOWER HULL, WHILE THIS IS IN EASY
REACH, BEFORE THE UPPER HULL PANELS
ARE FITTED (SEE PAGE

⑥ THE UPPER BULKHEADS AND FRAMES
ARE FITTED AND HELD SQUARE AND
UPRIGHT WITH THE TOPSIDE STRINGER
(SEE PAGE

⑥ THE UPPER HULLPANELS
ARE GLUED ON, AGAIN IN
EITHER ONE, TWO OR THREE
PIECES DEPENDING ON THE
NUMBER OF BUILDERS
(SEE PAGE

BUILDING SEQUENCE - HULL SHELLS

1

Tiki 38 building method

Then nearly ten years later we were approached by a New Zealander who was working with villagers in the Maskelynes, setting up a boatbuilding and navigation school. They wanted to build a sailing catamaran for inter-island sailing. To our delight, we discovered that these were the same people to whom we had sent the Melanesia plans. They had not forgotten us!

In 2006 we donated the project plans of my early Classic design, the 27ft Tanenui, as this would be the easiest design to build with mainly hand tools and minimum glues. All the materials were assembled in New Zealand and shipped to Vanuatu where the catamaran was built in just six weeks. They used a donated second hand Tornado catamaran rig.

Here are some comments we received from the build team:

The building of the boat is creating a lot of interest as it takes them a month to make a dugout. And they all think James Wharram is 'the man' for donating the design. So, 'tank yu tumas' from the people of Maskelynes.

Then a bit later:

I am pleased to report that 'Lanisif' (the good north wind that blows to the Maskelynes) was launched Wednesday 12 September and immediately sailed with 20 people to Avock Island in a brisk 15 knot easterly. She was fast on a reach—about 10 knots, despite the payload more than doubling the designer specs! The formal launching ceremony had the 103 year old 'Olfela Enrel'— Jack Enrel's dad, and the one who makes canoe models using the 'V' shaped sail plan—cutting the pandanus ribbon and giving a speech about his 'dream coming true' and recalling the last time that anybody in the Maskelynes had a bigger than 'canoe size' boat, being about 1920!

The local MP was there and a cast of 200 onlookers. This was a big day, the first in living memory for most, that a vessel as big as this has been built here.

And the women sailed it too—from Chief Willies mother—about 70, to the youngest about 12!

N.B. In the New Hebrides it had been against the law to travel to the other islands (missionaries liked to keep the plantation workers home and working).

By the time (2006) *Lanisif* was launched, we had sold around 650 Melanesia plans all over the world, showing that there was great interest in rediscovering Pacific canoe craft in the 'Western world'. The Melanesia was the first of several more Ethnic canoe craft we designed in subsequent years.

HANNEKE BOON.

30 Australia

I n July 1997 Hanneke, Jamie and I returned to Australia to complete our voyage round the world and bring *Gaia* back into European waters. Ruth was now seventy-six years old; she had fulfilled her dream of sailing the Pacific and felt she would now be more useful staying in Cornwall to keep the design business running.

Ruth was a very hard worker; she dealt with all our financial matters, organised the production and dispatch of design books, study plans and building plans, and spent many hours every day corresponding with Wharram builders and sailors, many of whom became her friends. She had two ladies working with her in her office, but she was the organising force that held it all together. She was the 'mother' of the Wharram world.

Don't forget that these were the days before internet and email. Payments were made by cheque in various currencies, requiring many visits to the bank. Communication was largely by 'snail mail', with fax only having come in during the previous few years.

❦

The boatyard in Brisbane had lifted *Gaia* out of the water and Steve Goodman, our agent in Australia, had organised a team of helpers to give her a serious overhaul. Masts were lifted out and revarnished, the hulls anti-fouled. Steve fitted solar panels. Beam lashings were checked and replaced and many other jobs done.

In order to repaint the orange hullsides, I had started to manually wet-and-dry sand them before the work team arrived. After several days of using my left arm (I am left-handed) in a circular motion, I had an aching shoulder and had to stop. I offered to do the simple task of washing up, not realising I was still using the shoulder. The pain got worse, several people tried their massage skills, without results. It was some years later that I was diagnosed with repetitive strain injury and my shoulder has never recovered, only got worse.

We had a long voyage ahead of us, around 10,000nm back to the Mediterranean, via Indonesia, Sri Lanka and the Red Sea. The plan was to do this in about ten months. We set out in early August with our work crew, to day-sail north.

It is often not realised how vast Australia is. The Queensland coast behind the Great Barrier Reef goes on for hundreds of miles; it is 1200nm in a straight line from Brisbane to Cape York at the northern tip of Australia, where one turns left through the Torres Straight, to reach Darwin another 700nm further on. There are miles of unpopulated coastline with long empty beaches. For a European it is hard to imagine this vastness and emptiness.

Because of the reefs, it is considered safer to sail only by day in the waters behind the Great Barrier Reef, though Joshua Slocum on his famous round-the-world voyage on *Spray* sailed there single-handed through the night—a brave man. Day sailing is far more tiring than ocean crossing. Having to raise anchor and hoist sails every day, anchoring again at night, is hard work. Navigation is more complicated, tidal currents have to be negotiated, and with a contrary wind one needs to tack in constricted waters.

It took us six weeks to sail the 800nm to Cairns, with longer stops at various places, a distance we can easily sail in the open ocean in a week. After entering behind Fraser Island through the Sandy Straights, our first important stop was in Hervey Bay to attend the sixth International Whale and Dolphin Conference. Sadly we arrived late and could only participate in the final party, where I met up again with Billy, my Aborigine friend, who in 1992 in Hawaii had asked me to perform in the dance to placate the ancestral spirits. It was an honour to welcome him on our boat.

After watching the humpback whales in Hervey Bay we stopped in Bundaberg where, on the recommendation of another sailor, we bought a new main anchor, a 65lb (30kg) Manson, a New Zealand-made version of a CQR (our Delta anchor had dragged on a number of occasions and we no longer trusted it). Another stop was in Gladstone where we bought and fitted an electric anchor capstan, so raising the anchor would be easier and Hanneke would be able to do so on her own.

For the last two weeks, from McKay to Cairns, we had a small crew of just me, Hanneke, Jamie and our friend Mike Ricks, a Cornishman living near Brisbane. Mike had build my Tiki 21 design many years ago and had built us a Melanesia while we were at home in England. It was now carried on the bow of Gaia.

We arrived in Cairns tired and were faced with a crew crisis. Our Canary Island

friend Sergio had been planning to fly out to us with his girlfriend, but they discovered she was pregnant and could not be vaccinated against various tropical diseases, so they could not come.

While contemplating our options, we met up with the owners of an unusual Wharram 35ft Tangaroa that was near us on the pile moorings. It was painted green all over, with elaborate seahorse carvings on both bows and a low central deck cabin.

The owners were unusual too. They had built their boat in a large agricultural shelter in the outback, close to a river, surrounded by tropical jungle. This wall-less roofed shelter was their home, the floor covered with a huge carpet from an old cinema, light bamboo roller blinds formed the walls. The tropical breeze cooled the interior.

Before building their Tangaroa, Ian and Rhonda had lived a nomadic life, sailing a Tornado catamaran along the Queensland beaches with their home-schooled children. People regularly visited their open house, which had become a meeting place for like minded 'New Age Christians'. Ian earned a living making beautiful airbrush paintings and harvesting marijuana growing wild in the nearby jungle.

After a week on the pile moorings, we discovered that our neighbour, an American of Dutch parentage, who was cruising on a beautiful 35ft classic yacht, was a yacht designer and a Wharram fan. He offered to crew with us to Darwin, while his wife stayed aboard waiting for paperwork necessary to sail to New Guinea.

At the same time two more crew offered. On a visit to Ian and Rhonda we met a young couple from near Brisbane, with no sailing experience, who shyly asked if maybe they could sail with us too?

With the crew problem solved, we left Cairns for the last stretch to Darwin. This was a voyage along an uninhabited coast, with Cooktown the last outpost of civilisation. Cooktown is where Captain Cook repaired his *Endeavour* after having been holed striking the Barrier reef. By the dinghy slip there was a large notice: 'Do not clean fish here, DANGER CROCODILES'.

We followed Captain Cook's route to Lizard Island and from there out into the open ocean for a shortcut outside the Barrier Reef where it curls into the coast. We reentered through Bligh Passage. It gave me an eerie feeling following where the famous Pacific explorers had sailed before.

Back behind the reef, on the last leg to Cape York, we had a hard-to-believe encounter. Seeing a sail ahead of us, with binoculars we realised it was a Wharram catamaran heading towards us. It was a 40ft Narai called *Stray*, and she had come from South Africa. Amazingly she was followed by another Wharram catamaran, a Pahi 42, called Little Blue. Both were sailing single handed, both were heading for New Zealand!

To me single-handed sailors are an inspiration. Though as a juvenile I wandered alone across the moors and mountains of northern Britain, sailing alone has never attracted me. Whether I might have learned the 'art' of single-handed ocean sailing had I not begun my sailing life with the wonderful German women, Ruth and Jutta, I do not know. But as these two 40ft Wharrams swept alongside me and on to their shouted destinations, I felt a sense of awe. Meanwhile we plodded on up the Australian coast.

Strong tides swept round Cape York, but *Gaia* with a brisk wind pushed through them. We worked our way through the Torres Straight and dropped anchor off Possession Island (another place named by Captain Cook). We went ashore on this uninhabited island and walked amongst the tall orange termite mounds and found turtle tracks on the beach.

From Possession Island we struck west in a direct line for Darwin, bypassing the inhospitable crocodile-infested shores of the Gulf of Carpentaria and Australian north coast. We have a video of this time, showing us as a happy crew, engaging with a pod of dolphins that swam under our bows for a long time.

When the wind dropped completely we swam naked between the hulls in the crystal clear sea, believing the two whale-like hulls of Gaia would protect us from any sharks or crocodiles. Not long afterwards we observed our first sharks in the distance, the only ones we ever saw. But a huge cane toad swam by, later followed by a black-and-white striped sea snake. We were not tempted to swim again.

Darwin lies behind some islands which are swept by strong tidal currents, at first against us at about 1½ knots, later sweeping us along at an extra 3½ knots with strong eddies 'boiling' around the boat. We dropped anchor in Fannie Bay, Darwin on 16 October.

The heat struck us, a very humid 33°C, day and night. It was almost unbearable; the seawater was lukewarm, and at night wafts of hot air would sweep over the boat, which felt like someone had opened the oven door. We anchored *Gaia* in the shallows where she went aground at low water, allowing us to walk ashore, carrying the dinghy

for our return. The season of the deadly box jellyfish had just started, so wading through the shallows carried a risk.

We had arranged to meet the explorer Bob Hobman in Darwin, who would sail with us across to Timor, to make preparations for the proposed raft voyage from Timor to Australia, which was planned for later in the year. This was the plan we had discussed in Auckland during the Vaka Moana Symposium the previous year, to reenact the voyage across the 'Wallace Line' of the first sailors to arrive in Australia around 60,000 years ago.

Back home we had made drawings of a proposed raft, constructed similar to the raft I had built in Trinidad in 1957 out of bundles of bamboo. Bob had been collecting bamboos to build it on the small island of Roti, south-west of Timor. Peter Welch, who had produced the film of Bob's voyage across the Indian Ocean in 1985, lived in Darwin and had been organising finance and support from the Aboriginal Trust. Two other crew of Bob's Indian Ocean voyage also lived in Darwin and came to meet us at the yacht club with disturbing news.

Bob was in marital trouble; he had left his Madagascar wife and two sons and was now living with a Dutch woman on Roti; he had not arrived back in Darwin yet. His friends were rallying around to try to make peace prior to his arrival. This was only the beginning of a saga that did not end well.

Waiting for Bob to turn up we got on with life in sweltering Darwin. We visited the Museum and Art Gallery of the Northern Territory and studied their wonderful boat collection. Problem was that one could only spend about fifteen minutes at a time in the swelteringly hot A-frame boat house. The aborigine art was housed in air-conditioned halls, but the boats were under an uninsulated tin roof.

Paul Clarke, the Museum director we had met in Auckland, welcomed us and arranged for me to give a lecture. We took Jamie into the air conditioned museum to catch up on some school work, sketching the skeleton of a turtle and writing about Australian wildlife.

Jamie also made friends with an aborigine lady on the beach and was invited to her house to play with her children. We were glad he had these experiences, very different to leaving him at home to go to school. We never regretted the decision to take him along.

The yacht club also gave us a welcome. Sitting there drinking a cold beer,

Hanneke suddenly exclaimed 'Have you noticed all those names around the top of the room?' I looked up and saw the name Wharam all around. These were people that had run the yacht club over the years. We asked at the bar and were given the phone number of the retired Wharam secretary, who lived nearby.

A phone call led to an invitation to meet Gerald Wharam and his wife Beryl, also a Wharam by birth. They were both into genealogy; Gerald had been born in Yorkshire and had come to Australia to meet his cousin Beryl, so both were delighted to meet another Wharram, even if he had one R too many. From them I discovered that one of their forebears had come to Australia as a convict, and not just for stealing a handkerchief, but for manslaughter. Did this make me an Australian aristocrat?

We spent three weeks in Darwin, waiting for our Indonesian 'Cruising Permit' to arrive from Jakarta. Bob and his new lady, Sylvia, turned up, together with a load of heavy gear Bob wanted to take to Roti on *Gaia*. This got dumped on the beach for us to ferry aboard in our dinghy in the broiling heat while he had 'other things to do'. This attitude did not bode well for our future cooperation.

31　The Indian Ocean

We were now in a new sector of the oceanic world, this was the Indian Ocean surrounded by south-east Asia, India and east Africa, a different world from the Pacific we had left behind.

The 500nm sail to Timor with Bob and Sylvia was slow in very little wind and great heat, using our motors some of the way. Kupang, our port of arrival in Timor, was a typical Indonesian city, a whirlwind of noise and people, where public transport is by 'Bemo'—decorated minibuses with blaring ghetto-blasters on the roof, packed full of people and vying to make the most noise.

Indonesia's bureaucracy had us visiting five offices in different parts of the city to clear into the country, requiring multiple copies of crew list and cruising permit, all needing to be rubber stamped. To our horror we learned that this would have to be repeated in every port.

One new crew member awaited us in Kupang; this was Italian Toto, who had sailed across the Indian Ocean with Rory McDougall the previous year on his Tiki 21. Peter Welch the film producer had flown in from Darwin and joined us on board.

We sailed to Bob's camp at the south end of Roti. I quickly saw that Roti was not a 'bamboo' island, the local people were not used to working with bamboo, they had one blunt machete between them. A large heap of bamboos had been gathered, all bent and twisted and not of large enough diameter. Many had split in the heat. I was very disappointed.

Our personal relations with Bob deteriorated. After three days we quit the project and departed for Bali, taking Peter with us, who had also been made unwelcome.

The end of this adventure was that a raft did get built, but as I had predicted, it lacked buoyancy and was ankle deep in water after just a few hours. The voyage to Australia was never made. Some years later another attempt was made, which was more successful and Bob is still building rafts to this day.

Replicating a voyage by raft across the 'Wallace Line' would have been a great adventure, and would have brought us closer to understanding the minds of early man who ventured by watercraft to unknown lands across the sea, but when personal relations break down, one is better off cutting one's losses.

Bali *is* the island of bamboo, where skilled craftsmen can make almost anything out of bamboo of many different species. This is where a raft should have been built and together with Peter Welch, who had invested a lot of his own money and time into the raft project, we researched the possibilities of building a better raft here. But for us the priority now was to sail home to Europe.

The island of Bali was lush and beautiful, but also hot and crowded. Its eastern shore is where fleets of distinctive, traditional double outrigger canoes, called 'jukung', are used for fishing. We could not leave without studying these.

The jukung have beautiful, skilfully carved dugout hulls with a beak-like stem resembling a swordfish. The buoyancy of the hull is carefully balanced to carry the weight of the crew aft. They are steered with a side rudder, ingeniously attached to the side of the hull with rope and a lever. The long thick bamboo outrigger floats are set on the ends of elegantly curved crossbeams, so the whole looks like a large water-bug. The sail is large and triangular with a spar on two sides, similar to sails used in the Western Pacific. The finishing touch is the colourful paintwork with 'eyes' that see the way ahead.

1997 was an *el Niño* year with very light winds; the forests of Sumatra were afire and spread a haze of smoke over the whole of Indonesia. Our disappointment in the raft project, together with the tedious bureaucracy of Indonesia and the sweltering humid heat, made us decide to leave the country and sail to Australian Christmas Island, which lies 190nm south of Java. From there we would sail round the outside of Indonesia, well clear of the coast of Sumatra, and on to Sri Lanka.

More German crew joined us in Bali: Lothar from our expedition in the Canary Islands, his friend Reiner, and Lothar's ten-year-old son Nico.

This was our first experience of a less than harmonious crew. Toto was a forty-year-old Sicilian spoiled by his Mama; the two Germans, from Berlin, worked to German discipline. Arguments soon erupted over the cleanliness of the washing up. As captain I stood back and let them find compromise.

Jamie, as a precocious twelve-year-old, didn't think Toto should smoke. They both liked playing chess, so Jamie challenged Toto to a game where if Toto lost three times in a row, he would have to stop smoking. Jamie won. But as could be expected, after a few days' confiscation (and hiding) of his cigarettes, Toto desperately needed his nicotine and we were glad we had not allowed Jamie to throw them overboard.

The voyage to Sri Lanka was mostly slow and hot. We celebrated Christmas in the doldrums while *Gaia* quietly ghosted along. Long silent nights were spent under a full moon on a gently undulating glassy ocean. At 4 degrees north of the equator, near the north end of Sumatra, the north-east monsoon came in and *Spirit of Gaia*, often accompanied by dolphins, sped the last 700nm at 7 to 10 knots in just four days. We had covered a distance of 1900nm in twenty days, an average of 95nm a day.

At dawn we approached the harbour of Galle, and out of the morning mist several large outrigger canoes quietly sailed towards us.

Two years earlier we had sailed into the Pacific with the dream to join a fleet of Polynesian double canoes, a meeting that turned out less than satisfying. We then discovered and studied the genuine working canoe craft of Melanesia and the beautiful canoes of Tikopia. From there we sailed to Indonesia and Bali, where we found many double outrigger canoes still had a working sailing life.

Arriving in Sri Lanka and to be met by several large sailing outrigger canoes, brought it home to me that canoe craft in all their forms are the generic sea craft of more than half the worlds oceans. These were craft developed by early man during his exploration of the world, and perfected over millennia, to become the ultimate Polynesian ocean exploration craft that had inspired me in my youth. Throughout my design life I have been able to tap into this archaic knowledge, and on our round the world voyage I was able to see and experience these craft in their various forms close up.

The Sri Lanka 'Oru' would not win any competition for elegance of form or finish. The first one we measured on the beach in Galle loomed over my head like an archaic sea animal. Its long dugout hull was pitted with age and mended with stitched-on tingles. Talking to fishermen on the beach I found out it was fifty years old.

Compared to the light woodwork elegance of the Balinese double outrigger jukung, this craft was brutally strong and easily repairable. The flat plank overhanging bows, which were sewn to the dug-out hull, had enormous lift, which could not only ride the surf on beaching, but also lift over stormy seas.

A road trip across the island to see the various tea plantations and temples ended on the beach at Ngombo, where there is still a large fleet of Oru, used for fishing.

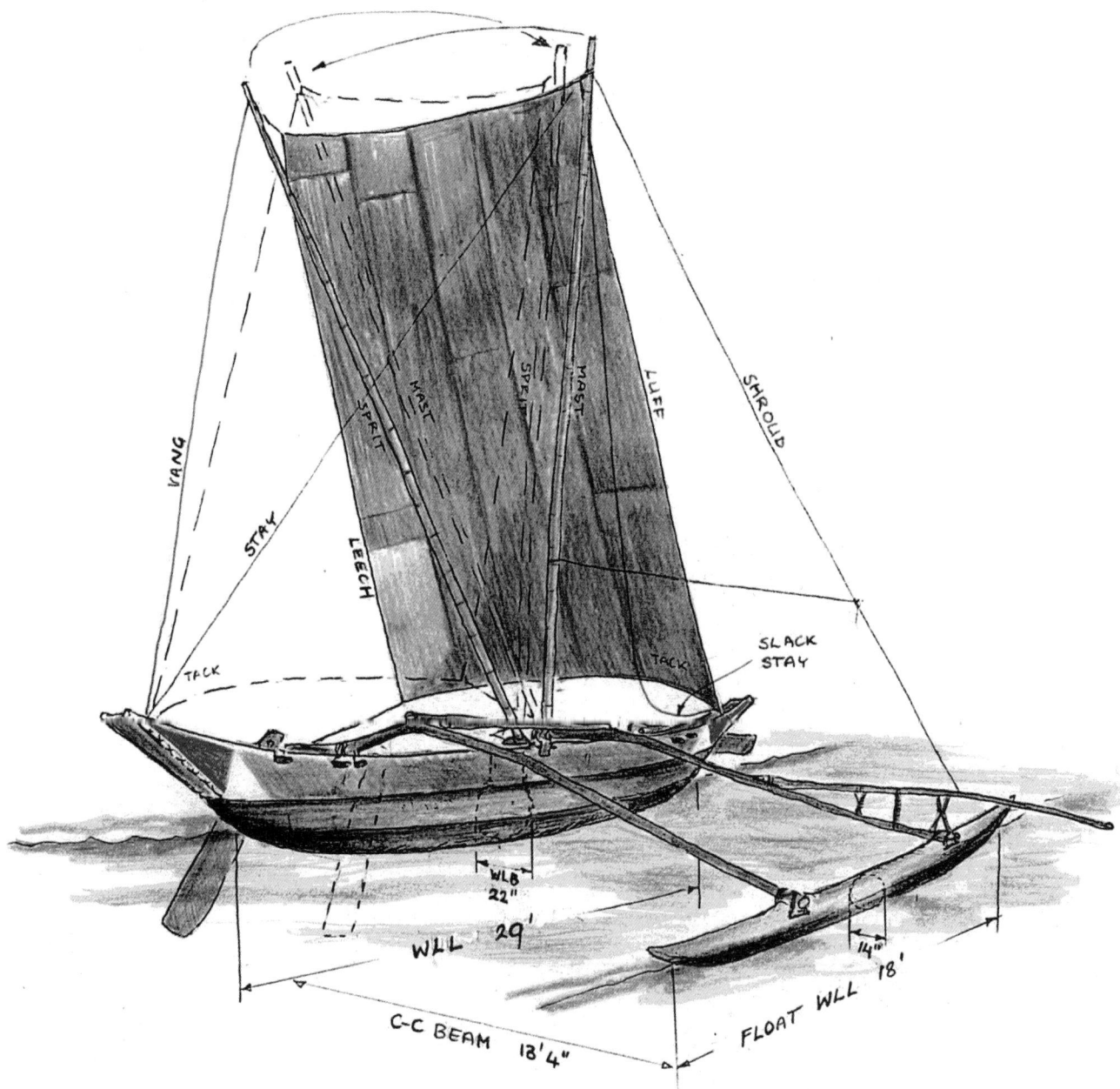

Oru, sailing outrigger of Sri Lanka

Here we got the chance to sail on one, not in strong wind conditions but in the lightest of airs.

The Oru use a large square sail which is set on a bamboo mast and sprit in a unique manner. To tack, the canoe is reversed end-for-end like a Micronesian proa, with outrigger float always kept to windward. During the tack the mast becomes the sprit and the sprit the mast by the simple adjustments of some ropes, an easier tacking method than swinging the whole triangular rig around, as is done on the Micronesian proas, which requires a big strong crew (we had seen this in operation in New Zealand, where the museum had a proa from the Marshall Islands, which was sailed during the Vaka Moana Symposium). The Oru are steered by a crude plank side rudder, tied on with rope; there is one at each end and a similar board midway, which acts as a leeboard.

Six of us pushed the craft down the beach, and in the glassy calm she ghosted out to sea. When the first wind ripples began showing on the water, the absurd rectangular sail filled like a spinnaker, and the craft was moving at 3–4 knots 45 degrees off the wind.

Light weather sailing ability is as important as strong wind ability. This archaic looking craft moved well in the lightest of winds. From the crews' description of where their offshore fishing areas were and the time they took to get there, this craft could average 7 knots. Other fishermen reported 10 knot averages in winds which are described as 1, 2, 3 or 4 men winds, i.e. attained with the number of people out on the outrigger beam to add stability.

These large sailing outrigger canoes at first sight looked crude, but if subjected to some hydrodynamic comparisons, they prove to be a lot more sophisticated than they seem. The 15-to-1 main hull length/beam ratio and float length/beam ratio equals many modern high-speed multihulls. The blunt ends of the dugout log Oru give a high prismatic coefficient, again considered an important aspect of modern multihull design. Their semi circular cross section gives minimum wetted surface for maximum speed.

In 1998 Sri Lanka was fighting an ongoing civil war in the north between the northern Tamils and the majority southern Sinhala, the former feeling discriminated against by the latter. A few days after we visited Kandy a truck bomb was exploded, damaging the

'Temple of the Tooth', one of the holiest Buddhist shrines in the world.

Sri Lanka, formerly Ceylon, has been a trading hub of the Indian Ocean for at least two thousand years. The seasonal changing monsoon winds have driven ships from the Arab world to south-east Asia and back again, with Sri Lanka and southern India as the meeting place of the sea routes. I could see why—our crossing of the Arabian Sea was the easiest ocean voyage I have ever made. The north-east monsoon was a gentle Force 2–4, and no spray ever broke over the decks.

We had a new crew member, our old friend Ernald, who had played a major part in the launching of *Gaia*. Ernald arrived on his sixtieth birthday. He was born in Ceylon where his father had been a rubber planter. In a phone call to his mother in England, Ernald got directions to find the plantation, which he last visited at the age of seven (like many British children at that time he was sent to school in England). At the plantation we met some of the old people that remembered his father with fondness and respect. This was very emotional for Ernald, to whom he had been a severe and distant figure.

We also took on board two young Dutch crew. Eric had worked in our office as a naval architect student and helped us build the Melanesia. He had asked if he could bring his sister. During the two week crossing to Oman, young Alexa spent most of her time sitting astride the stem head, wearing nothing but a hat and a belt pocket with a 'Walkman' and earphones, getting browner and browner.

We were entering the Muslim world. After a brief stop at the Maldives our landfall was in southern Oman at the port of Salalah. The Sultanate of Oman is an absolute monarchy and has been run by a benevolent ruler for many years. The country is rich in oil and a lot of the country's wealth has been spent on infrastructure, roads, public buildings, and so on. Under Muslim rules of hospitality we were treated as honoured guests. With the town some distance from the harbour, we were offered a lift by a naval officer, who then got a man to drive us everywhere we needed to go.

At the post office Ernald received a shock. News awaited him that his mother had died and he needed to return to England as soon as possible. He was sad to go, but also glad that his last conversation with his mother had been about the visit to the family rubber plantation.

Before leaving Sri Lanka we had considered Muslim etiquette. For the next three months the girls would need to dress discreetly and cover up most of their bodies. This included our painted naked girls that decorate *Gaia*'s bows. Long gowns cut from self adhesive plastic did the job. It saddened me to see their beautiful naked curves hidden by ugly blue plastic.

We urged Dutch Alexa to 'fully cover up'. We lent her a sarong and long-sleeved man's shirt as her own clothes were far too skimpy. We urged her to button up the shirt and not show a bare midriff. Difficult, as she was used to the relaxed attitudes of liberal Holland.

In the harbour of Salalah we found many dhows, large timber-built ships with powerful phallic stem-heads. In the past they would have carried large lateen sails, but now they were driven by motors. Many were built in Pakistan.

Also in the harbour were several other round-the-world yachts, who like us were heading for the Red Sea and the Suez Canal. Possible piracy was discussed among the crews, but that year things were quiet and the risk was considered low. Piracy around the coast of Somalia only became a serious problem in later years. However we would take the precaution of staying well clear off the coast on both sides of the Gulf of Aden and make a first stop in Djibouti.

Half way along the 760nm voyage to Djibouti the waves built up, followed by the first strong wind since Australia. After such a long time of calms and light winds this caught us unprepared. Items on deck needed to be stowed away or secured, and hatches shut.

Djibouti was a chaotic remnant of French colonialism, half African, half French, with dusty outdoor markets full of colourfully dressed Africans, goats and heaps of rubbish, alongside modern supermarkets full of expensive foodstuffs imported from France, where pale elegant French ladies shopped. On the streets were noisy generators to cut in when the unreliable electric supply cut out.

At the anchorage off the run-down 'Club Nautique' we were subjected to the noise of the city, with every few hours calls to Muslim prayer from the many mosques, starting at 4.30 in the morning, blasted through amplifiers in clashing melancholy.

Eric and his sister Alexa went exploring. In town they met a friendly young Ethiopian, who went by the name of 'Baby', who told them he was a DJ at a night club. Through him they also met some nice Ethiopian girls. Eric and Alexa invited them all to come and see our boat. They arrived dressed elegantly in Western clothes. Over cups of tea and biscuits, in return they invited us for a traditional Ethiopian meal and coffee ceremony at their place.

The meal was served on the stairwell landing of their apartment block, where they had set up a table. It was delicious, a traditional huge pancake, shared by all, on which tasty morsels of spicy food were served.

After the meal the girls invited us into their room to introduce us to a traditional Ethiopian coffee ceremony. On a bed was a girl with both legs in plaster casts. Her story was that she had fallen in love with a French Foreign Legionnaire who was going to take her to France. Only he didn't, and in addition he had walked off with her music stereo. In despair she had jumped out of the window. It was on the first floor so it had only broken her legs. Young Jamie sat on the edge of her bed, showed her card tricks and made her smile.

'Baby' invited our group to 'his' nightclub for a free drink one early evening. It was quiet when we arrived and we, including twelve-year-old Jamie, sat there sipping Fanta.

Some bored looking girls gently swayed to the music in front of a mirrored wall, while an older French woman with a hatchet face was busy behind the bar. It was not long before the first customers arrived, young French Foreign Legionnaires, dressed in their (very small) uniform shorts, they sat on the bar stools drawing the girls into their arms. It dawned on me then, how the kind and lovely girls we had met made their living.

On arrival in Djibouti Eric had checked his diary and realised he did not have enough time to sail all the way up the Red Sea with us. He had pending exams for his naval architecture course and would have to fly home to Holland.

But a new crew member was at hand. Back home with Ruth at our office John Barker, an experienced engineer who had previously worked in Southampton building hovercraft, was helping us with drawing plans for our new Tiki 46 and helping Ruth with answering technical design questions. He had come to us as a volunteer building *Gaia* and later to help build the Melanesia. We discovered his drawing and engineering skills and employed him to do drawing and design work. John deserved a break and some sailing time on *Gaia*, and he jumped at the chance to join us in Djibouti.

32   The Red Sea

The Red Sea is the natural geographical divide between Africa and Eurasia; it is a huge stretch of water, over 1000nm long and between 120 and 200 wide. Since the opening of the Suez Canal it has become a busy shipping route from Europe to India and the Far East. On the chart, on one side is the beguiling coastline of Sudan with many reef-protected inlets, on the opposite side is the coast of Saudi Arabia with Jeddah, the port to Mecca, a sacred place of history. Sudan had, and still has, constant turmoil in its politics. Saudi Arabia had, and still has, a male dominated society where attitudes, particularly towards women, are dictatorially repressive. They do not welcome yachts in the very few ports on its Red Sea coast.

According to my *Atlas of Ancient History*, in the days of the Egyptian, Greek and Persian empires the Red Sea was not one of the regular trade routes. These then flowed from India and Oman up the Persian Gulf to Mesopotamia and then overland to the Levant and the Mediterranean. Or in Egypt they followed the course of the Nile.

Having sailed up the Red Sea, I understand why. For in our 30,000nm voyage round the world, the slog of 1000nm up the Red Sea to Suez, entrance to the Suez Canal, was the hardest.

Running north to south with a hot desert surrounding its southern end, air from the Mediterranean gets sucked down its length as the heated air in the south rises. The effect of this is frequent very strong northerly winds in the upper half of the Red Sea. To travel north in a sailing ship one has to fight these winds.

In early history sailing ships often had poor windward ability, so trying to sail up the Red Sea would have been very hard, with a great risk of shipwreck. The ancient trade routes followed the much gentler winds in the Persian Gulf or the sailing route up and down the Nile where the northerly winds were counter-balanced by the flow of the river. Later in history camel caravans carried trade up the Arabian peninsula. They must have considered this arduous overland travel preferable to sailing up the Red Sea.

The only account we have of voyaging on the Red Sea in ancient times is the expedition of a fleet of five ships built by Queen Hatsepsut, the female Pharaoh who ruled Egypt from 1481 to 1472 BCE, that travelled to the land of Punt, bringing back exotic goods like myrrh and frankincense. These ships had sails and oars, so they could have coast-hopped under oars in the quieter spells (like many yachts do nowadays, using engines). No-one is sure where Punt is located, but it is assumed to be at the bottom end of the Red Sea. Oman, nowadays, is still famous for its myrrh and frankincense.

One of the first sailing accounts I read in my teens was *Sailing All Seas in the 'Idle Hour'* by Dwight Long, the voyage of a 32ft gaff-rigged ketch from the west coast of America to Britain. Dwight Long's account of his voyage up the Red Sea in 1937 was of hardships, fighting their way to windward, reef-strewn coastal waters, encounters with unfriendly Arab tribesmen, and having to stop to make repairs to the engine in Jeddah at the risk of being arrested and put in jail! Sixty years later little had changed. The Saudi Arabian side of the Red Sea is still as dangerous with its off-lying reefs, and according to the pilot book a no-go coast for yachtsmen. There had been incidents of piracy in recent years, and—the northerly wind still blows as hard.

After entering the Red Sea through the famous Bab-el-Mandeb (Gate of Tears), the southern half with favourable winds was easy sailing, but after six days, with Port Sudan on one side and Jeddah on the other, the northern winds hit us with a force 7 hard on the nose and waves building up quickly.

Seams in the foresail started to fail; we took it down and sewed them up with our hand-cranked sewing machine on the platform. The next day, sailing heavily reefed, the staysail seams started to go. Six years of sailing in strong ultraviolet light had degraded all the stitching.

We spent a day hove to whilst Hanneke and John took the staysail down into the galley where Hanneke restitched every seam with triple stitching and John mended the luff wire, which was breaking at the reef. Without our staysail we would not be able to fight our way to windward; it was vital to repair this sail.

The next day, with the staysail reset and a reef tied in, they focussed on the foresail, which was equally essential to make way to windward. With the sewing machine on the roof of the deckpod, and Alexa to help haul the sail around, Hanneke and John stitched as much of every seam as they could reach.

Then the hard slog started. The next twelve days were spent beating to windward in

John and Hanneke repair sails – Alexa and Jamie in the cockpit

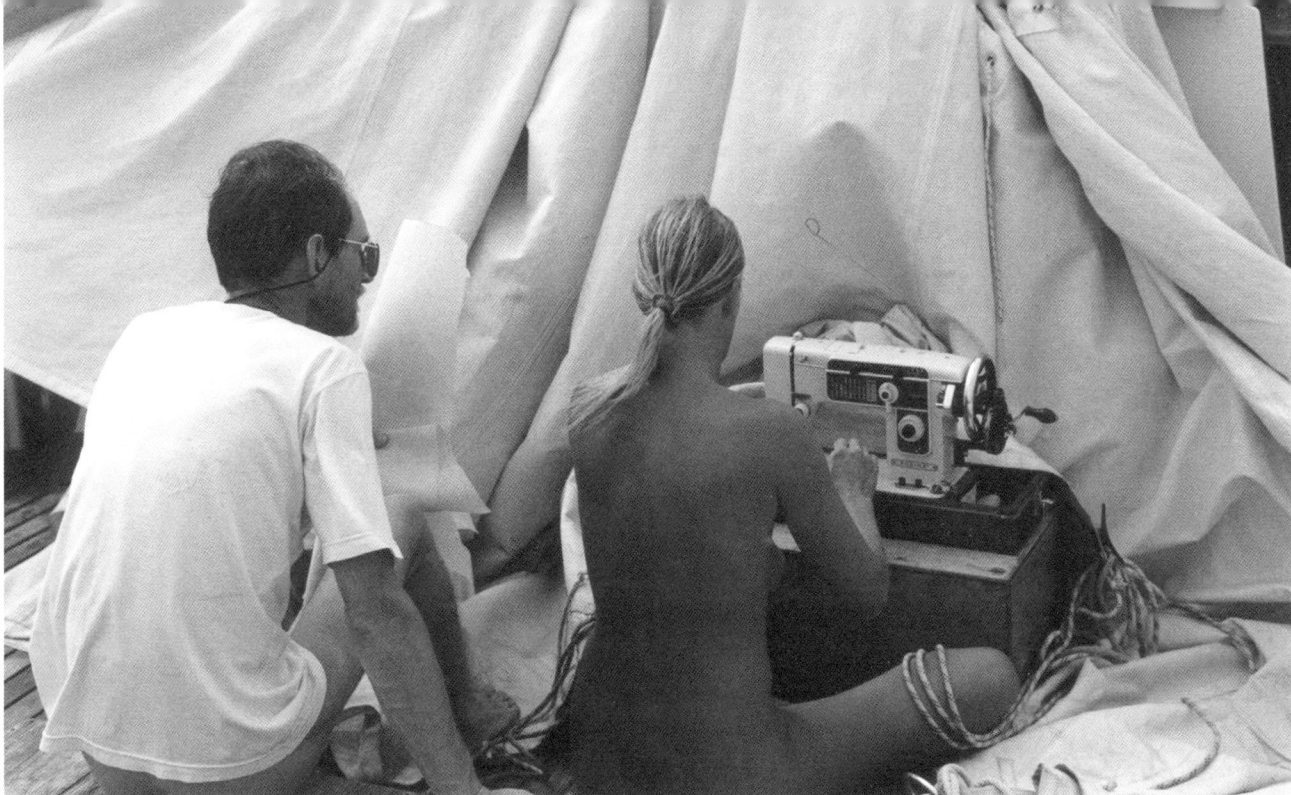

winds between force 6 and 8, with waves as high as four metres, the sky a clear blue, the wind warm, but unrelenting. *Gaia* valiantly fought her way over the steep waves, the self-steering wind-vane keeping her pointing at around 50 degrees off the wind. Under deep-reefed sails we kept the speed down to around 5 knots, tacking through 120 degrees (by the chart). Any faster and the motion would have been unbearable. Waves regularly hit the bows and threw a cascade of water over the ship. Others leapt on board over the stern decks. Wave crests burst up through the platform slats. The beam-lashings creaked as they absorbed the fierce shock loads. This was the first time I ever saw the whole front half on one hull suspended in the air, before crashing down into the trough.

We made around 55-60 miles northing every 24 hours, which was good progress under the circumstances; the *Idle Hour* had often only made a very disappointing 5–10 miles northing a day and frequently anchored at night to not lose any ground. The *Idle Hour* was a much smaller boat, but I was proud of our Polynesian double canoe, with her shallow draught, as she ploughed on hour after hour, day after day, eating up miles to windward.

There were short spells of lighter winds, when we quickly let out reefs and made the most of the smoother seas. But there was no telling when the strong wind would return, there was no warning, it often started again at sunset and would blow hard throughout the night. The crew stayed positive, often coming on deck with the cheery greeting of: 'And another day of beating up the Red Sea!'

We were never tempted to anchor. One is not allowed to anchor on the Saudi Arabian side and the Sudan/Egypt side lies towards the sun during the afternoon and evening, making it hard to see the reefs. Our two 9.9hp outboard motors were too weak to push us against the strong wind and we weren't sure they would work after their regular dowsing in seawater. So we tacked well clear of the shore and any reefs approximately every twelve hours. Somehow shipping was mainly encountered at night as we crossed the shipping lane, requiring a careful watch, with VHF radio at the ready, and bright torch to make sure we were seen.

After eleven days tacking to windward, and a last day of very strong wind, we were within reach of the first Egyptian port of Safaga. The wind eased as we sailed towards the reef passage leading to the harbour late in the afternoon. But the Red Sea wasn't going to give up. As the sun dropped towards the horizon the wind picked up again and started to head us. After nearly three weeks of inactivity one outboard refused to start and the other would not provide any drive. It was hopeless and we headed back out to spend another night bouncing up and down hove to in a howling wind, to try again the next morning.

On the morning of 9 April, with a more moderate wind, we tacked up behind the off-lying island to the harbour of Safaga. Another large yacht entered harbour ahead of us heeled over hard under sail, a 65ft Swan called *Tangaroa*. Later we discovered they were in fact motor sailing. With both outboards out of action we dropped anchor under sail. Exhausted, we cleared customs together with the crew of *Tangaroa* and another yacht called *Halcyon of Hebe* who, with a much stronger motor, had coast-hopped from inlet to inlet. They gave us a tow through the narrow passage to the anchorage, which was full of yachts waiting for lighter winds to travel north. We were the only yacht at that time that had made the whole voyage up the Red Sea under sail alone.

It is 'Sod's Law' that the moment we came to anchor at Safaga the strong northerlies eased and many of the yachts departed. But we needed a rest and spent time ashore by the pool of the Holiday Inn enjoying cool drinks. Sometimes it is nice to be a tourist. We also wanted to see Egypt, so after sorting out the ship and getting the outboards working again, we boarded a bus to travel through the desert to the Nile at Luxor.

Luxor was very quiet and desperate for tourists, after a busload of German tourists had been massacred by Muslim extremists the previous year. We spent four nights at a small hotel at very little cost. We visited all the famous ancient sites and temples, but the highlight for us were the feluccas that sail the Nile.

On our first evening we walked down to the river and booked a sunset sail. After eighteen days' hard sailing on the Red Sea, sailing this felucca was a delight. Crewed by an older man and his nephew, we set off upriver with the wind behind. The felucca is broad and shallow and has a large lateen sail. It is steered with a long shallow rudder with a massive tiller. On either side of the river we passed green fields with people working the land as they had done for the last 3000 years. It was a scene from antiquity.

On the return trip we had to tack into the northerly wind, but the current was behind us and progress was good. We helped in the sailing, moving from side to side and hauling on the sheet at every 'ready about'. The two men enjoyed having some real sailors on board. Seeing the skill with which these two handled their felucca when mooring was a lesson in boat handling. The skipper made precise use of wind and current whilst the younger man climbed the yard and gradually furled the sail from the top downwards, slowing the boat, then jumped onto the little pier just as the boat came to a stop.

The next day we returned to the river and while the young crew brewed tea on a Primus stove they kept under the foredeck, we discussed boat design with our skipper and other experienced felucca sailors.

The last part of the voyage up the Gulf of Suez was less challenging, the wind and waves more moderate. We sailed by day and anchored at night as there is a lot of shipping along with the oil rigs.

The two days' passage through the Suez Canal was a challenge in its own right. Our two 9.9hp Yamaha outboard motors pushed us fine in the light wind of early morning, but as the wind increased with the heat of the day, our speed became slower and slower and the pilot more and more agitated. The canal is quite wide and we suggested we could hoist some sail and go faster by motor sailing. With permission granted, we 'tacked' up the Suez Canal. One very long slant and then a short tack across followed by another slant.

Half way through the second day one motor suddenly lost all drive. We could no longer make progress against the strong northerly wind and the pilot told us to moor up to make repairs. Tied alongside a floating pontoon bridge we were put under armed guard and the pilot disappeared. The rubber hub that encased the propellor bearing had sheared, so the prop slipped on the drive shaft. We had no spare propellor, so made the best repairs we could, using thick bronze nails as retaining pins glued in with epoxy. As we worked the two young soldiers on the pontoon kept annoying us. They asked to see passports, but spoke no English, nor could read Roman script. The focus of their attention was Alexa with her long dark hair, until even she got fed up. I told her she should try covering her head with a scarf, which miraculously worked.

The next day, after a struggle to find another pilot, we reached Port Said, and minutes after the pilot left us the propellor sheared again. We limped out of the canal into the wide Mediterranean under jib and one motor. The wind was light, the air humid and hazy; we hoisted full sail for the first time in weeks. The aft sail crackled with encrusted salt as it stretched to its full height, the humid air dissolving the salt which quietly dripped on to the deck.

In the early hours of the second night we reached Ashkelon in southern Israel and its beautiful modern marina. We were back in our own more familiar Western World. We relaxed in the comfortable marina, walked in the modern town, and peeled the ugly dresses from the naked girls painted on *Gaia*'s bows. I celebrated my seventieth birthday in Ashkelon and looked back on a lifetime in which I had been surrounded by liberated women who have lived the life of sea people with me. Such a life would not have been possible in the world we had just passed through.

I was aware of stresses building between the Israelis and Palestinians in Gaza, just to the south of Ashkelon. It made me uncomfortable and in spite of the friendly welcome and hospitable marina, I did not want to leave our *Gaia* there for long.

We flew home to be reunited with Ruth, whom we had missed. Three months later, after a spell catching up with work in Cornwall, we returned to Ashkelon to sail *Spirit of Gaia* on to Greece, where a new life awaited her in Corfu.

From Ashkelon we sailed north-west towards the islands of the eastern Mediterranean. After a short stop in the old harbour of Rhodes, whose entrance was once guarded by the famous Colossus, one of the Wonders of the World, we reached the large island of Crete. Sailing in the Mediterranean gave me a quiet inner joy. I could sense history everywhere. Crete has always interested me. Though a long way from the mainland of Greece or Africa, it was populated by humans very early in the history of mankind. There have been recent archaeological finds that indicate that people were living in Crete 130,000 years ago, meaning they must have crossed the sea in some form of watercraft to reach the island. This can be compared to early man reaching the Indonesian Island of Flores by watercraft around the same period.

Cretan 'culture' emerged around the seventh century BCE, culminating in the sophisticated Minoan civilisation around 4000 years ago, which had regular contact by boat with mainland Greece. This ancient culture expressed itself in the beautiful frescos of human figures and dolphins discovered at the palace of Knossos.

To me there is an emotional connection between the islands of the Greek Mediterranean and the Polynesian islands, in their close connection to the sea, their appreciation of the human form, and their use of stone in a mystical way (in the Cretan palace platforms and Polynesian Marae).

My other emotional connection is through my adopted trademark. On an earlier visit to Crete in the 1970s I discovered in the Heraklion Archeological Museum a tiny cylinder seal engraved with the 'Eye-symbol' that I had adopted in the 1960s as my meditation focus and design trademark. This symbol of the female bird goddess (as two eyes with eyebrows connected into the shape of birds' wings) originated in the Balkans during the Neolithic, when people worshipped the 'mother goddess', and was used by seafaring peoples that travelled along the coasts of the Mediterranean and Atlantic Europe, where the symbol has been found carved on stones in Portugal, Ireland, Britain (the Folkton Drums, a unique set of decorated chalk objects found in northern England) and as far north as Denmark.

From Crete we sailed on, up the west coast of Greece to Corfu, to a new life of quiet sailing in sheltered waters, surrounded by the beautiful Greek islands and remains of an ancient culture.

Recently Hanneke has been researching my ancestry, going back down the Wharram line. There she found my great great grandfather, George Wharram, born in 1808, who became a soldier in the Royal Sappers and Miners (later to become the Royal Engineers). To my surprise I discovered that he had been stationed in Corfu for nine years in the 1830s. He must have lived at the old fort in Corfu town, which during our years in Corfu we regularly sailed past. He must have known the island well, having worked on various engineering projects; maybe he even learned to speak Greek.

We had completed our round the world voyage. *Spirit of Gaia* had safely taken us across three oceans, through storms and the hard sail up the Red Sea. What was remarkable was that in the six years since her launching we had no structural problems—nothing that we had designed and built had broken. Her 'simplicity' had been at the core of this success. There were no complicated 'systems' to break down. *Gaia*'s simple structure of ply, epoxy, glass and rope lashings proved strong and durable. What had caused us trouble were the outboard motors, and our electronic wind instrument had failed while sailing up the Red Sea.

Epilogue

In 1998 I had achieved my ambition to sail to the Pacific, to study the boats that had inspired me as a young man, and to sail round the world. There are still twenty years of my life after this date, but I will not write about these in detail as this period has been covered on my website in regular news items. We sailed for many years in the Mediterranean, in Greek waters, as well as a longer voyage to Venice and Croatia in 2001. I also sailed with Hanneke in the cold waters of the northern Atlantic for a month in 1999, on the Pahi 42 *Toroa*, a voyage from Scotland to Iceland on an expedition researching Viking navigation.

My last serious sailing expedition was in 2008–9 when Hanneke, together with our German partner Klaus Hympendahl, organized the 'Lapita Voyage' to sail two 38ft Ethnic Tama Moana designs from the Philippines to the remote Polynesian islands of Tikopia and Anuta, situated at the eastern end of the Solomon Islands—a voyage of 4500nm. I was eighty when I made this voyage and it was the hardest I ever sailed and physically the most strenuous. As it was Hanneke's project I will leave any writing about it to her. I left the expedition a month before its ending with an ongoing stomach complaint, which was later diagnosed as bowel cancer.

Though many of the memories of this voyage are unpleasant, I am glad I made it. With it my life's work of rediscovering the sailing craft of the Polynesians came full circle after fifty years. It was my final way of showing that Thor Heyerdahl's theory of Polynesian migrations from South America was wrong. The double canoes with hulls modelled on the Tikopia canoe in Auckland Museum, and using traditional Polynesian rigs and steering paddles, were able to sail successfully to windward and proved themselves capable of the type of migratory voyages made by the early Polynesians.

My success as a designer in introducing the Polynesian double canoe into Western sailing culture would not have been possible without the many builders and sailors of my craft. Already in the early years of my design life people believed in me and were prepared to put their life's savings into building a boat I had designed. They were then prepared to sail their boat across oceans and through storms.

There are a number of these sailors who stand out in my memory. Two of the first Wharram catamarans that sailed round the world were built in British Columbia in the early 1970s. There was *Kiskadee*, a 46ft Oro, built and sailed by Harold and Wendy Goddard and their children. Their friends the Hembroff brothers built *Piggy*, a 46ft Ariki. The two boats were launched around the same time and both were sailed around the world.

Another sailor who stands out for his incredible voyage is Dutchman Henk de Velde, who in 1978 together with his wife Ginny sailed their 46ft Oro *Orowa* across the Atlantic and into the Pacific. On the way to Easter Island Henk became seriously ill. During this voyage his heavily pregnant wife had to sail the boat as well as nurse her sick husband. On arrival in Easter Island the population carried *Orowa* ashore for safety and their son was the first child to be born to outsiders on Easter Island. Later when sailing across the Indian Ocean *Orowa* was overtaken by cyclone Oscar. The boat and crew survived this very severe storm and reached South Africa. The last leg of the voyage back to Europe was sailed by Henk alone. Ginny was no longer prepared to sail on. Henk on *Orowa* arrived in Falmouth in 1985, where we welcomed him just weeks after my son Jamie was born.

But my small designs also made remarkable voyages. In 1975 American Tom Jones and his wife Carol were caught in hurricane Blanche between Bermuda and the US east coast in their 23ft Hinemoa *Two Rabbits*. They retreated to their tiny cabins and sat it out, their boat taking them through some of the worst storm conditions, proving the incredible seaworthiness of the Polynesian double canoe. Another Hinemoa sailed from California to Hawaii.

Many examples of my 27ft Tane design also made long ocean crossings in the 1970s. Annie Hill, now famous for her book *Voyaging on a Small Budget*, started her sailing life on a Wharram Tane across the Atlantic.

Glenn Tieman, another American, built one of my Pahi 26 designs on a shoestring in the 1980s and roamed the Pacific on *Peregrin* for many years, ending in the Philippines. Then in 2003 he asked us for a slightly bigger design with the simplicity of his *Peregrin,* to roam the Pacific once more. For him we designed the pure Ethnic Tama Moana, based on the Tikopia canoe. Now with more money, he built it beautifully, called her *Manu Lele,* and has been sailing the Pacific on her for the last thirteen years.

The smallest of my designs to sail round the world was the Tiki 21 *Cooking Fat* sailed by Rory McDougall. He singlehanded large stretches of the voyage and had a companion on others. Rory set off from the UK in 1991 and completed his voyage, after a long stop in New Zealand, in 1997 (one year before we did on *Spirit of Gaia*) by sailing up that dreaded Red Sea on his own, without a motor!

In 2010 Rory sailed *Cookie* in the singlehanded trans-Atlantic 'Jester Challenge' and came a close second behind a larger Russian monohull. He then turned round and sailed back to the UK in just twenty-two days, the same route that we sailed fifty-one years earlier on *Rongo*, taking twice as long. He is a remarkable sailor, better than I ever was.

These are just a very few of the thousands of Wharram catamarans that have been built and sailed all over the world. Many of their amazing stories have never been told. Without all these people believing in me and putting their trust in my designs, I would not have achieved the recognition I have, and I would be just another ocean sailor amongst many unsung others.

During my early career as a designer, as a man from the North of England who designed unusual sailing boats and led an unusual lifestyle, I experienced a lot of antipathy within the established yachting circles. However with the achievements and enthusiasm of the many builders and sailors of my designs (over 10,000 building plans have been sold) I have gained, in my old age, recognition within the British (yachting) establishment.

In 2009, after completing the Lapita Voyage, I was offered Fellowship of the Royal Geographical Society for my canoe craft studies in the Pacific. Then in 2012 the Ocean Cruising Club awarded me their prestigious 'Award of Merit' for my contributions to ocean sailing. In 2013 the French multihull group 'The Golden Oldies' made me their 'parrain' (godfather) and in 2018 I was given a 'Lifetime Achievement Award' by *Classic Boat* magazine. I value these recognitions.

People of the Sea

The Ocean is a deep element of our consciousness. It is in spirit our mother. It is a regulator of the oxygen we breath. It is life.

Our planet is 75% ocean. Its true name should be Oceania. Some people believe that our ancestors were semi-aquatic primates who adapted to live in the sea along the sea shore.

More certain is that 50-60,000 years ago Man of the modern species was leaving the sight of land on basic watercraft and discovered the Australian continent.

Half of Oceanus' surface is called by Man the 'Pacific Ocean'.

5,000 years ago EuroAsian land men were developing Armies, Slavery, Rigid Social Systems, Enclosing Cities—beginning concepts which entrap us today.

At the same time, families of Man living in small social groups left the EuroAsian land-mass and took to life on the island studded Pacific Ocean. They became People of the Sea.

They adapted themselves to the ocean, using subtle design in assembling sailing rafts, sailing canoes balanced by an outrigger, sailing double-canoes, which had the advantages of both raft and canoe.

With shells, stones, bones and sharkskin, they shaped trees and bamboos into rafts, dug-outs, plank built craft. From coconut fibres they hand spun twine and rope and lashed the craft together, giving them flexibility to yield to the forces of the ocean seas. From fibrous leaves they wove with supple fingers sails that could drive these Pacific Sea Craft thousands of miles against the ocean currents into the heart of the Pacific and beyond.

They reached briefly the Americas. Their legends recount they sailed to the Antarctic. The spatial wonder of their achievements will be equalled only when small groups of Man fly into space to 'seed the stars'.

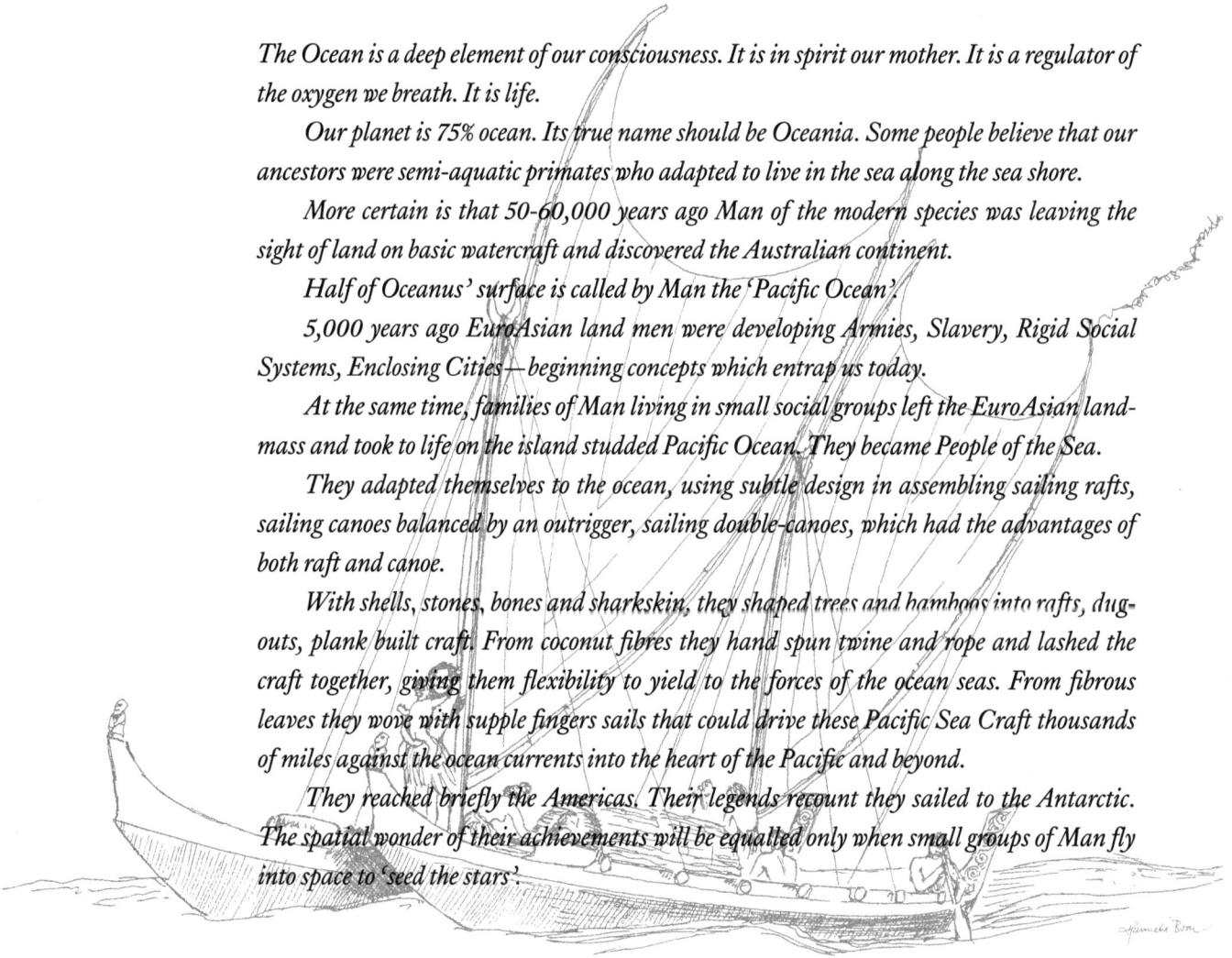

300 years ago, this world of blue ocean seas, small green islets, larger high volcanic islands was 're-united' with explorers of the EuroAsian Landmass Man. Men like de Bougainville of France, who wrote enthusiastically at having discovered 'Man of the Golden Age'.

Unfortunately, within the bodies of the men of the Landmass was disease. Afloat in the blue ocean, the Sea People had no diseases, no resistance to diseases, and they began to die like wild flowers under the poisonous herbicides of Modern Man.

Within the minds of the men of the Landmass were harsh religious doctrines, which enslaved the saddened survivors of the joyous Sea People.

Bodies die—Ideas live. The joyous ideas of the Sea People have lived and now enrich the lives of the Landmass people.

In their tens of thousands, the young of the Landmass people now ride, in poetic harmony with their surfboards, where ocean waves crash onto the land. How many of them know, that it was the sport of the Sea People?

The luxury holiday sailing catamaran. How many know, that their basic design was developed by the Sea People?

The graceful women who swim or play topless or naked on the beaches of Europe. How many of them know they are living in the image of their Sea People sisters?

Sea People women had the right to choose their lovers, the right to sexual fulfilment. Now, it is the growing expectation of women of the Landmass.

How many Lands Women know their 'expectations' were once the Sea Women's rights?

From the Sea People of the past have come many of today's joys. We need the Sea People to sail again.

James Wharram, 1995

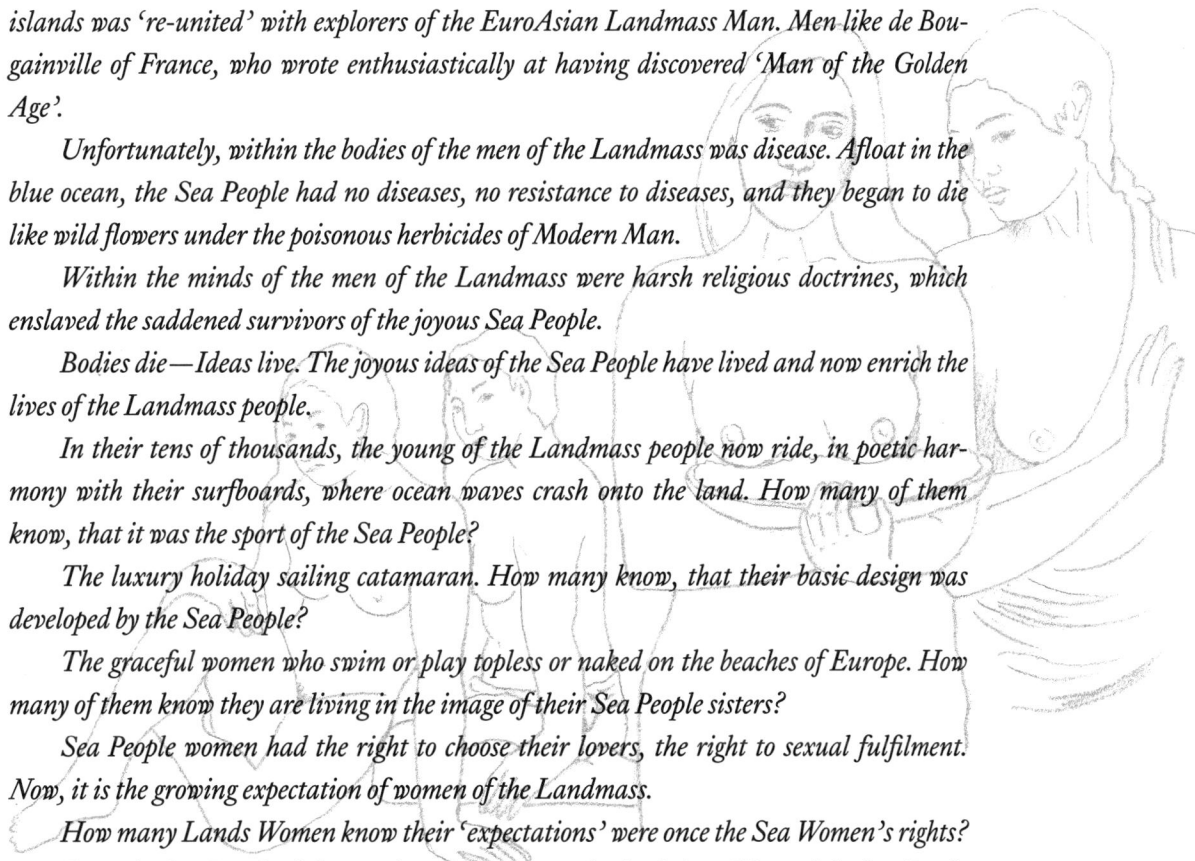

Single Outrigger Proa

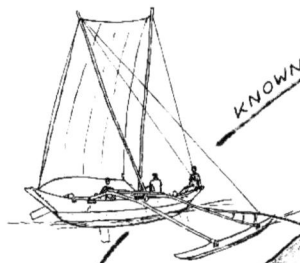

Double Outrigger Canoe

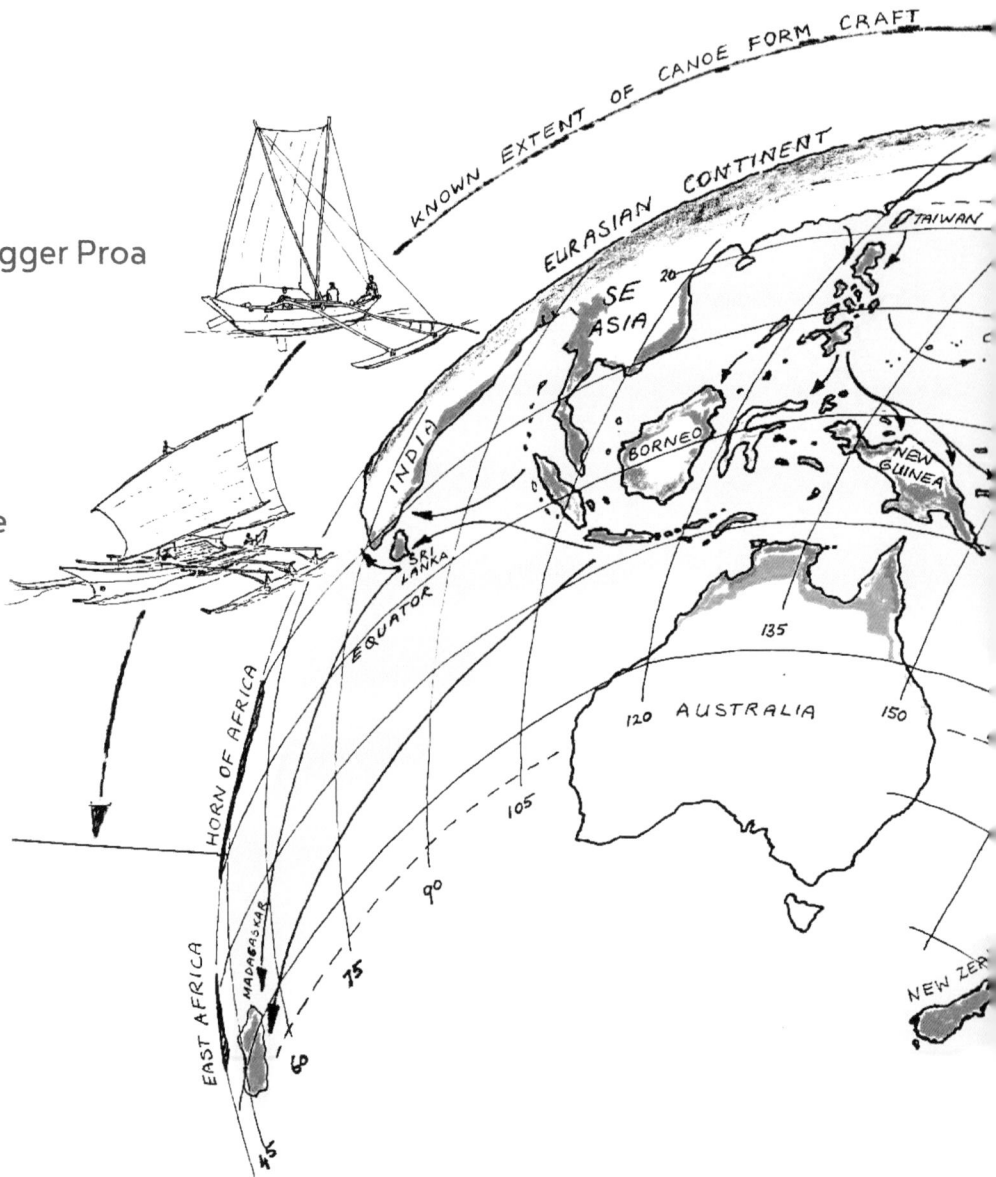

Sailing waters of Canoeform Craft

Single Outrigger Proa

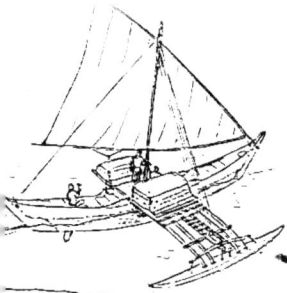

Single Outrigger Canoe

Double Canoe

JAPAN

165 E

180

MARIANAS

MARSHALLS

SOLOMONS

KIRIBATI

VANUATU

ELLICE

EQUATOR

HAWAII

150

10.800 Nm

HALF EARTH CIRCUMFERENCE

NORTH AMERICA

FIJI

SAMOA

TONGA

COOKS

SOCIETY

TUAMOTUS

MARQUESAS

20

10

40

135

1500 Nm TO EASTER ISL.

0

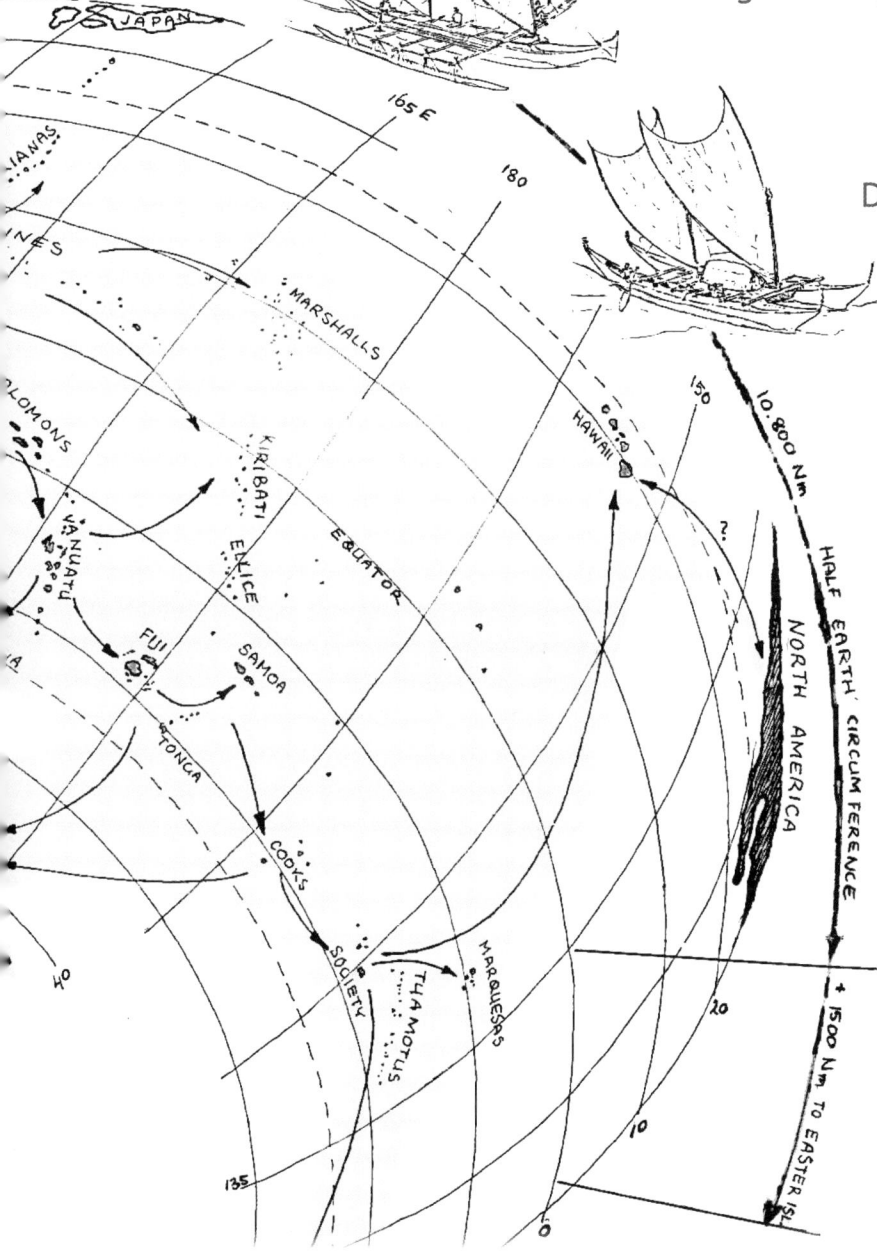

Drawn by Hanneke Boon

Acknowledgements

My dear Ruth died in 2013 at the age of 92, after two years of reduced capacity due to a stroke, which robbed her of her ability to read. She could no longer communicate by letter or email with her many friends and Wharram builders round the world. To them she had been the 'mother' of the Wharram world. My life would not have been the same if she had not joined me in 1951 and helped me throughout our sixty-four years together.

It was she who preserved and archived the documents that recorded my life, old diaries, letters and logbooks. She also kept a visual record of my life in hundreds of black and white photographs, which she developed and printed herself, as well as boxes full of colour slides, recording our voyages on *Rongo* and *Tehini*.

However it was Hanneke, my other life partner, without whom this book would never have been finished. She pushed me to keep writing, researched facts, read through diaries and letters, and kept my memory alive of the shared events of our life. We worked as a team. Her artwork has been a very valuable part of the Wharram myth. She took most of the photos during our round the world voyage on *Spirit of Gaia* that illustrate this book.

I must also thank the various ladies that typed parts of my handwritten manuscript, which I would read out to them, as my handwriting is too hard too decipher. The first to read the unfinished manuscript was Dennis Gorman, a single-handed sailor and author of his own auto-biography. He gave us some very constructive criticism, which helped us make improvements.

We would like to thank the BBC for the use of Alison Chisholm's beautiful Cento on page 12, which she composed for a publicity video for the programs produced by BBC2. It so well describes the many aspects of my life that it could have been written specially for me. Alison herself has expressed delight at it's use in this book and we thank her for composing it.

A year ago, when about two thirds the book was written and edited, the author Sam Llewellyn was prepared to read it and gave me great encouragement to keep writing. Both he and my other yachting writer friend Tom Cunliffe guided me to my publisher, Richard Wynne, who has prepared this book for publication in record time, for which I am grateful, as I did want to see the book in print before my life will also come to an end, which at 92 cannot be too far away.

James Wharram
June, 2020

Bibliography

Bader, Hans-Dieter & McCurdy, Peter, 1999, *Proceedings of the Waka Moana Symposium 1996.* New Zealand National Maritime Museum. Auckland, New Zealand.

Bednarik, Robert G., 2014, *The First Mariners,* Lambert Academic Publishing, Germany.

Best, Elsdon, 1976, *The Maori Canoe.* Dominion Museum Bulletin No. 7. A.R. Shearer, Government Printer. Wellington, New Zealand.

Bisschop, Éric de, 1940, *The Voyage of the Kaimiloa.* G. Bell and Sons Ltd. London.

Bisschop, Éric de, 1959, *Tahiti-Nui. By Raft from Tahiti to Chile.* Collins. London.

Brand, Steward, 1968–72, *Whole Earth Catalog.* USA.

Buck, Peter H., 1959, *Vikings of the Pacific.* The University of Chicago Press. Chicago.

Danielsson, Bengt, 1956, *Love in the South Seas.* George Allen and Unwin Ltd. London.

Danielsson, Bengt, 1957, *Forgotten Islands of the South Seas.* George Allen and Unwin Ltd. London.

Diamond, Jared, 2005, *Collapse—How Societies Choose to Fail or Survive.* Allen Lane. London.

Doak, Wade, 1985, *Dolphin Dolphin,* Sheridan House Inc. USA

Doak, Wade, 1990, *Encounters with Whales and Dolphins,* Hodder & Stoughton. London.

Dobbs, Horace, 1977, *Follow a Wild Dolphin,* Souvenir Press. London.

Dodd, Edward, 1972, *Polynesian Seafaring.* Dodd, Mead & Company. New York.

Duhm, Dieter, 2010, *Eros Unredeemed.* Verlag Meiga.

Feinberg, Richard, 1988, *Polynesian Seafaring and Navigation.* The Kent State University Press. Kent, Ohio.

Finney, Ben R., 1979, *Hokule'a, The Way to Tahiti.* Dodd, Mead & Company. New York.

Firth, Raymond W., *We the Tikopia,* George Allen & Unwin Ltd. London.

Gatty, Harold, 1943, *The Raft Book.* George Grady Press. New York.

Gladwin, T., 1970, *East Is a Big Bird*. Harvard University Press. Cambridge, Massachusetts.

Griffith, Nancy, 1979, *Blue Water: A Guide to Self-Reliant Sailboat Cruising*. Sail, USA.

Haddon, A.C. & Hornell, J, 1975, *Canoes of Oceania*. Bishop Museum Press. Honolulu, Hawaii.

Heyerdahl, Thor, 1950, *The Kon-Tiki Expedition*. George Allen & Unwin Ltd. London.

Heyerdahl, Thor, 1952, *American Indians in the Pacific*. Bokförlaget Forum AB. Stockholm.

Heyerdahl, Thor, 1974, *Fatu Hiva*. George Allen & Unwin Ltd. London.

Hill, Annie, 2001, *Voyaging on a Small Income,* Tiller Publishing, USA.

Holmes, Tommy, 1981, *The Hawaiian Canoe*. Editions Limited. Kauai, Hawaii.

Howlett, John, 1956, *Mostly about Boats,* Edward Arnold Ltd. UK.

Irwin, Geoffrey, 1992, *The Prehistoric Exploration and Colonisation of the Pacific*. Cambridge University Press.

Hesselberg, Erik, 1950, *Kon-Tiki and I,* George Allen & Unwin Ltd. London.

Jones, Thomas F., 1994, *Multihull Voyaging,* Sheridan House. USA.

Jung, Carl G., 1964, *Man and his Symbols*. Doubleday. New York.

Jung, Carl G., 1969, *The Archetypes and the Collective Unconscious*. Princeton University Press.

Kane, Herb K., 1976, *Voyage. The Discovery of Hawaii*. Island Heritage Limited. Honolulu.

Kane, Herb K., 1991, *Voyagers*. WhaleSong, Incorporated. Washington.

Krockow, Christian von, 1991, *Hour of the Women,* Harper Collins. London.

Lewis, Dr David, 1972, *We, the Navigators*. The University Press of Hawaii. Honolulu, Hawaii.

Lichy, Dr Roger & Herzberg, Eileen, 1993, *The Waterbirth Handbook,* Gateway Books. UK.

Lilly, John C, M.D., 1978, *Communication between Man and Dolphin,* Julian Press. New York.

Long, Dwight, 1938, *Sailing the Seas in the 'Idle Hour'*. Hodder & Stoughton. London.

Malinowski, Bronisław, 1922, *Argonauts of the Western Pacific*. E. P. Dutton & Co., Inc. New York.

McIntyre, Joan, 1974, *Mind in the Waters,* Charles Scribner's Sons. New York; Sierra Club Books. San Francisco.

Morgan, Elaine, 1972, *The Descent of Woman,* Souvenir Press. London.

Morgan, Elaine, 1982, *The Aquatic Ape,* Souvenir Press. London.

Neyret, J., *1976, Pirogues Océaniennes, Tome I&II.* Association des Amis des Musées de la Marine. Paris.

Rabl, S.S., 1947, *Boat Building in Your Own Backyard.* Cornell Maritime Press. USA.

Savoy, Gene, 1974, *On the Trail of the Feathered Serpent.* International Community of Christ. USA.

Sharp, Andrew, 1957, *Ancient Voyagers in the Pacific.* Penguin Books.

Siers, James, 1977, *Taratai—A Pacific Adventure,* Millwood Press Ltd. New Zealand.

Sidenbladh, Erik, 1983, *Waterbabies.* A & C Black Ltd. U.K.

Silk, Don, 1994, *From kauri trees to sunlit seas: Shoestring shipping in the South Pacific.* Godwit Press, New Zealand.

Slocum, Joshua, 1900, *Sailing Alone around the World.* The Century Company. Canada.

Velde, Henk de, 1987, *Ganzen Trekken in Troepen,* Albatross, Netherlands.

Wesley, Mary, 1984, *The Camomile Lawn,* MacMillan. UK.

Wharram, James, 1969, *Two Girls Two Catamarans.* 2001, Crociera Totale Edizione. Bologna.

Wharram, James, 1977, 'History & Problems of Design of Modern Multihulls'. HISWA Symposium. Netherlands.

Wharram, James, 1994, 'Nomads of the Wind'. *Practical Boat Owner*, October 1994.

Wharram, James, 2000, 'Lessons from the Stone Age Sailors'. *Water Craft*, July-October 2000.

Wharram, James, 2006, 'The Pacific Migrations by Canoe-form Craft'. *Proceedings of the Tenth International Symposium on Boat and Ship Archaeology*, Roskilde 2003. Oxbow Books.

Williams, Heathcote, 1988, *Falling for a Dolphin,* Jonathan Cape, London.

Index

Published by
Lodestar Books
71 Boveney Road, London, SE23 3NL, United Kingdom
lodestarbooks.com

A CIP catalogue record for this book is available from the British Library

ISBN 978-1-907206-50-4

Typeset by Lodestar Books in Equity Text and Noyh Geometric

Printed in Wales by Gomer Press
All papers used by Lodestar Books are sourced responsibly

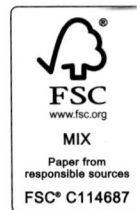

FSC
www.fsc.org
MIX
Paper from
responsible sources
FSC® C114687

Lapita Anuta off the coast of New Guinea – Hanneke steering into Rabaul

Tiki 38 **Pilgrim** *crossed the Atlantic – Don Brazier on his Narai MkIV in the Pacific*